THE LETTERS OF ABELARD AND HELOISE

THE LETTERS OF ABELARD AND HELOISE

Translated from the latin by

C. K. SCOTT MONCRIEFF

GYAN

Published by

Gyan Publishing House
5, Ansari Road
Daryaganj, New Delhi-110002
Phone: 011-47034999, 9811692060
E-mail: books@gyanbooks.com

Distribution Network
gyanbooks.com
India, USA, Canada, UK, Australia

ISBN: 978-81-212-6552-2 (HB)
First Published, 1926

2nd Impression 2024

Printed at: Gyan Press, Delhi.

THE LETTERS OF ABELARD AND HELOISE
Author: PETER ABELARD, Translator: C. K. SCOTT MONCRIEFF

THE LETTERS OF ABELARD AND HELOISE

BLUE JADE LIBRARY

THE BLUE JADE LIBRARY

THE ADVENTURES OF HAJJÎ BABA OF ISPAHAN
By James Morier

THE LETTERS OF ABELARD AND HELOÏSE
Translated by C. K. Scott Moncrieff

THE WOOINGS OF JEZEBEL PETTYFER
By Haldane Macfall

THE MEMOIRS OF CARLO GOLDONI
Written by Himself

THE TWILIGHT OF THE GODS
By Richard Garnett

THE LIFE OF HENRI BRULARD
By Henri Boyle-Stendhal

CAPTAIN COOK'S VOYAGES
By Andrew Kippis

HADRIAN THE SEVENTH
By Frederick Baron Corvo

A ROMANTIC IN SPAIN
By Théophile Gautier

SAÏD THE FISHERMAN
By Marmaduke Pickthall

SIR WALTER RALEGH
By Martin A. S. Hume

PABLO DE SEGOVIA
By Francisco de Quevedo-Villegas

THE DIABOLIQUES
By Barbey d'Aurevilly

RACHEL MARR
By Morley Roberts

THE LETTERS OF ABELARD AND HELOISE

Translated from the Latin by
C. K. SCOTT MONCRIEFF

NEW YORK
ALFRED A. KNOPF
1926

To my friend

GEORGE MOORE

Who has made these dry

bones live

CONTENTS

My dear George Moore,

IT would obviously be impossible for any translation of these Letters to be published in England without some reference, whether by dedication or otherwise, to the one man using our language who has taken the matter up within living memory, and the only man who at any time has made the dry bones of ABELARD and HELOISE reincarnate themselves in a far livelier garment of romantic flesh, I fancy, than was ever theirs in their twelfth century existence: but there is an especial reason why I must dedicate this translation to you, as, although I hasten to acquit you of any responsibility for the actual volume, it was over your table in Ebury Street that I had it suggested to me, for the first and (I would now wager) the last time, that I might write a book—one of the literary-historical kind—about the cloistered lovers and their correspondence.

What you told me then, had the speaker been any but yourself, must have fallen upon deaf ears; for, to tell the truth, I had never read the Letters, I had no intention of reading them, and I assumed that their problems were sufficiently well-known already to persons less illiterate than myself: but I do remember your telling me that the First Letter was, in your opinion, from the hand of Jean de Meung, a literary forgery, designed to create a background and a justification for the rest. You then knocked down the whole card castle by reminding (you were really informing) me that the whole of the evidence for the story of the lovers was contained in this First Letter, as indeed the whole compass of your own marvellous romance is contained in the period before Heloise went to Paraclete, that is a year at least before even the First Letter purports to have been written. But you did not then tell me, of what I discovered only after Mr Chapman had coerced me into undertaking this version, of a far greater and more impudent forgery, the English "translation" (still on sale) of the Letters published some two hundred years ago. Whether this work was forged in England, or, as seems to me likely, is translated from a French forgery of the late seventeenth century, I have no means, here in Pisa, of discovering. It consists of six letters, the first of them, entitled Abelard to Philintus, following more or less the lines of the History of the Calamities, though with such startling interpolations as the following:

"I was infinitely perplexed what course to take; at last I applied myself to Heloise's singing master. The shining metal, which had no effect on Agaton, charmed him: he was excellently qualified for conveying a *billet* with the greatest dexterity and secrecy. He delivered one of mine to Heloise, who, according to my appointment, met me at the end of the garden, I having scaled the wall with a ladder of ropes. I confess to you all my failings, Philintus; how would my enemies, Champeaux and Anselm, have triumphed, had they seen this redoubted philosopher in such a wretched condition. Well! I met my soul's joy—my Heloise! I shall not transcribe our transports, they were not long, for the first news Heloise acquainted me with plunged me into a thousand distractions. A floating Delos was to be sought for, where she might be safely delivered of a burden she began already to feel. Without losing much time in debating, I made her presently quit the Canon's house and at break of day depart for Brittany; where she, like another goddess, gave the world another Apollo, which my sister took care of."

Of this specimen of twelfth century literature its most recent editor (a lady who seems not to have studied the inside of the Latin volume) writes: "Of course the authenticity of the letters has been questioned, but no human being can read them and not know them to be genuine."

This may not seem a very serious matter, but it is serious in this respect, that people who have read only the traditional English version of the Letters must have formed a wholly different conception of the character of the lovers from theirs who have studied, however casually, the Latin text. The former kind will be surprised to learn that Abelard did not inspire a hopeless passion in Heloise's maid, already courted as she was by a rich abbot and a courtier, "to say nothing of a young officer"; that he never said: "Pyramus and Thisbe's discovery of the crack in the wall was but a slight representation of our love and its sagacity"; and that the irregularities of conventual life at Paraclete did not oblige Heloise to write: "I walk my rounds every night and make those I catch abroad return to their chambers; for I remember all the adventures that happened in the monasteries near Paris."

But let us return to the question of the First Letter, which you regard, you tell me, as "a piece of book making," and of the Second, which you say was "certainly touched to make it fit on." It seems to me that here there are two things to be said: first, that if the Letter to a Friend be a forgery, it is a remarkably clever impersonation on the forger's part of Abelard as he reveals himself in the later Letters. Only the irrepressible young prig who insisted on lecturing impromptu upon the interpretation of Ezekiel, and expected his better instructed seniors then to sit under him, could have grown into the intolerable old egoist who could write to his wife (in the Fifth Letter) of his own emasculation: "Neither grieve that thou wert the cause of so great a good, for which thou needst not doubt that thou wert principally created by God." And what artistry to make him seek to comfort his friend in an unnamed affliction by writing exclusively about his own affairs. On the other hand, it was careless on the forger's part, if he composed the First Letter, having already the text of the other seven to his hand, to make Abelard say that he had frequently visited Heloise and her companions at Paraclete, when Heloise's chief ground of complaint against her husband, and one that he admits to be valid in the opening lines of the Third Letter, is that he has never come to see her since their conversion.

Then you made the point, in writing to me, that there was, or had been, some obscurity in the public mind as to the reason for Abelard's sending Heloise back to Argenteuil after their marriage. But as to this, I think, he makes himself clear enough in the First, and again in the Fifth Letters. He first offered to marry Heloise, in order to pacify her uncle. He married her, against her will and advice, but, as he thought always of his own interests only, made her keep their marriage secret, so that his career as a teacher and potential churchman might not be jeopardised. The uncle, unfortunately, makes the fact of the marriage known; Heloise denies it; the uncle maltreats her; Abelard removes her from his custody and sends her back, as a *pensionnaire,* to Argenteuil. He has no thought, however, of breaking off his relations with her, and in the Fifth Letter reminds her how those relations were resumed (uncomfortably enough, one would think, not to say sacrilegiously) in the refectory at Argenteuil. The uncle, however, whose sole and very natural motive is hatred of Abelard, concludes that he is "putting away" his wife with the intention of himself also seeking orders, and takes the one step, short of murder, which must make it impossible for Abelard ever to be admitted to the priesthood. From this point, our hero's life may be summed up in the poignant words of the fair-complexioned man in *Candide:* "O che sciagura d'essere senza coglioni!"

There is an inevitable change in his nature. First of all, his whole affection, which seems never to have deserved a politer name than lust, for Heloise abruptly ceases. As her husband, he compels her to take the veil at Argenteuil before he himself retires to the Abbey of Saint-Denis. And when, in later years, she writes him her three immortal letters, his irritation and boredom are manifest in every line of his replies. In his final letter, when dealing with the use of wine in convents, he actually transcribes several pages of her previous letter to him, as though forgetting that it was she who had written them. In his other relations also, his character is enfeebled. True, the young prig who lectured his seniors upon Ezekiel survives in the middle-aged prig (how curiously like certain

Anglican prelates of to-day) who points out to his fellow monks of Saint-Denis that their founder may not, after all, have been the Areopagite; but the young cocksure who confuted William of Champeau and laughed in the venerable beard of Anselm has dwindled into a querulous craven, constantly in terror of persecution, poison and the rest, magnifying his dangers with a buoyant indifference to his correspondent's natural anxiety, and piteously appealing to her for an eventual Christian burial. His once famous teaching, too, has become a string of garrulous quotations, many of them singularly inept.

There is nothing more to be said, except that the lovers, I find, owe some part, at least, of their reputation in our Island to the assumption that they were never legally married; a British spinster, resident for many years in the Antipodes, to whom I was speaking recently about the Letters, was genuinely shocked to learn that their writers repose beneath the same covering in Père Lachaise. When I assured her that, before burial, they had been man and wife, her face fell still farther. But the great majority of people in England think, if they think about the matter at all, that Abelard and Heloise are fictional characters invented, my dear George Moore, and very beneficially invented by yourself. This volume will, as I need not assure you, do little or nothing to dispel their illusion, or to diminish the reputation of *Heloise and Abelard*. Such as it is, pray accept the offering of my part in it, with every good wish, upon this your *onomastico*,

From

Charles Scott Moncrieff

Lung'arno Regio, Pisa.
Saint George's Day, 1925.

THE FIRST LETTER WHICH IS A HISTORY OF THE CALAMITIES OF ABELARD, WRITTEN TO A FRIEND

Argument: *This letter, from the monastery of Saint Gildas, in Brittany, which at that time* Peter Abelard *was governing as Abbot, he writes to a friend whose name, neither in the whole course of the letter, long as it is, does he himself mention, nor does* Heloise *when in the following letter she refers to this. It is in narrative form. For throughout the whole text of the letter he diligently narrates the story of his past life from his infancy to the time at which he is writing; and yet makes no mention of* John Rosselin, *which most learned philosopher* Otho, *Bishop of Freising, a writer of authority who lived at the same time, assures us was* Abelard's *teacher. Nevertheless he gives a graphic description of the feelings that governed his actions and writings, of his sufferings, of the envy with which his rivals were consumed, and takes the opportunity of replying briefly and with point to his detractors. In fine, he appears to have written this letter rather for his own comfort than for his friend's, that is to say, with a view to lightening the burden of his present misfortunes by recalling those in the past, and to banishing more easily the fear of imminent perils. For he draws no comparison between his friend's troubles and his own, so as to make them appear more serious by contrast.*

OFTEN examples serve better than words to excite or to mitigate human passions. Wherefore, after certain comfort offered thee in speech in thy presence, I have decided in absence to write by way of comfort the experience of my own calamities, that in comparison with mine thou mayest see thy trials to be none at all, or but slight matters, and may be better able to endure them.

Chapter I. Of the birthplace of Peter Abelard *and of his parentage.*

I THEN was born in a certain town which, situated at the entering into Brittany, distant from the city of Nantes about eight miles, I believe, in an easterly direction, is properly known as Palatium. As by the nature of the soil or of my blood I am light of heart, so also I grew up with an aptitude for the study of letters. A father, moreover, I had who was to no small extent imbued with letters before he girded on himself the soldier's belt. Whence, at a later time, he was seized with so great a love of letters that whatever sons he had he was disposed to instruct in letters rather than in arms. And so it befell us. I too, being the first-born, in so far as I was dearer to him than the rest, so much the more diligently did he care for my education. And I, when I advanced farther and had more facility in the study of letters, so much the more ardently did I adhere to it, and with such love of that study was I consumed that, abandoning the pomp of military glory with the inheritance and the privileges of a first-born son to my brother, I finally relinquished the court of Mars that I might be educated in the lap of Minerva. And inasmuch as I preferred the equipment of dialectic to all the teachings of philosophy, I exchanged those weapons for these and to the trophies of war preferred the conflicts of discussion. Thereafter, perambulating divers provinces in search of discussion, wherever I had heard the study of this art to flourish, I became an emulator of the Peripatetics.

Chapter II. Of the persecution of him by his master William. *Of his mastership at Melun, at Corbeil and in Paris. Of his retirement from the city of Paris to Melun, his return to Mont Sainte-Genevieve and to his own country.*

I CAME at length to Paris, where this study had long been greatly flourishing, to *William* styled "of Champeau," my preceptor, a man at that time pre-eminent, rightly and by common repute, in this teaching: with whom I stayed for a while, welcomed by him at first but afterwards a grave burden to him, since I endeavoured to refute certain of his opinions and often ventured to reason with him, and at times shewed myself his superior in debate. Which things indeed those who among our fellow-scholars were esteemed the foremost suffered with all the more indignation in that I was junior to them in age and in length of study. Hence arose the beginnings of my calamities which have continued up to the present time, and the more widely my fame extended, the more the envy of others was kindled against me. At length it came to pass that, presuming upon my talents beyond the capacity of my years, I aspired, boy as I was, to the mastership of a school, and found myself a place in which to practise, namely Melun, at that time a town of note and a royal abode. My master afore-named suspected this plan and, seeking to remove my school as far as possible from his own, secretly employed all the means in his power to contrive that before I left his school he might take from me mine and the place that I had selected. But inasmuch as among the powerful in the land he numbered several there who were jealous of him, relying upon their help I succeeded in obtaining my desire and won the support of many for myself by the manifest display of his envy. And from this beginning of my school, so much did my name in the art of dialectic begin to be magnified that not only the repute of my fellow-scholars but that of the master himself began to decline and was gradually extinguished. Hence it came about that, presuming more largely upon myself, I made haste to transfer my school to the town of Corbeil, which is nearer to the city of Paris, so that there opportunity might furnish more frequent contests of disputation. Not long afterwards, however, being stricken with an infirmity by the immoderate burden of my studies, I was obliged to return home, and for some years, being banished, so to speak, from France, I was sought out more ardently by those to whom the teaching of dialectic appealed.

But a few years having gone by, when for some time I had recovered from my infirmity, that teacher of mine, *William*, Archdeacon of Paris, laying aside his former habit transferred himself to the order of the regular clergy, with the intèntion, as was said, that being thought to be more religious he might be promoted to a higher grade in the prelacy, as shortly happened, he being made Bishop of Chalons. Nor did this change of habit call him away either from the city of Paris or from his wonted study of philosophy; but in that same monastery to which for religion's sake he had repaired, he at once opened public classes in his accustomed manner. Then I returning to him that from his lips I might learn rhetoric, among the other efforts of our disputations, contrived, by the clearest chain of argument, to make him alter, nay shatter, his former opinion with regard to universals. For he had been of this opinion touching the community of universals, that he maintained a thing as a whole to be essentially the same in each of its individuals, among which, forsooth, there was no difference in essence but only variety in the multitude of their accidents. He now so corrected this opinion that thereafter he proclaimed the thing to be the same not essentially, but indiscriminately. And inasmuch as this has always been the main question among dialecticians concerning universals so much so that even *Porphyry* in his Isagoga, when he treats of universals, does not presume to define it, saying: "For this is a most weighty business," after he had corrected and then perforce abandoned his opinion, into such neglect did his instruction fall that he was scarcely admitted to be a teacher of dialectic at all; as if in this opinion about universals consisted the sum total of that art. Hence did my teaching acquire so great strength and authority that they who formerly adhered most vehemently to our said master and attacked my doctrine most strongly now flocked to my school, and he who had succeeded to our master's chair in the school of Paris offered me his own place, that there among the rest he might submit himself to my teaching where formerly his master and mine had flourished.

And so after a few days, I reigning there in the study of dialectic, with what envy our master began to consume away, with what rage to boil, is not easily expressed. Nor long sustaining the heat of the affliction that had seized him, he cunningly attempted to remove me once again. And because in my conduct there was nothing whereon he could openly act, he laboured to remove the school from him who had yielded up his chair to me (charging him with the vilest accusations), and to substitute a certain other, one of my jealous rivals, in his place. Then I, returning to Melun, established my school there as before; and the more openly his jealousy pursued me, the more widely it enlarged my authority, according to the words of the poet:

> Envy seeketh the heights, the winds blow on the mountain-tops.

Not long after this, when it came to his knowledge that well-nigh all his disciples were in the utmost hesitation as to his religion, and were murmuring vehemently as to his conversion, in that evidently he had not retired from the city, he transferred himself and his conventicle of brethren, with his school, to a certain village at some distance from the city. And immediately I returned from Melun to Paris, hoping that thenceforth I should have peace from him. But seeing that, as I have said, he had caused my place there to be filled by one of my rivals, outside the city on the Mount of Saint

Genevieve I pitched the camp of our school, as though to beleaguer him who had occupied my place. Hearing which, our master straightway returning unashamed to the city, brought back such pupils as he might still have, and the conventicle of brethren to their former monastery, as though to deliver his soldier, whom he had abandoned, from our siege. In truth, whereas he intended to advantage him, he greatly harmed him. He, forsooth, had until then retained sundry disciples, principally for the lectures on *Priscian* in which he was considered to excel. But after the master arrived he lost them one and all, and so was compelled to cease from the tenour of his school. And not long after this, as though despairing for the future of any worldly fame, he too was converted to the monastic life. Now after the return of our master to the city, the conflicts of discussion which our scholars waged as well with him as with his disciples, and the results which fortune in these wars gave to my people, nay to myself in them, thou thyself hast long known as matters of fact. But this saying of *Ajax* I may with more modesty than he repeat and more boldly utter:

> Shouldst thou demand the issue of this fight,
> I was not vanquished by mine enemy.

As to which, were I silent, the facts themselves speak and its outcome indicates the whole matter. But while these things were happening my dearest mother *Lucy* obliged me to return home. Who, to wit, after the conversion of *Berenger*, my father, to the monastic profession, was preparing to do likewise. Which being accomplished, I returned to France, principally that I might learn divinity, when our afore-mentioned master *William* attained to the Bishopric of Chalons. In this study, moreover, his own master, *Anselm* of Laon, was of great and long-established authority.

Chapter III. How he came to Laon to the master Anselm.

I CAME therefore to this old man, who owed his name rather to long familiarity than to his intelligence or his memory. To whom if any came knocking upon his door in uncertainty as to some question, he departed more uncertain still. Indeed, he was admirable in the eyes of his hearers, but of no account in the sight of questioners. His fluency of words was admirable but in sense they were contemptible and devoid of reason. When he kindled a fire he filled his house with smoke, rather than lighted it with the blaze. His tree, in full life, was conspicuous from afar to all beholders, but by those who stood near and diligently examined the same it was found to be barren. To this tree therefore when I had come that I might gather fruit from it, I understood that it was the fig-tree which the Lord cursed, or that old oak to which *Lucan* compares *Pompey*, saying:

> There stands the shadow of a mighty name,
> Like to a tall oak in a fruitful field.

Having discovered this, not for many days did I lie idle in his shadow. But as I gradually began to come to his lectures more rarely, certain among the more forward of his disciples took it amiss, as though I were shewing contempt for so great a master. Thereafter him also secretly exciting against me with vile suggestions, they made me offensive in his sight. But it fell upon a day that after certain controversies of opinion we scholars were disporting ourselves. When, after a certain one had inquired of me with menacing intent what I thought as to the reading of the Holy Scriptures, I, who had as yet studied nothing save physics only, replied that it was indeed most salutary, the study of this lore in which the salvation of the soul is revealed, but that I marvelled greatly that, to them who were literate men, the Scriptures themselves or the glosses upon them should not be sufficient, so that they should require no other instruction. Many of those present, laughing at me, asked whether I was able and presumed to approach this task. I replied that I was ready to try it if they wished. Then, shouting together and laughing all the more: "Certainly," they said, "we agree. Let some one find, therefore, and bring to us here an expositor of some little read Scripture, and let us put what you promise to the proof."

And they all agreed upon the most obscure prophecy of *Ezekiel*. And so, taking up the expositor, I at once invited them to attend my lecture on the morrow, who, pouring counsels into my unwilling ears, said that in so weighty a matter there was nothing to be gained by haste, but that seeing my inexperience I must give longer thought to the examination and strengthening of my exposition. But I indignantly replied that it was not my custom to advance by practice but rather by intelligence; and added that either I abandoned the contest altogether or they, abiding by my judgment, must come to my lecture without delay. And my first lecture indeed few attended, since that to all it seemed ridiculous that I, who hitherto had been almost wholly unacquainted with Holy Writ, should so hastily approach it. To all, however, who did attend, that lecture was so pleasing that they extolled it with singular commendation, and compelled me to furnish further glosses in the style of my first lecture. Which becoming known, those who had not been present began to flock eagerly to my second lecture and my third, and all alike were solicitous at the start of each to take down in writing the glosses which I had begun on the first day.

Chapter IV. Of the persecution of him by his master Anselm.

WHEREFORE the old man aforesaid, being stirred by vehement envy, and having already been stimulated against me by the persuasion of divers persons, as I have before recounted, began no less to persecute me over the Holy Scriptures than our *William* had aforetime done over philosophy. Now there were at the time in this old man's school two who appeared to predominate over the rest, namely *Alberic* of Rheims and *Lotulph*, a Lombard: who, the more they presumed upon themselves, were the more kindled against me. And so, his mind greatly perturbed by their suggestions, as later it came to light, this old man boldly forbade me to continue further the work of interpretation which I had begun in his place of teaching. Advancing this pretext forsooth, that if perchance I were to write anything in error in my work, being still untrained in that study, it might be imputed to him. This coming to the ears of the scholars, they were moved with the utmost indignation against so manifest a calumny of envy, the like of which had never befallen any man yet. Which, the more manifest it was, the more honourable was it to me, and so by persecution my fame increased.

Chapter V. How, having returned to Paris, he completed the interpretations which he had begun to deliver at Laon.

So, after a few days, returning to Paris, the schools that had long before been intended for me and offered to me, from which I had at first been driven out, I held for some years in quiet, and there at the opening of my course I strove to complete those interpretations of *Ezekiel* which I had begun at Laon. Which indeed were so acceptable to their readers that they believed me to be no less adept in the Holy Scriptures than they had seen me to be in philosophy. Whence in both kinds of study our school vehemently multiplying, what pecuniary gain and what reputation it brought me cannot have failed to reach your ears. But inasmuch as prosperity ever puffs up fools, and worldly tranquillity enervates the vigour of the mind, and easily loosens it by carnal allurements, when now I esteemed myself as reigning alone in the world as a philosopher, nor was afraid of any further disturbance, I began to give rein to my lust, who hitherto had lived in the greatest continence. And the farther I advanced in philosophy or in the Holy Scriptures, the farther I receded by the impurity of my life from philosophers and divines. For it is well known that philosophers, not to say divines, that is to say men intent on the exhortations of Holy Scripture, have excelled principally by the grace of continence. When, therefore, I was labouring wholly in pride and lechery, the remedy for either malady was by divine grace conferred on me, albeit unwilling; and first for lechery, then for pride. For lechery, indeed, by depriving me of those parts with which I practised it; but for the pride which was born in me from my surpassing knowledge of letters, as is said by the Apostle: "Knowledge puffeth up"—by humiliating me by the burning of that book in which most I gloried. The story of both which things I wish you now to learn more accurately from a statement of the facts than by common hearsay, in the order in which they befell me. Since, therefore, I ever abhorred the uncleanness of harlots, and was withheld from the society of noble women by the assiduity of my studies, nor had ever held much conversation with those of the common sort, lewd fortune, as the saying is, caressing me, found a more convenient opportunity whereby she might the more easily dash me down from the pinnacle of this sublimity; so that in my overweening pride, and unmindful of the grace I had received, divine pity might recall me humbled to itself.

Chapter VI. How having fallen in love with Heloise *he was thereby wounded as well in body as in mind.*

Now there was in this city of Paris a certain young maiden by the name of *Heloise,* the niece of a certain Canon who was called *Fulbert,* who, so great was his love for her, was all the more diligent in his zeal to instruct her, so far as was in his power, in the knowledge of letters. Who, while in face she was not inferior to other women, in the abundance of her learning was supreme. For inasmuch as this advantage, namely literary knowledge, is rare in women, so much the more did it commend the girl and had won her the greatest renown throughout the realm. Seeing in her, therefore, all those things which are wont to attract lovers, I thought it suitable to join her with myself in love, and believed that I could effect this most easily. For such renown had I then, and so excelled in grace of youth and form, that I feared no refusal from whatever woman I might deem worthy of my love. All the more easily did I believe that this girl would consent to me in that I knew her both to possess and to delight in the knowledge of letters; even in absence it would be possible for us to reach one another's presence by written intermediaries, and to express many things more boldly in writing than in speech, and so ever to indulge in pleasing discussions.

So, being wholly inflamed with love for this girl, I sought an opportunity whereby I might make her familiar with me in intimate and daily conversation, and so the more easily lead her to consent. With which object in view, I came to terms with the aforesaid uncle of the girl, certain of his friends intervening, that he should take me into his house, which was hard by our school, at whatever price he might ask. Putting forward this pretext, that the management of our household gravely hindered my studies, and that the expense of it was too great a burden on me. Now he was avaricious, and most solicitous with regard to his niece that she should ever progress in the study of letters. For which two reasons I easily secured his consent and obtained what I desired, he being all agape for my money, and believing that his niece would gain something from my teaching. Whereupon earnestly beseeching me, he acceded to my wishes farther than I might presume to hope and served the purpose of my love: committing her wholly to my mastership, that as often as I returned from my school, whether by day or by night, I might devote my leisure to her instruction, and, if I found her idle, vehemently chastise her. In which matter, while marvelling greatly at his simplicity, I was no less stupefied within myself than if he had entrusted a tender lamb to a ravening wolf. For in giving her to me, not only to be taught but to be vehemently chastised, what else was he doing than giving every licence to my desires and providing an opportunity whereby, even if I did not wish, if I could not move her by blandishments I might the more easily bend her by threats and blows. But there were two things which kept him most of all from base suspicions, namely his love for his niece and the fame of my continence in the past.

What more need I say? First in one house we are united, then in one mind. So, under the pretext of discipline, we abandoned ourselves utterly to love, and those secret retreats which love demands, the study of our texts afforded us. And so, our books lying open before us, more words of love rose to our lips than of literature, kisses were more frequent than speech. Oftener went our hands to each other's bosom than to the pages; love turned our eyes more frequently to itself than it directed them to the study of the texts. That we might be the less suspected, blows were given at times, by love, not by anger, affection, not indignation, which surpassed all ointments in their sweetness. What more shall I say? No stage of love was omitted by us in our cupidity, and, if love could elaborate anything new, that we took in addition. The less experienced we were in these joys, the more ardently we persisted in them and the less satiety did they bring us. And the more this pleasure occupied me the less leisure could I find for my philosophy and to attend to my school. Most tedious was it for me to go to the school or to stay there; laborious likewise when I was keeping nightly vigils of love and daily of study. Which also so negligently and tepidly I now performed that I produced nothing from my mind but everything from memory; nor was I anything now save a reciter of things learned in the past, and if I found time to compose a few verses, they were amorous, and not secret hymns of philosophy. Of which songs the greater part are to this day, as thou knowest, repeated and sung in many parts, principally by those to whom a like manner of life appeals.

What was the sorrow, what the complaints, what the lamentations of my scholars when they became aware of this preoccupation, nay perturbation of my mind, it is not easy even to imagine. For few could fail to perceive a thing so manifest, and none, I believe, did fail save he to whose shame it principally reflected, namely the girl's uncle himself. Who indeed, when divers persons had at divers times suggested this to him, had been unable to believe it, both, as I have said above, on account of his unbounded affection for his niece and on account also of the well known continence of my previous life. For not readily do we suspect baseness in those whom we most love. Nor into vehement love can the base taint of suspicion find a way. Whence cometh the saying of Saint *Jerome* in his Epistle to *Sabinian* (the eight-and-fortieth): "We are always the last to learn of the evils of our own house, and remain ignorant of the vices of our children and wives when they are a song among the neighbours. But what one is the last to know one does at any rate come to know in time, and what all have learned it is not easy to keep hidden from one." And thus, several months having elapsed, it befell us also. Oh, what was the uncle's grief at this discovery!

What was the grief of the lovers themselves at their parting! What blushing and confusion for me! With what contrition for the girl's affliction was I afflicted! What floods of sorrow had she to bear at my shame! Neither complained of what had befallen himself, but each the other's misfortune. But this separation of our bodies was the greatest possible coupling of our minds, the denial of its satisfaction inflamed our love still further, the shame we had undergone made us more shameless, and the less we felt our shame the more expedient our action appeared. And so there occurred in us what the poets relate of Mars and Venus when they were taken. Not long after this, the girl found that she had conceived, and with the greatest exultation wrote to me on the matter at once, consulting me as to what I should decide to do; and so on a certain night, her uncle being absent, as we had planned together I took her by stealth from her uncle's house and carried her to my own country without delay. Where, in my sister's house, she stayed until such time as she was delivered of a man child whom she named *Astrolabe.*

Her uncle, however, after her flight, being almost driven mad, with what grief he boiled, with what shame he was overwhelmed no one who had not beheld him could imagine. How he should act towards me, what snares he should lay for me he knew not. If he were to kill me, or to injure my body in any way, he feared greatly lest his beloved niece might be made to pay the penalty in my country. To seize my person and coerce me anywhere against my will was of no avail, seeing that I was constantly on my guard in this respect, because I had no doubt that he would speedily assault me if it were worth his while or if he dared. At length I, in some compassion for his exceeding anxiety and vehemently accusing myself of the fraud which my love had committed, as though of the basest treachery, went to supplicate the man, promising him also such further amends as he himself should prescribe. Nor, I asserted, did it appear remarkable to any who had experienced the force of love and retained a memory of the ruin to which even the greatest men, from the very beginning of the human race, had been brought down by women. And, that I might conciliate him beyond all that he could hope, I offered him the satisfaction of joining her whom I had corrupted to myself in marriage, provided that this were done in secret lest I incurred any detriment to my reputation. He assented, and with his own word and kiss, as well as with those of his household, sealed the concord that I had required of him, the more easily to betray me.

Chapter VII. The afore-mentioned girl's dissuasion of him from marriage. He takes her, however, to wife.

STRAIGHTWAY I, returning to my country, brought back my mistress that I might make her my wife. She, however, did not at all approve this action, nay utterly deprecated it for two reasons, namely the danger as well as the disgrace to myself. She vowed that he could never be placated by any satisfaction in the matter, as the event proved. She asked me, also, what glory she was like to have from me when she made me inglorious and equally humiliated herself and me. What a penalty this world would be entitled to exact from her if she took from it so bright a lantern, what maledictions, what prejudice to the Church, what tears of philosophers would follow such a marriage. How indecorous, how lamentable it would be were I to dedicate myself, whom nature had created for all mankind, to a single woman, and subject myself to so base a condition. She vehemently detested this marriage, because it was in every respect a shame and a burden to me. She set before me at the same time my own disgrace and the difficulties of matrimony which the Apostle exhorts us to avoid when he says: "Art thou loosed from a wife? Seek not a wife. But and if thou marry, thou hast not sinned; and if a virgin marry, she hath not sinned. Nevertheless such shall have trouble in the flesh: but I spare you." And again: "But I would have you without carefulness."

But if I accepted neither the counsel of the Apostle nor the exhortations of the Saints as to the heavy yoke of marriage, at least, she said, I should hearken to the philosophers, and pay regard to what things were written by them or concerning them on this matter. Which in great measure the Saints also diligently do for our censure. As in that passage of Saint *Jerome* in his First Book against *Jovinian*, where he recalls that *Theophrastus*, after diligently expounding in great detail the intolerable annoyances of marriage, and its perpetual disquietudes, shewed by the clearest reasoning that a wise man ought not to take a wife, where he himself also ends these reasonings of philosophic exhortation with the following conclusion: "What Christian does not *Theophrastus* confound, arguing thus?" In the same book, she went on, "*Cicero*," saith *Jerome*, "being asked by *Hircius* that after the repudiation of *Terentia* he would marry his sister, absolutely refused to do so, saying that he could not give his attention at the same time to a wife and to philosophy. He does not say, 'give attention,' but he adds what is tantamount that he does not wish to do anything which can be reckoned equal with the study of philosophy." But, to say no more of this obstacle to philosophic study, consider the state itself of honourable conversation. For what concord is there between pupils and serving-maids, desks and cradles, books or tablets and distaves, styles or pens and spindles? Who, either, intent upon sacred or philosophic meditations can endure the wailing of children, the lullabies of the nurses soothing them, the tumultuous mob of the household, male as well as female? Who, moreover, will have strength to tolerate the foul and incessant squalor of babes? The rich, you will say, can, whose palaces or ample abodes contain retreats, of which their opulence does not feel the cost nor is it tormented by daily worries. But the condition of philosophers is not, I say, as that of the rich, nor do those who seek wealth or involve themselves in secular cares devote themselves to divine or philosophic duties. Wherefore also the eminent philosophers of yore, utterly despising the world, not so much leaving the age as flying from it, forbade themselves all kinds of pleasure, that they might rest in the embrace of their philosophy alone. One of whom, and the greatest, *Seneca*, instructing *Lucilius*, saith (in his three-and-seventh epistle): "When thou mayest be idle is no time for philosophy, we must neglect all else that we may devote ourselves to this for which no time is long enough." It matters little whether one omit or be intermittent in the study of philosophy; for where it is interrupted it does not remain. We must resist other occupations, and not extend them but put them away. What now among us they endure who rightly are called monks, those endured also from desire for philosophy who stood out among the Gentiles as noble philosophers.

For among every people, Gentile as well as Jewish or Christian, some men have always stood out by faith or by the respectability of their morals, taking pre-eminence over the rest, and segregating themselves from the people by some singularity of continence or abstinence. Among the Jews, indeed, in ancient times, the Nazarites, who consecrated themselves to the Lord according to the Law, or the Sons of the Prophets, followers of *Elias* or *Eliseus*, of whom (as witnesseth Saint *Jerome*, in his fourth and thirteenth epistles) we read in the Old Testament as monks. More recently, also, those three sects of philosophy which *Josephus* distinguishes in the Eighteenth Book of Antiquities, some Pharisees, others Sadducees and others Essenes. But among us, the monks, who imitate either the common life of the Apostles or that earlier and solitary life of *John*. And among the Gentiles, as has been said, the philosophers. For the name Wisdom or Philosophy they applied not so much to the perception of learning as to strictness of life, as we learn from the derivation of the word itself, and also from the testimony of the Saints. Of which is that passage of Saint *Augustine* in the eighth book, Of the City of God, where he distinguishes the races of philosophers: "The Italian race had as their founder *Pythagoras* the Samian, from whom the very name Philosophy is said to have been derived. For whereas before him they were called wise who appeared to outshine the rest by some manner of praiseworthy living, he being asked what was his profession replied that he was a philosopher, that is a student or lover of wisdom, for to profess oneself wise seemed to him the height of arrogance." So in the passage where it is said: "who appeared to outshine the rest by some manner of praiseworthy living," it is clearly shewn that the wise men of the Gentiles, that is to say the philosophers, were so named rather in praise of their lives than of their learning. How soberly, though, and continently these lived it is not for me now to shew by examples, lest I seem to be offering instruction to Minerva herself. If, however, laymen and Gentiles lived thus, bound by no profession of religion, how does it behove thee, who art a clerk and a canon, to act, that thou prefer not base pleasures to thy sacred duties, that this Charybdis swallow thee not quick, that thou immerse not thyself shamelessly and irrevocably in these obscenities? Nay, if thou care not for the prerogative of the clerk, do thou at least defend the dignity of the philosopher. If the reverence due to God be contemned, at least let the love of honour temper thy shamelessness. Remember that *Socrates* was wedded, and with how sordid a case he first purged that stain on philosophy, that thereafter other men might by his example be made more prudent. Which is not overlooked by *Jerome*, writing of the said *Socrates* in his first against *Jovinian:* "Once upon a time, when he had withstood the endless invective poured upon him by *Xanthippe* from an upper storey, being drenched with unclean water he made no more answer than, as he wiped his head: 'I knew that rain must follow all that thunder.'" Finally she observed both how dangerous it would be for me to bring her back, and how much dearer it would be to her, and more honourable to me, to be called mistress than wife, that affection alone might hold me, not any force of the nuptial bond fasten me to her; and that we ourselves, being parted for a time, would find the joy of meeting all the keener, the rarer our meetings were.

With these and similar arguments seeking to persuade or dissuade me, since she could not bend my obstinacy, nor bear to offend me, sighing vehemently and weeping, she brought her exhortation to an end in this manner. One thing, she said, remains to the last, that after the ruin of us both our suffering may be no less than the love before it. Nor in this speech, as the whole world was to know, was the spirit of prophecy lacking. And so, commending our infant son to my sister, we returned privily to Paris, and a few days later, having kept secret vigils of prayer by night in a certain church, there at the point of dawn, in the presence of her uncle and divers of our own and his friends, we were plighted together by the nuptial benediction.

Presently we withdrew privily apart, nor did we see each other afterwards save seldom and by stealth, concealing as far as possible what we had done. Her uncle, however, and his servants, seeking a solace for their ignominy began to divulge the marriage that had been celebrated, and to break the promise they had given me on that head. But she began to anathematise to the contrary, and to swear that their story was altogether false. Whereby he being vehemently moved began to visit her with frequent contumely.

On learning of this I removed her to a certain Abbey of nuns near Paris, which is called Argenteuil, where she herself as a young girl had been bred up and schooled. The garments also of religion, which befitted the monastic profession, except the veil, I had fashioned for her and put them on her. Hearing which, the uncle and his kinsmen and associates were of the opinion that I had played a trick on them, and had taken an easy way to rid myself of *Heloise*, making her a nun. Whereat vehemently indignant, and conspiring together against me, on a certain night while I slumbered and slept in an inner room of my lodging, having corrupted a servant of mine with money, they punished me with a most cruel and shameful vengeance, and one that the world received with the utmost amazement: amputating, to wit, those parts of my body wherewith I had committed that of which they complained. Who presently taking flight, two of them who could be caught were deprived of their eyes and genitals. One of whom was the servant afore-mentioned, who while he remained with me in my service was by cupidity led to my betrayal.

Chapter VIII. Of the injury to his body. He becomes a monk in the Monastery of Saint Denis: Heloise a nun at Argenteuil.

BUT day coming the whole town congregating round about me, with what amazement they were transfixed, with what an outcry they lamented, with what clamour they wearied me, with what tribulations disturbed me it would be difficult, nay impossible to relate. The clergy principally, and most of all my scholars tormented me with intolerable lamentations and wailings, so that I was hurt far more by their compassion than by the passion of my wound, felt more occasion to blush than to bleed, and was troubled rather by modesty than by pain. It occurred to my mind with what glory I had but recently shone, how easily and in a moment this had been brought low, nay, utterly extinguished. By how just a judgment of God was I stricken in that portion of my body wherein I had sinned. With how just a betrayal had the man repaid me for my former betrayal of him. With what shouts of praise would my rivals extol so manifest an equity. What contrition of perpetual grief would this stroke bring to my family and friends. With what expansion would this matchless infamy occupy the minds of the whole world. What way would lie open to me thereafter, with what face would I appear in public, to be pointed out by every finger, scarified by every tongue, doomed to be a monstrous spectacle to all.

Nor did it less confound me that, according to the letter of the Law, that killeth, there is so great abomination of eunuchs before God that men who have been made eunuchs by the amputation or bruising of their stones are forbidden to enter the Church, as though they were stinking and unclean, and that in the sacrifice even animals of that sort are utterly rejected. As it is written in Leviticus, the twenty-second chapter and twenty-fourth verse: "Ye shall not offer unto the Lord that which is bruised, or crushed, or broken, or cut;" and in Deuteronomy, the twenty-third chapter and first verse: "He that is wounded in the stones, or hath his privy member cut off, shall not enter into the congregation of the Lord." Plunged in so wretched a contrition, it was the confusion of shame, I confess, rather than the devotion of conversion that drove me to the retirement of a monastic cloister. She, moreover, had already at my command willingly taken the veil and entered a convent. And so both the two of us at one time put on the sacred habit, I in the Abbey of Saint Denis and she in the Convent of Argenteuil aforesaid. Who indeed, I remember, when divers in compassion of her tried vainly to deter so young a woman from the yoke of the monastic rule, as from an intolerable burden, breaking out, as best she could amid her tears and sobs, into that famous complaint of *Cornelia*, answered:

> Great husband, undeserving of my bed!
> What right had I to bow so lofty a head?
> Why, impious female, did I marry thee,
> To cause thy hurt? Accept the penalty
> That of my own free will I'll undergo . . .

And with these words she hastened to the altar and straightway, before the Bishop, took the blessed veil from the altar and publicly bound herself to the monastic profession.

Meanwhile I had scarcely recovered from my injury when the clergy, pouring in upon me, began to make incessant demands both of our Abbot and of myself, that what hitherto I had done from eagerness for wealth or praise I should study now to do for the love of God, considering that the talent which had been entrusted to me by God would be demanded of me by Him with usury, and that I who hitherto had aimed principally at the rich should henceforth devote myself to the education of the poor. And to this end chiefly, I should know that the hand of the Lord had touched me, namely that being naturally set free from carnal snares and withdrawn from the turmoil of secular life, I might devote myself to the study of letters. Nor should I become a philosopher of the world so much as of God.

Now this Abbey of ours to which I had repaired was entirely abandoned to the secular life, and that of the lewdest. Whereof the Abbot himself exceeded the rest of us no more in rank than in the dissoluteness and notorious infamy of his life. Their intolerable filthiness I frequently and vehemently, now in private now publicly attacking, made myself burdensome and odious beyond measure to them all. And so, greatly rejoicing at the daily importunities of my pupils, they sought an opportunity whereby they might remove me from their midst. And so my pupils long continuing to insist, and importuning the Abbot also, and the brethren intervening, I withdrew to a certain cell, to devote myself as of old to my school. Thereto indeed so great a multitude of scholars poured in that neither was the place sufficient for their lodging nor the soil for their sustenance. There, as more became my profession, giving my attention principally to the Holy Scriptures, I did not altogether lay aside the teaching of the secular arts in which I was more fully versed, and which they demanded most of me; but made of them, as it were, a hook wherewith I might draw them, enticed by the philosophic savour, to the study of the true philosophy, as (the Ecclesiastical History reminds us) was the custom of the greatest of the Christian philosophers, *Origen.* Inasmuch, therefore, as the Lord appeared to have conferred on me no less of His grace in the Holy Scriptures than in profane letters, our school began to multiply exceedingly in both classes, and all the rest to be greatly attenuated. Whereby I aroused the envy and hatred of the other masters against myself. Who detracting me in every way possible, two of them in particular were always objecting to me in my absence that it was evidently contrary to the profession of a monk to be detained by the study of secular books, and that, without myself having had a master, I had presumed to aspire to a mastership in the Holy Scripture, seeking evidently thus to interdict me from every exercise of scholastic teaching, whereto they incessantly incited Bishops, Archbishops, Abbots and whatever persons bearing a name in religion they might approach.

Chapter IX. Of the book of his Theology, and of the persecution which he bore from his fellow-students. A Council is held against him.

Now it so happened that I applied myself first to lecturing on the fundamentals of our faith by the analogy of human reason, and composed a certain tractate of theology, Of Unity and the Holy Trinity, for our scholars, who were asking for human and philosophical reasons, and demanded rather what could be understood than what could be stated, saying indeed that the utterance of words was superfluous which the intelligence did not follow, nor could anything be believed unless first it had been understood, and that it was ridiculous for anyone to preach to others what neither he himself nor they whom he taught could comprehend with their intellect, Our Lord Himself complaining that such were "blind leaders of the blind." Which tractate indeed, when numbers had seen and read it, began generally to please its readers, because it appeared to satisfy all alike upon these questions. And inasmuch as these questions appeared difficult beyond all others, the more their gravity was admitted, the more subtle my solution of them was considered to be, whereupon my rivals, vehemently incensed, assembled a Council against me, principally those two old plotters, namely *Alberic* and *Lotulph*, who now that their and my masters, to wit *William* and *Anselm*, were defunct, sought as it were to reign alone in their room and also to succeed them as if they had been their heirs. Since moreover both of them were conducting schools at Rheims, by repeated suggestions they moved their Archbishop *Rodulph* against me, that associating with himself *Cono* Bishop of Palestrina, who then held the office of Legate in France, he should assemble a conventicle under the name of Council in the city of Soissons, and should invite me to appear there, bringing with me that famous work which I had written about the Holy Trinity. And so it came to pass. But before I came there, those two rivals of mine so diffamed me among the clergy and the people, that almost the people stoned me and the few of my disciples who had come with me on the first day of our arrival; saying that I preached and had written that there were three Gods, as they themselves had been assured.

I, however, as soon as I had reached the town sought out the Legate; I gave him my book for his perusal and judgment, and declared myself, if I had written anything that was dissentient from the Catholic Faith, ready to receive correction or to give satisfaction. But he at once enjoined me to take the book to the Archbishop and to my two rivals, that they themselves might judge me who were my accusers on that count, that it might be fulfilled in me: "even our enemies themselves being judges." They, however, repeatedly perusing and searching the book, and finding nothing that they dared bring forward against me in the audience, adjourned to the end of the Council the condemnation of the book for which they were panting. But I, on each several day before the Council sat, publicly expounded the Catholic Faith to all according to what I had written, and all who heard me with great admiration commended both my exposition of the words and my sense. Which when the people and the clergy saw they began in turn to say: "Lo, now he speaks in public and no one answers him anything. And the Council is coming rapidly to an end, that was convened principally, as we have heard, against him. Can it be that his judges have recognised that they, rather than he, are in error?" Wherefore my rivals were daily more and more inflamed.

And so one day *Alberic* coming to me with evil intent, and certain of his disciples, after divers bland words said that he marvelled at one thing which he had noticed in that book: namely that whereas God begat God, and there was but one God, I denied that God had begotten Himself. To which straightway I replied: "On this point, if you wish it, I will reason." "We pay no heed," said he, "to human reason, nor to our own sense in such matters, but only to the words of authority." To which I: "Turn the page of the book, and you will find the authority." And there was a copy of the book at hand, which he had brought with him. I turned to the place, which I knew, and which he had failed to observe, or else he sought there only what might harm me. And there was a sentence entitled: *Augustine* On the Trinity, Book I, Chapter 1: "Whoso supposes God to be so powerful as Himself to have begotten Himself, errs the more greatly in that not only God is not so; but no creature, either spiritual or corporeal. For there is nothing whatsoever that may beget itself." Which when his disciples, who were present, had heard, they were stupefied and blushed. But he, that he might cover himself as best he could, said: "It is well that it should be understood." To which I subjoined that this was nothing new, but for the present it was of little import, since he had required of me words only, and not sense. If, however, he wished me to give him sense and reason, I declared myself ready to shew him, according to his own opinion, that he had fallen into that heresy by which the Father is His own Son.

Which when he had heard, as though straightway made furious, he turned to threats, asserting that neither my reasons nor the authorities would avail me in this case. And so he withdrew. But on the last day of the Council, before they took their seats, the Legate and the Archbishop began to discuss at length with my rivals, and with divers persons, what should be decided about me and my book, the matter for which principally they had been called together. And as neither in my speech nor in the writings that were before them had they aught that they might charge against me, all being silent for a little space, or less open in their detraction of me, *Geoffrey*, Bishop of Chartres, who had precedence over the other Bishops by the fame of his piety and the dignity of his see, thus began: "All of you, Sirs, that are here present know that this man's teaching, whatsoever it be, and his intellect have had many supporters and followers in whatsoever he has studied, that he has greatly diminished the fame as well of his own masters as of ours, and that, so to speak, his vine has spread its branches from sea to sea. If, as I do not think, ye condemn him by prejudice, even rightly, ye must know that ye will offend many, and there will not be wanting those who will wish to defend him; especially as in the writing here present we see nothing which may deserve any open calumny; and as is said by *Jerome*: 'Strength that is manifest ever excites jealousy, and the lightnings strike the highest mountain peaks.' Take heed lest ye confer more renown on him by violent action, and lest we earn more reproach for ourselves by the envy than for him by the justice of the charge. For a false rumour, as the aforesaid Doctor, in his Tenth Epistle, reminds us, is quickly stifled, and a man's later life pronounces judgment on his past. But if ye are disposed to act canonically against him, let his dogma or his writing be brought into our midst, and let him be questioned and allowed freely to reply, that convicted or confessing his error he be henceforward silent. Following at least those words of Saint *Nicodemus*, when, desirous of setting Our Lord Himself at liberty, he said: 'Doth our law judge any man before it hear him and know what he doeth?' "

Hearing which straightway my rivals interrupting him cried out: "O wise counsel, that we should contend against his verbosity whose arguments or sophisms the entire world could not withstand!" But of a surety it was far more difficult to contend with Christ Himself, and yet *Nicodemus* invited that He should be heard according to the sanction of the law. When therefore the Bishop could not induce their minds to consent to what he had proposed, he tried by another way to restrain their envy; saying that for the discussion of so weighty a matter the few who were present could not suffice, and that this case needed a greater examination. His advice was, further, that to my Abbey, that is the monastery of Saint Denis, my Abbot, who was there present, should recall me; and that there, a greater number of more learned persons being called together, by a more diligent examination it should be decided what was to be done in the matter. The Legate assented to this last counsel, and so all the rest. Thereafter presently the Legate rose that he might celebrate Mass, before he entered the Council, and sent to me by the Bishop the licence that had been granted, namely to return to my monastery, and there to await what should be determined.

Then my rivals, considering that they had achieved nothing if this business should be carried on outside their diocese, where forsooth they would not be able to sit in judgment, little trusting evidently in justice, persuaded the Archbishop that it was assuredly ignominious to himself if this case were to be transferred to another audience, and that it would be most dangerous if in that way I escaped. And straightway hastening to the Legate, they succeeded in altering his opinion and brought him reluctantly to the position that he should condemn the book without any inquiry, and at once burn it in the sight of all, and condemn me to perpetual enclosure in a strange monastery. For they said that for the condemnation of the book this ought to be sufficient, that I had ventured publicly to read it, though commended by the authority neither of the Roman Pontiff nor of the Church, and had given it to be copied by many. And this would be of great benefit to the Christian faith, if by my example a similar presumption were prevented in others. And because the Legate was less a scholar than he should have been he relied principally on the Archbishop's advice, as the Archbishop on theirs. Which the Bishop of Chartres foreseeing straightway reported these machinations to me, and vehemently exhorted me that I should suffer them the more quietly, the more violently it was evident to all that they were acting. And that I must not doubt that this violence of so manifest an envy would go greatly against them and in my favour. Nor should I be at all perturbed over my confinement in a monastery, knowing that the Legate himself, who was doing this under compulsion, after a few days, when he had removed from the place, would set me wholly at liberty. And so he gave me what comfort he might, and to himself also, both of us in tears.

Chapter X. Of the burning of his book. Of his persecution by the Abbot and his brethren.

AND so being summoned I went straightway before the Council, and without any process of discussion they compelled me to cast my aforesaid book upon the fire. And thus it was burned, when, as they seemed to be saying nothing, one of my adversaries was heard to murmur that he understood it to be written in the book that God the Father alone was Almighty. Which when the Legate understood, greatly marvelling, he answered him that it was not to be believed of any little child that he would so err: "When our common Faith," he said, "holds and professes that there are Three Almighty." Hearing which a certain *Terric*, a master of a school, laughingly quoted the words of *Athanasius* (in the Creed): "yet there are not Three Almighties but One Almighty." And, when the Bishop began to chide and reprove him as one guilty of speaking against authority, boldly gainsaid him and, recalling the words of *Daniel*, said: "Thus, ye foolish children of Israel, neither judging nor knowing the truth, ye have condemned the daughter of Israel. Return to judgment," and judge the judge himself, ye who have set up such a judge for the instruction of the Faith and the correction of error: who when he ought to judge out of his own mouth hath condemned himself. This day, by divine mercy, deliver him who is plainly innocent, like Susanna of old, from his false accusers.

Then the Archbishop rising confirmed the sentence of the Legate, changing the words as was required. "Verily, Sir," he said, "the Father is Almighty, the Son is Almighty and the Holy Ghost is Almighty, and whoso dissenteth from this is evidently in error, nor is he to be heard. And yet, if it please thee, it is well that this our brother expound his faith before us all, that it be either approved or disapproved and corrected, as may be fitting." But when I rose to profess and expound my faith, that what I felt, I might express in my own words; my adversaries said that nothing else was necessary than that I should recite the Creed of *Athanasius*, which any boy could have done as well as I. And lest I should put forward the excuse of ignorance, as though I were not familiar with the words they had the written text brought for me to read.

I read it amid sighs, sobs and tears as best I could. Then like a criminal and a convict I was handed over to the Abbot of Saint Medard, who was present, and committed to his cloister as though to a gaol. And straightway the Council was dissolved. Now the Abbot and monks of that monastery, thinking that I was to remain longer with them, received me with the greatest exultation and using every diligence tried in vain to comfort me. God, Who judgest equity, with what gall then, with what bitterness of mind did I, wretch that I was, challenge Thee, did I finally accuse Thee, constantly repeating that plaint of Saint *Anthony*: "Good Jesus, where wert Thou?" But with what grief I boiled, with what blushing I was confounded, with what desperation perturbed, I then could feel, I cannot now express. I compared with what I had aforetime suffered in my body what I was now enduring, and of all men reckoned myself the most unhappy. That other I regarded as a small betrayal in comparison with this outrage, and lamented far more the detriment to my fame than that to my body: since to the former I had come through my own fault, but to this so open a violence, a sincere intent and love of our Faith had brought me which had compelled me to write. But when all those to whom the report of it came vehemently protested that this had been cruelly and inconsiderately done, the several persons who had taken part in it, repelling the blame from themselves, heaped it each on the others, so much so that my rivals themselves denied that it had been done by their counsel, and the Legate publicly deplored the jealousy of the French in this matter. Who being straightway moved to repentance, after some days, since at the time under compulsion he had given satisfaction to their jealousy, transferred me from the strange monastery to my own, where almost all the monks that had been there before were now, as I have already said, my enemies, for the vileness of their lives and their shameless conversation made suspect to them a man whose reproaches they could ill endure. And a few months having elapsed, fortune furnished them with an opportunity whereby they strove to undo me.

For it happened one day when I was lecturing that there came up a certain saying of *Bede*, when in expounding the Acts of the Apostles he asserts that *Denys* the Areopagite was Bishop of Corinth and not of Athens. Which seemed contrary to their taste, who boast that the famous Areopagite was their own *Denys*, whom his Acts profess to have been Bishop of Athens. Coming upon this I shewed it, as though jestingly, to certain of the brethren who were standing by. But they, greatly indignant, said that *Bede* was a most mendacious writer, and that they had a more truthful witness in *Hilduin*, their Abbot, who to investigate this matter had travelled long in Greece, and, having acquainted himself with the facts, had in the Acts of that Saint, which he compiled, veraciously removed all doubt. Whereupon one of them challenged me with an importunate question: what seemed to me the truth in this controversy, namely between *Bede* and *Hilduin?* I replied that the authority of *Bede*, whose writings the entire body of the Latin Churches consult, seemed to me the more acceptable. Whereat they, vehemently incensed, began to cry out, that now I had openly shewn that I had ever been the enemy of that our monastery, and that now I had greatly detracted from the whole realm, taking from it that honour wherein it singularly gloried when I denied that their Patron had been the Areopagite. I replied that neither had I denied this, nor was it any great matter whether he had been the Areopagite or had come from elsewhere, since he had won so bright a crown before God.

But they hastening straightway to the Abbot told him what they had made me say. Who readily gave ear to them, rejoicing to find any occasion whereby he might oppress me, fearing me the more as he himself lived so much more vilely than the rest. Then, his chapter summoned and the brethren congregated, he threatened me severely and said that he would send me immediately before the King. And I offered myself to the discipline of the rule, if I had in any way offended, but in vain. Then, horrified at their villainy and having borne for so long such adverse fortune, utterly despairing as though the whole world had conspired against me, with the help of a certain consensus of the brethren who took pity on me, and of certain of my disciples, I stole out secretly by night and made for the neighbouring lands of Count *Theobald*, where formerly I had sojourned in a cell. He moreover was both somewhat acquainted with me and was full of compassion for my oppressions, whereof he had heard. And so there I began to dwell in the town of Provins, to wit in a certain cell of monks of Troyes whose Prior had formerly been my bosom friend, and loved me dearly. Who, greatly rejoicing at my advent, cared for me with the utmost diligence.

Now it fell upon a day that our Abbot came to that town, to the aforesaid Count, upon certain business. Hearing of which, I went to the Count with this Prior, asking him to intercede for me with our Abbot, that he should pardon me and give me leave to live monastically wheresoever a suitable place might be found. And he and they that were with him took the matter into consideration, promising to reply to the Count that same day before they departed. But when they began their discussion, they decided that I wished to transfer myself to another Abbey, and that this would be a great disgrace to them. For they regarded it as the greatest glory to themselves that I had come to them on my conversion, as though despising all other Abbeys; and now they said that it would be the greatest reproach to them if, casting them off, I went elsewhere. Hence they would listen to nothing from me or from the Count on this matter. Nay, they straightway threatened me that if I did not speedily return they would excommunicate me. And that Prior, with whom I had taken refuge, they forbade in every way that he should not harbour me any longer, else he must share my excommunication. Hearing which, both the Prior and I were greatly troubled. But the Abbot departing in this obstinacy, a few days later died. And when another had succeeded him, I approached him with the Bishop of Meaux, that he might grant me what I had sought from his predecessor. And as he too did not at first acquiesce in the matter, certain of my friends thereafter intervening, I appealed to the King and his Council, and so obtained what I desired.

A certain *Stephen* who was the King's Steward at that time, summoning the Abbot and his friends, inquired of them why they wished to retain me against my will, whereby they might easily incur scandal and could gain nothing, since my life and theirs could in no way be made to agree. And I knew the opinion of the King's Council in the matter to be this, that the less regular that Abbey was the more it should be subject to the King and profitable, that is to say in temporal wealth. Wherefore I had believed that I should easily secure the consent of the King and his servants. And so it came to pass. But lest the monastery should lose the glorification which it had from me, they conceded me the right to remove to what wilderness I would, provided that I placed myself under the yoke of no Abbey. And this, in the presence of the King and his servants, was agreed and confirmed on either side.

I therefore took myself to a certain wilderness in the Troyes country which was known to me aforetime, and there, land having been given to me by certain persons with the assent of the Bishop of the place, built an oratory in the name of the Holy Trinity, making it at first of reeds and thatch. Where lying hidden with one of my clerks, I could truly declaim with the Lord: "Lo then did I wander far off and remain in the wilderness."

Chapter XI.

WHEN the scholars knew this they began to hasten in from all parts and, leaving cities and towns, to inhabit the wilderness; instead of their roomy homes, to construct for themselves little huts; instead of delicate viands, to live upon wild herbs and coarse bread; instead of soft beds, to lay down thatch for themselves and straw; and instead of tables to heap banks of turf; and verily you would have thought that they were imitating the early philosophers whom *Jerome* in his Second Book against *Jovinian* commemorates in these words: "Through the senses as it were through windows the vices gain entrance to the soul. The metropolis and citadel of the mind cannot be taken, unless a hostile army have broken in by the gates. If any delight in the circus, if in the contests of athletes, if in the agility of mummers, if in the beauty of women, if in the splendour of jewels, garments and other things of the sort, by the windows of the eyes is captured the liberty of the soul, and that prophecy is fulfilled: 'For death is come up into our windows.' When therefore by these gates wedged columns as it were of perturbation have entered the citadel of our mind, where shall its liberty be, where its fortitude, where its thoughts of God? Especially when the touch depicts to itself also past pleasures and forces the soul to suffer the memory of its vices, and in a sense to experience what it refrains from doing. Invited then by these considerations, many philosophers have left the crowded cities and suburban gardens, where the watered meadows, the foliage of trees, the twittering of birds, the mirror of the spring murmuring with rivulets are so many snares of eyes and ears, lest the strength of their souls should grow soft through the luxury and abundance of their resources, and their modesty be debauched. Indeed, it is of no profit to see often the things whereby thou mayest at any time be caught, and to commit thyself to an experience of things which thou canst with difficulty forego. For the Pythagoreans also, declining associations of this sort, were wont to dwell in the wilderness and the solitary place." But *Plato* himself also, albeit he was a rich man and *Diogenes* trampled his bed with muddy feet, that he might find time for philosophy chose for academy a villa remote from the city, in a place not only deserted but pestilential also, in order that by the trouble and assiduity of sickness the assaults of lust might be broken, and that his disciples might feel no other delight save in those things which they studied. Such a life also the Sons of the Prophets, the followers of *Elisha*, are reported to have led, of whom also *Jerome*, as of the monks of that time, writes among other things to the monk *Rusticus:* "The Sons of the Prophets, who are described as monks in the Old Testament, built for themselves huts by the river Jordan, and turning away from cities lived upon meal and wild herbs." Such huts our disciples built for themselves by the river Arduzon, seeming hermits rather than scholars.

But the greater the confluence of scholars thither, and the harder the life they endured under my teaching, the more glorious my rivals reckoned it to me, and to themselves ignominious. Who, when they had done all that they could against me, were pained to see everything work together for my good, and so I, in the words of *Jerome*, remote from cities, markets, courts and crowds was sought out even in my retreat, as *Quintilian* says, by jealousy. Complaining privily among themselves and lamenting, they began to say:

"Lo, the whole world has gone away after him, we have gained nothing by persecuting him but have made him the more glorious. We sought to extinguish his fame, we have but made it shine the brighter. Lo, in the cities scholars have all things necessary at hand, and scorning civilised delights they flock to the poverty of the wilderness and of their own accord become wretched."

Now at that time it was intolerable poverty that principally drove me to the governance of a school, since dig I could not and to beg I was ashamed. And so reverting to the art which I knew, instead of the labour of my hands I was driven to the office of my tongue. But my scholars of their own accord prepared what was necessary for me, as well in food as in raiment or the tilling of the fields, or again in the expense of building, so that no domestic cares should hinder me from study. But as our oratory could not hold even a modest part of them, of necessity they enlarged it and building with stone and timber made it more seemly. Which though it was founded and afterwards dedicated in the name of the Holy Trinity, yet because I was a fugitive there and, when in such despair, had by the grace of divine comfort drawn breath a little, in memory of that benefit I named Paraclete. And many hearing of this received the news with great astonishment, and several vehemently denounced my action, saying that it was not lawful that any church should be assigned to the Holy Spirit especially, more than to God the Father, but either to the Son alone or to the whole Trinity at once, according to ancient custom.

To which calumny this error, doubtless, chiefly led them, that they believed there to be no distinction between the Paraclete and the Ghost Paraclete. Whereas the Trinity itself also, and any Person of the Trinity, as He is called God or Helper, so may rightly be named Paraclete, that is Comforter, as is said by the Apostle: "Blessed be God, even the Father of our Lord Jesus Christ, the Father of mercies, and the God of all comfort; who comforteth us in all our tribulation," and according to what the Truth saith: "And He shall give you another Comforter." What is to prevent, therefore, when the whole Church is consecrated alike in the Name of the Father and of the Son and of the Holy Ghost, nor doth any of Them possess anything separately, that the house of the Lord be so ascribed to the Father or to the Holy Ghost as to the Son? Who will presume to erase from the front of the porch the title of Him Whose is the house itself. Or, since the Son has offered Himself as a sacrifice to the Father, and for that reason in the celebration of masses prayers are addressed especially to the Father and an immolation is made of the Host, why may the altar not appear to be principally His, to Whom supplication and sacrifice are mainly offered? Cannot the altar be said rightly to be more His to Whom, than His of Whom the sacrifice is made? Or will any profess that the altar is rather that of the Lord's Cross, or of the Sepulchre, or Holy *Michael*'s or *John*'s or *Peter*'s, or any other saint's, who neither are sacrificed there nor is sacrifice made to them nor are prayers addressed to them? Surely not even among idolaters were altars or temples said be to be any's save theirs to whom they intended to offer the sacrifice and service.

But haply some one may say that for this reason neither church nor altars should be dedicated to the Father, because no action by Him exists which may entitle Him to a special solemnity. But this argument detracts from the Trinity Itself, while from the Holy Ghost it does not detract. Since the Holy Ghost Himself by His coming hath the solemnity of Pentecost, as the Son by His hath the feast of the Nativity. For as the Son was sent into the world, so the Holy Ghost coming to the Disciples claims His proper solemnity. To Whom also a temple seems more fitly ascribed than to either of the other Persons, if we diligently attend to Apostolic authority and to the Holy Ghost Himself. For to none of the Three Persons does the Apostle specially ascribe a temple, save to the Holy Ghost. For he says, not the temple of the Father nor the temple of the Son but the temple of the Holy Ghost, writing thus in the First Epistle to the Corinthians: "But he that is joined unto the Lord is one Spirit." And again: "Know ye not that your body is the temple of the Holy Ghost which is in you, which ye have of God, and ye are not your own?" Who, moreover, does not know that the sacraments of divine benefits which are brought to pass in the Church are ascribed specially to the operation of Divine Grace, whereby is understood the Holy Ghost? For by water and the Holy Ghost are we reborn in baptism, and then first are we constituted as a special temple for God. In confirmation also the sevenfold Grace of the Holy Ghost is conferred, whereby the temple of God itself is adorned and dedicated. What wonder then if to that Person to whom the Apostle specially attributes the spiritual temple we ascribe a corporal? Or to what Person can the Church be said more rightly to belong than to Him to Whose operation all the benefits that are administered in the Church are specially assigned? Not thus, however, were we reasoning if, when we first named our oratory Paraclete, we professed to have dedicated it to one Person, but for that reason which we have stated above, to wit in memory of the comfort afforded us. Although if we had done it in that manner which is commonly believed it would not be against reason, albeit unknown to custom.

Chapter XII. Of his persecution by certain seeming new apostles.

AND so my body lay hidden in this place but my fame went out through the entire world, and, like that poetical figment which is called *Echo*, sounded far and wide. It is so called because it hath much voice but no substance. My former rivals, since in themselves they were now of less account, stirred up against me certain new apostles, in whom the world greatly believed. Of whom one boasted that he had reformed the life of the Canons Regular, the other that of the monks. These men, as they went preaching about the world and shamelessly slandering me in whatever way they could, made me for the time not a little contemptible as well to certain ecclesiastical as to the secular powers, and of my faith as of my life disseminated reports so sinister that they turned from me even the chief of my own friends, and those who hitherto had retained some of their old affection for me dissimulated this in every way from fear of them. God Himself is my witness, as often as I heard that any gathering of ecclesiastical persons had assembled, I imagined it to be purposing my condemnation. Stupefied as by the impact of a thunderbolt, I expected to be brought as a heretic or profane person before councils or synagogues. And, to compare the flea with the lion, the ant with the elephant, with no gentler spirit did my rivals persecute me than, of old, the heretics *Athanasius.* And often (God wot) I fell into such despair that, crossing the bounds of Christendom, I was ready to remove among the heathen, and there in quiet, by some arrangement of tribute, to live christianly among the enemies of Christ. Who, I believed, would be entirely propitious to me, since from the charge levelled against me they would suspect me to be the less a Christian, and on that account would believe that I could be the more readily inclined towards their sect.

Chapter XIII. Of the Abbey to which he was called, and of his persecution as well by his sons, that is the monks, as by the tyrant.

But while I was being incessantly afflicted by so great perturbations, and had come to this last resort, that among Christ's enemies I should flee to Christ: seizing a certain opportunity whereby I believed that I might escape a little from those toils, I fell among Christians, and monks, far more savage than the heathen, and worse. There was in Brittany, in the Bishopric of Vannes, a certain Abbey of Saint Gildas called de Ruys, left desolate by the death of its shepherd. To which the unanimous election of the brethren with the assent of the lord of the place summoned me, and from our Abbot and brethren demanded and easily won permission. Thus the jealousy of the French drove me to the West as that of the Romans drove *Jerome* to the East. For never

(God wot) would I have acquiesced in this except that I might escape from those oppressions which, as I have said, I had incessantly to endure. The country was barbarous and the speech of the country strange to me; the vile and intractable life of these monks was known to all, and the people of the country were inhuman and uncouth. So, like a man who terrified by a sword that is hanging over him dashes towards a precipice, and just as in the nick of time he avoids one death incurs another, so I from one danger to another knowingly bore myself, and there by the waves of the roaring Ocean, since the ultimate ends of the Earth allowed me to flee no farther, often in my prayers repeated these words: "From the end of the earth will I cry unto Thee, when my heart is overwhelmed."

For of the anguish wherewith that undisciplined congregation of brethren, over whom I had undertaken to rule, lacerated my heart by day and night, when I thought of the dangers as well to my soul as to my body, no one I think is now unaware. I was certain, at least, that if I tried to compel them to the regular life which they had professed, it would cost me my own life. Whereas if I did not attempt this, to the utmost extent of my power, I was damned. The Abbey itself also a certain tyrant of great power in that country had long since subjugated to himself, taking the opportunity, in the disorder of the monastery, to appropriate all the lands adjoining it to his own uses and to grind down the monks themselves with heavier extortions than his Jewish tributaries. The monks came clamouring to me for their daily necessities, since then had nothing in common which I might administer to them, for each of them from his own purse supported himself and his concubine, their sons and daughters. They took delight in vexing me in this manner, and they themselves also stole and carried off what they could, so that falling short in the administration of what there was I might be compelled either to abandon my discipline or to retire altogether. And since the whole barbarian populace was similarly lawless and undisciplined, there were no men to whose aid I might resort, inasmuch as I dissented equally from the conduct of them all. Without, this tyrant and his satellites assiduously oppressed me; within, the brethren incessantly laid snares for me, until the state of things shewed that the words of the Apostle had been said specially of me: "Without were fightings, within were fears."

I considered, weeping, how useless and miserable a life I was leading, and how fruitlessly to myself as to others I was living, and how much I had formerly profited my clerks, whereas now that I had deserted them for the monks neither in them nor in the monks was I bearing any fruit, and how impotent I had proved in all my undertakings and endeavours, that now it might most properly be said of me by all men: "This man began to build and was not able to finish." I was in profound despair when I remembered from what I had escaped and considered what I was incurring, and esteeming my former troubles now as nothing often said to myself with sighs and groans: "Deservedly am I suffering thus, who deserting the Paraclete, that is the Comforter, thrust myself into certain desolation, and to escape from threats fled eagerly among certain dangers."

But this most of all tormented me, namely that having left our oratory I could not provide for the celebration of the Divine Office as was meet, inasmuch as the exceeding poverty of the place barely sufficed for the needs of one man. But the true Paraclete Himself brought me true comfort for this grief, and provided for His own oratory as was fitting. For it happened that our Abbot of Saint Denis acquired by fair means or foul that Abbey of Argenteuil wherein *Heloise*, my sister in Christ now rather than my wife, had taken the religious habit, as belonging by ancient right to his monastery, and forcibly expelled from it the convent of nuns over which my comrade held the priorship. When these were scattered in exile into divers places I realised that an opportunity had been furnished me by the Lord whereby I might provide for our oratory. For returning thither I invited her with certain others of the same congregation who had clung to her to the aforesaid oratory. And they being conveyed thither the oratory itself with all things pertaining thereto I surrendered and gave to them, and that donation of mine, with the assent and by the intervention of the Bishop of the place, Pope *Innocent* the Second corroborated to them and their successors by privilege in perpetuity.

At first indeed they endured there a life of hardship, and were for a time in great desolation, but shortly the protection of God's mercy, Whom they devoutly served, brought them comfort, and He shewed Himself to them a true Paraclete, and made the neighbouring peoples compassionate to them and propitious. And I think that they were more greatly (God wot) increased in one year in the fruits of the earth than I had been in a hundred had I remained there. For inasmuch as the feminine sex is feebler, so does their more wretched poverty more easily move the human heart, and their virtue is more pleasing to God as to man. And such grace in the eyes of men did the Lord bestow on that our sister, who was over the rest, that the Bishops loved her as a daughter, the Abbots as a sister, the laity as a mother; and all alike marvelled at her piety, her prudence, and in all things the incomparable meekness of her patience. And the more rarely she let herself be seen, that in a closed cell she might devote herself more purely to sacred meditations and prayers, the more ardently did those who dwelt without demand her presence and the admonitions of her spiritual conversation.

Chapter XIV. Of the scandal of his lewdness.

But when all the neighbours vehemently reproached me because I gave less succour to these women's poverty than I could and ought, and might easily, if only by my preaching, have earned this for them, I began to resort to them more often, that I might help them in what manner I could. Whereat the murmur of jealousy was not lacking, and what a sincere charity compelled me to do my detractors with their accustomed depravity most shamelessly denounced, saying that I was driven thither by some attraction of carnal concupiscence, and could hardly or never suffer the absence of the woman I had aforetime loved. I frequently repeated to myself that complaint of Saint *Jerome* who, in writing to *Asella* of feigned friends (in his nine-and-ninetieth Epistle), saith: "No fault is found in me save my sex, nor in that would fault ever be found save when *Paula* comes to Jerusalem." And again: "Before I knew the house of the holy *Paula*, my praises were sounded throughout the city, in the judgment of well-nigh all I was deemed worthy of the supreme Pontificate. But I know that through good and evil report we attain to the Kingdom of Heaven."

When, I say, I had called to mind this insult of detraction levelled at so great a man I derived from it no mean comfort, saying: "Oh, if my rivals found in me as great cause for suspicion, with what detraction would they oppress me! But now, when I, by divine mercy, have been set free from that suspicion, how, when the means of perpetrating this lewdness have been taken from me, does this suspicion remain? What is this latest and so shameless incrimination? For the state in which I am so removes the suspicion of lewdness from all men's minds that those who seek to keep a stricter watch on their wives attach eunuchs to them, as sacred history tells us of *Esther* and the other damsels of King *Ahasuerus*. We read also that that powerful eunuch of Queen *Candace* was over all her treasure. To whom, for his conversion and baptism, *Philip* the Apostle was directed by an angel. And if such men have ever obtained greater dignity and familiarity among modest and honourable women, how far have they been removed from this suspicion. To the entire removal of which that greatest of the Christian philosophers, *Origen*, when he was minded to undertake the instruction of women also in sacred matters, laid violent hands on himself, as is contained in the sixth book of the Ecclesiastical History."

Yet I thought that in this divine mercy had been propitious to me rather than to him, in that whereas he is reputed to have acted with little forethought, and thereby to have incurred no small reproach, the same was done to me by another's fault, that he might set me free for a similar work, and with so much the less pain as it was more brief and sudden, since, heavy with sleep, when hands were laid upon me I felt little pain or none. But what then I had perhaps felt less from my wound now I must at greater leisure deplore from calumny, and I am tormented more by the detriment to my reputation than by the diminution of my body. As it is written: "A good name is rather to be chosen than great riches." And, as Saint *Augustine* reminds us in a sermon On the Life and Morals of the Clergy: "Whoso trusting in his conscience neglects his reputation is cruel." And before that, he says: "Let us provide things honest, as the Apostle says, not only in the sight of God but in the sight of all men. For ourselves our conscience sufficeth in us. For ourselves our reputation ought not to be polluted, but rather polished in us. Conscience and reputation are twain. Conscience for thyself; reputation for thy neighbour." But what would their jealousy have said to Christ himself, or to His members, His Prophets that is as well as His Apostles, or to the other holy Fathers, if it had existed in their time, when it saw them, though entire in body, associate in such familiar conversation with women. As to which also Saint *Augustine* in his book, Of the Work of Monks, shews that women adhered to the Lord Jesus Christ and to His Apostles as such inseparable companions that they went with them even to their preaching. "For to this end," he says, "faithful women also, having worldly substance, went with them, and ministered to them of their substance, that they might lack none of those things which pertain to the substance of this life."

And whoso does not think that it was the way of the Apostles, that with them women of godly conversation consorted wherever they preached the Gospel, let him hear the Gospel and know how they acted thus after the example of the Lord Himself. For in the Gospel it is written: "And it came to pass afterward, that He went throughout every city and village, preaching and shewing the glad tidings of the kingdom of God: and the twelve were with Him. And certain women, which had been healed of evil spirits and infirmities, *Mary* called *Magdalene*, out of whom went seven devils, and *Joanna* the wife of *Chuza Herod*'s steward, and *Susanna*, and many others, which ministered unto Him of their substance." And *Leo* the Ninth, in reply to the Epistle of *Parmenian* On the Zeal for the Monastic Life, says: "We absolutely profess that it is not lawful for bishop, priest, deacon or subdeacon to cast away his wife from his care for the sake of religion, and not to bestow on her food and raiment, but only that he should lie not with her carnally.

"So also we read that the Holy Apostles acted, as Saint *Paul* saith: 'Have we not power to lead about a sister, a wife, as the brethren of the Lord, and *Cephas*?' Observe, fool, that he did not say: 'Have we not power to embrace,' but 'to lead about,' to wit that their wives might be maintained by them out of the reward of their preaching, but not that there might be carnal intercourse between them." Of a surety that Pharisee who spake within himself, saying of the Lord: "This man, if he were a prophet, would have known who and what manner of woman this is that toucheth him; for she is a sinner," could far more easily, so far as concerns human judgment, conceive a lewd conjecture of the Lord than of me, or whoso behold His Mother commended to the care of a young man, or the Prophets dwelling in the hospitality and conversation of widows could contract a far more probable suspicion from those things. And what would those my detractors have said if they had seen that servile monk *Malchus*, of whom Saint *Jerome* writes, living in the same chamber with his wife. How they would have condemned what that holy Doctor, when he had seen it, greatly commended, saying: "There was there a certain old man named *Malchus*, a native of that place, and an old woman also in his chamber. Both of them zealous after religion, and so wearing out the threshold of the church that you would have thought them to be *Zacharias* and *Elisabeth* out of the Gospel, save that *John* was not between them."

Why lastly do they refrain from the detraction of the holy Fathers, of whom we often read, or have even seen them founding monasteries of women also, and ministering to them, following the example indeed of the seven Deacons whom the Apostles appointed instead of themselves to serve tables and for the ministration of their wives? For so much does the weaker sex need the aid of the stronger that the Apostle lays down that the man is ever over the woman, as her head. In token of which also he commands that she must ever have her head covered. Wherefore I marvel not a little that these customs should long since have crept into monasteries, whereby as Abbots are set over men so are Abbesses over women, and women as men bind themselves by profession of the same rule. And yet in that rule are contained many things which can in no way be performed by women, whether superior or subordinate. And in many places also the natural order of things is overturned, and we see these Abbesses and nuns prevailing even over the clergy themselves, to whom the people is subject, and so much the more easily able to lead them to lewd desires as they have a greater power over them, and govern them by so heavy a yoke. Which the satiric poet has in mind when he says:

> Nothing is more intolerable than a rich woman.

Chapter XV.

DELIBERATING these things often with myself, I was disposed to provide for those sisters, so far as was allowed me, and to manage their affairs; and that they might revere me the more to watch over them with my bodily presence also. And since my persecution by my sons was then more frequent and greater than that by my brethren aforetime, I would turn to them from the raging of that tempest as to a haven of tranquillity, and would rest there awhile, and at least cultivate some fruit in them who had gathered none from the monks. And the more salutary that would be to me, the more necessary was it to their infirmity. But now Satan has so hindered me that I may not find a place wherein I can rest or even dwell, but fugitive and a vagabond, like the accursed *Cain* I am borne hither and thither: as I have said above, "without fightings, within fears" incessantly torment me, nay both without and within fears incessantly, and fightings as much as fears. And far more perilous and continual is my persecution by my sons than by my enemies. For them I have always with me and their devices I must bear close at hand. The violence of my enemies, to the peril of my body, I behold, if I leave the cloister. But within the cloister my sons, that is the monks committed to me as their Abbot, that is their father, trouble me with ceaseless machinations as violent as they are deceitful. Oh, how often have they sought to destroy me by poison! As was done to Saint *Benedict.* As if the same reason for which he abandoned his perverse sons openly encouraged me to do the same, by the example of so great a Father; lest by opposing myself to a certain peril I become a rash tempter rather than a lover of God, nay, be considered my own murderer.

And as in the administration of my food and drink I provided as best I could against their daily pitfalls, in the very sacrifice of the altar they endeavoured to destroy me, putting poison in the chalice. And on another day, when I had gone to Nantes to visit the Count in his sickness, and was lodged there with one of my brothers after the flesh, they tried to slay me with poison through him who was the servant in my train, where they believed that I would be less on my guard against such a machination. But by divine intervention it was then brought to pass that while I did not touch the food which had been made ready for me, a certain brother, one of the monks, whom I had brought with me, having taken that food in ignorance fell down dead, and the servant who had prepared it, terrified as much by his own conscience as by the evidence of what had occurred, took to flight. And so thenceforward, their villainy being manifest to all, I began openly to avoid their pitfalls as best I could, to withdraw from the congregation of the Abbey and to live in cells with a few brethren. And the rest if they expected that I was to be travelling anywhere set robbers, whom they had corrupted with money, upon the highways or paths, to slay me.

And while I was labouring amid these perils, one day falling from my saddle the Hand of the Lord vehemently struck me, to wit breaking the column of my neck. And this fracture afflicted and weakened me far more than my former injury. At times, coercing their unchecked rebellion by excommunication, certain of them whom I dreaded more than the rest I compelled so far as to promise me, on their own word or by oaths publicly sworn, that they would remove altogether from the Abbey, nor disturb me in any way further. Who publicly and most shamelessly violating both the word that they had given and the oaths that they had sworn, at length by the authority of the Roman Pontiff *Innocent*, through a Legate sent to me for the purpose, were compelled in the presence of the Count and the Bishop to swear this and many other things. Yet not even then did they remain quiet. And recently when, those aforesaid having been expelled, I returned to the Abbey and entrusted myself to the remaining brethren whom I suspected less, I found these far worse than the others. From whom, dealing now not with poison indeed but with a sword put to my throat, under the protection of a lord of that country I with difficulty escaped. In which peril I still labour, and daily suspect as it were a sword hanging over my head, so that at table I can scarcely breathe; as we read of him who, when he imagined the greatest happiness to be contained in the power and treasure of the tyrant *Dionysius*, noticing a sword that hung privily over him by a thread, learned what happiness it is that follows earthly power. Which now I also, from a poor monk promoted Abbot, experience without ceasing, being so much more wretched as I am become more rich, that by my example their ambition who seek the same goal may be restrained.

Now, dearly beloved brother in Christ, and from our long

conversation most familiar friend, let this story of my calamities, in which almost from the cradle I have closely toiled, be sufficient for me to have written in the thought of thy affliction and the wrong that has been done thee, that, as I said at the beginning of my letter, thou mayest judge thy oppression, in comparison with mine, to be none at all or but a slight matter, and so much the more patiently endure it the less you esteem it to be. Taking that ever for thy comfort which the Lord foretold to His members of the devil: "If they have persecuted me, they will also persecute you. If the world hate you, ye know that it hated Me before it hated you. If ye were of the world, the world would love his own." And "Yea," writes the Apostle, "all that will live godly in Christ Jesus shall suffer persecution." And again: "Do I seek to please men? For if I yet pleased men, I should not be the servant of Christ." And the Psalmist saith that they are put to shame who please men, "because God hath despised them." Diligently studying which Saint *Jerome*, whose inheritor I esteem myself in the slander of detraction, writing to *Nepotian*, in his Second Epistle, saith: "If I yet pleased men, I should not be the servant of Christ. He ceaseth to please men, and is become the servant of Christ." The same writing to *Asella* of feigned friends: "I thank my God that I am worthy, whom the world hateth." And to *Heliodorus* the monk in his First Epistle: "Thou errest, brother, thou errest, if thou thinkest that the Christian can ever not suffer persecution. For our adversary, as a roaring lion, walketh about seeking whom he may devour, and dost thou think it peace? He sitteth in the lurking places with the rich."

Encouraged therefore by these documents and examples, let us endure those things with greater confidence the more injuriously they befall us. Which, if they add not to our merit, at least let us not doubt that they avail somewhat for our purgation. And as all things are governed by divine ordinance, in this at least let each of the faithful be comforted in every strait place, that the supreme bounty of God permits nothing ever to happen inordinately, and that whatsoever things happen perversely He Himself brings to the best conclusion. Wherefore also is it said to Him rightly in all circumstances: "Thy Will be done." What comfort, moreover, cometh to them that love God from that Apostolic authority: "We know that all things work together for good to them that love God." Which the wisest of men diligently considered when he said in the Proverbs: "There shall no evil happen to the just." Whereby manifestly he sheweth that those depart from justice who are angered by any oppression of themselves, which they doubt not is directed against them by divine ordinance; and subject themselves to their own rather than to the Divine Will, and revolt in their secret desires against that which is uttered in the words: "Thy Will be done," placing their own will before the Will of God. Farewell.

THE SECOND LETTER WHICH IS FROM HELOISE TO ABELARD, INTERCEDING WITH HIM

Argument: Heloise, *first* Abelard's *mistress, then his wife, and later set by him over the monastery of Paraclete, which he for himself with the wealth of his disciples had raised from its foundations, having read his letter to his friend, writes him this, praying that he will write back to her of his perils or deliverance, whereby she may be made a partner in his sorrow or in his joy. She expostulates also that he has not written to her since her monastic profession, when previously he had sent her many letters of love. She expounds her love for him, both in time past when it was base and carnal, and at the present time when it is chaste and spiritual: and bitterly complains that she is not loved equally by him in return. It is a letter full of great affection and querulous complaints, in the feminine way, a letter in which a woman's heart may be discerned, abounding in great erudition.*

To her master, nay father, to her husband, nay brother; his handmaid, nay daughter, his spouse, nay sister: to ABELARD, HELOISE.

Your letter written to a friend for his comfort, beloved, was lately brought to me by chance. Seeing at once from the title that it was yours, I began the more ardently to read it in that the writer was so dear to me, that I might at least be refreshed by his words as by a picture of him whose presence I have lost. Almost every line of that letter, I remember, was filled with gall and wormwood, to wit those that related the miserable story of our conversion, and thy unceasing crosses, my all. Thou didst indeed fulfil in that letter what at the beginning of it thou hadst promised thy friend, namely that in comparison with thy troubles he should deem his own to be nothing or but a small matter. After setting forth thy former persecution by thy masters, then the outrage of supreme treachery upon thy body, thou hast turned thy pen to the execrable jealousy and inordinate assaults of thy fellow-pupils also, namely *Alberic* of Rheims and *Lotulph* the Lombard; and what by their instigation was done to that famous work of thy theology, and what to thyself, as it were condemned to prison, thou hast not omitted.

From these thou comest to the machinations of thine Abbot and false brethren, and the grave detraction of thee by those two pseudo-apostles, stirred up against thee by the aforesaid rivals, and to the scandal raised by many of the name of Paraclete given to the oratory in departure from custom: and then, coming to those intolerable and still continuing persecutions of thy life, thou hast carried to the end the miserable story of that cruellest of extortioners and those wickedest of monks, whom thou callest thy sons. Which things I deem that no one can read or hear with dry eyes, for they renewed in fuller measure my griefs, so diligently did they express each several part, and increased them the more, in that thou relatedst that thy perils are still growing, so that we are all alike driven to despair of thy life, and every day our trembling hearts and throbbing bosoms await the latest rumour of thy death.

And so in His Name Who still protects thee in a certain measure for Himself, in the Name of Christ, as His handmaids and thine, we beseech thee to deign to inform us by frequent letters of those shipwrecks in which thou still art tossed, that thou mayest have us at least, who alone have remained to thee, as partners in thy grief or joy. For they are wont to bring some comfort to a grieving man who grieve with him, and any burden that is laid on several is borne more easily, or transferred. And if this tempest should have been stilled for a space, then all the more hasten thou to write, the more pleasant thy letter will be. But whatsoever it be of which thou mayest write to us, thou wilt confer no small remedy on us; if only in this that thou wilt shew thyself to be keeping us in mind.

For how pleasant are the letters of absent friends *Seneca* himself by his own example teaches us, writing thus in a certain passage to his friend *Lucilius*: "Because thou writest to me often, I thank thee. For in the one way possible thou shewest thyself to me. Never do I receive a letter from thee, but immediately we are together." If the portraits of our absent friends are pleasant to us, which renew our memory of them and relieve our regret for their absence by a false and empty consolation, how much more pleasant are letters which bring us the written characters of the absent friend. But thanks be to God, that in this way at least no jealousy prevents thee from restoring to us thy presence, no difficulty impedes thee, no neglect (I beseech thee) need delay thee.

Thou hast written to thy friend the comfort of a long letter, considering his difficulties, no doubt, but treating of thine own. Which diligently recording, whereas thou didst intend them for his comfort, thou hast added greatly to our desolation, and while thou wert anxious to heal his wounds hast inflicted fresh wounds of grief on us and made our former wounds to ache again. Heal, I beseech thee, the wounds that thou thyself hast given, who art so busily engaged in healing the wounds given by others. Thou hast indeed humoured thy friend and comrade, and paid the debt as well of friendship as of comradeship; but by a greater debt thou hast bound thyself to us, whom it behoves thee to call not friends but dearest friends, not comrades but daughters, or by a sweeter and a holier name, if any can be conceived.

As to the greatness of the debt which binds thee to us neither argument nor evidence is lacking, that any doubt be removed; and if all men be silent the fact itself cries aloud. For of this place thou, after God, art the sole founder, the sole architect of this oratory, the sole builder of this congregation. Nothing didst thou build here on the foundations of others. All that is here is thy creation. This wilderness, ranged only by wild beasts or by robbers, had known no habitation of men, had contained no dwelling. In the very lairs of the beasts, in the very lurking places of the robbers, where the name of God is not heard, thou didst erect a divine tabernacle, and didst dedicate the Holy Ghost's own temple. Nothing didst thou borrow from the wealth of kings or princes, when thou couldst have obtained so much and from so many, that whatsoever was wrought here might be ascribed to thee alone. Clerks or scholars flocking in haste to thy teaching ministered to thee all things needful, and they who lived upon ecclesiastical benefices, who khew not how to make but only how to receive oblations, and had hands for receiving, not for giving, became lavish and importunate here in the offering of oblations.

Thine, therefore, truly thine is this new plantation in the divine plan, for the plants of which, still most tender, frequent irrigation is necessary that they may grow. Frail enough, from the weakness of the feminine nature, is this plantation; it is infirm, even were it not new. Wherefore it demands more diligent cultivation and more frequent, after the words of the Apostle: "I have planted, *Apollos* watered; but God gave the increase." The Apostle had planted, by the doctrines of his preaching, and had established in the Faith the Corinthians, to whom he wrote. Thereafter *Apollos*, the Apostle's own disciple, had watered them with sacred exhortations, and so by divine grace the increment of virtues was bestowed on them. Thou art tending the vineyard of another's vine which thou didst not plant, which is turned to thine own bitterness, with admonitions often wasted and holy sermons preached in vain. Think of what thou owest to thine own, who thus spendest thy care on another's. Thou teachest and reprovest rebels, nor gainest than aught. In vain before the swine dost thou scatter the pearls of divine eloquence. Who givest so much thought to the obstinate, consider what thou owest to the obedient. Who bestowest so much on thine enemies, meditate what thou owest to thy daughters. And, to say nothing of the rest, think by what a debt thou art bound to me, that what thou owest to the community of devoted women thou mayest pay more devotedly to her who is thine alone.

How many grave treatises in the teaching, or in the exhortation, or for the comfort of holy women the holy Fathers composed, and with what diligence they composed them, thine excellence knows better than our humility. Wherefore to no little amazement thine oblivion moves the tender beginnings of our conversion, that neither by reverence for God, nor by love of us, nor by the examples of the holy Fathers hast thou been admonished to attempt to comfort me, as I waver and am already crushed by prolonged grief, either by speech in thy presence or by a letter in thine absence. And yet thou knowest thyself to be bound to me by a debt so much greater in that thou art tied to me more closely by the pact of the nuptial sacrament; and that thou art the more beholden to me in that I ever, as is known to all, embraced thee with an unbounded love. Thou knowest, dearest, all men know what I have lost in thee, and in how wretched a case that supreme and notorious betrayal took me myself also from me with thee, and that my grief is immeasurably greater from the manner in which I lost thee than from the loss of thee.

And the greater the cause of grief, the greater the remedies of comfort to be applied. Not, however, by another, but by thee thyself, that thou who art alone in the cause of my grief may be alone in the grace of my comfort. For it is thou alone that canst make me sad, canst make me joyful or canst comfort me. And it is thou alone that owest me this great debt, and for this reason above all that I have at once performed all things that you didst order, till that when I could not offend thee in anything I had the strength to lose myself at thy behest. And what is more, and strange it is to relate, to such madness did my love turn that what alone it sought it cast from itself without hope of recovery when, straightway obeying thy command, I changed both my habit and my heart, that I might shew thee to be the one possessor both of my body and of my mind. Nothing have I ever (God wot) required of thee save thyself, desiring thee purely, not what was thine. Not for the pledge of matrimony, nor for any dowry did I look, nor my own passions or wishes but thine (as thou thyself knowest) was I zealous to gratify.

And if the name of wife appears more sacred and more valid, sweeter to me is ever the word friend, or, if thou be not ashamed, concubine or whore. To wit that the more I humbled myself before thee the fuller grace I might obtain from thee, and so also damage less the fame of thine excellence. And thou thyself wert not wholly unmindful of that kindness in the letter of which I have spoken, written to thy friend for his comfort. Wherein thou hast not disdained to set forth sundry reasons by which I tried to dissuade thee from our marriage, from an ill-starred bed; but wert silent as to many, in which I preferred love to wedlock, freedom to a bond. I call God to witness, if *Augustus*, ruling over the whole world, were to deem me worthy of the honour of marriage, and to confirm the whole world to me, to be ruled by me for ever, dearer to me and of greater dignity would it seem to be called thy strumpet than his empress.

For it is not by being richer or more powerful that a man becomes better; one is a matter of fortune, the other of virtue. Nor should she deem herself other than venal who weds a rich man rather than a poor, and desires more things in her husband than himself. Assuredly, whomsoever this concupiscence leads into marriage deserves payment rather than affection; for it is evident that she goes after his wealth and not the man, and is willing to prostitute herself, if she can, to a richer. As the argument advanced (in *Aeschines*) by the wise *Aspasia to Xenophon* and his wife plainly convinces us. When the wise woman aforesaid had propounded this argument for their reconciliation, she concluded as follows: "For when ye have understood this, that there is not a better man nor a happier woman on the face of the earth; then ye will ever and above all things seek that which ye think the best; thou to be the husband of so excellent a wife, and she to be married to so excellent a husband." A blessed sentiment, assuredly, and more than philosophic, expressing wisdom itself rather than philosophy. A holy error and a blessed fallacy among the married, that a perfect love should preserve their bond of matrimony unbroken, not so much by the continence of their bodies as by the purity of their hearts. But what error shews to the rest of women the truth has made manifest to me. Since what they thought of their husbands, that I, that the entire world not so much believed as knew of thee. So that the more genuine my love was for thee, the further it was removed from error.

For who among kings or philosophers could equal thee in fame? What kingdom or city or village did not burn to see thee? Who, I ask, did not hasten to gaze upon thee when thou appearedst in public, nor on thy departure with straining neck and fixed eye follow thee? What wife, what maiden did not yearn for thee in thine absence, nor burn in thy presence? What queen or powerful lady did not envy me my joys and my bed? There were two things, I confess, in thee especially, wherewith thou couldst at once captivate the heart of any woman; namely the arts of making songs and of singing them. Which we know that other philosophers have seldom followed. Wherewith as with a game, refreshing the labour of philosophic exercise, thou hast left many songs composed in amatory measure or rhythm, which for the suavity both of words and of tune being oft repeated, have kept thy name without ceasing on the lips of all; since even illiterates the sweetness of thy melodies did not allow to forget thee. It was on this account chiefly that women sighed for love of thee. And as the greater part of thy songs descanted of our love, they spread my fame in a short time through many lands, and inflamed the jealousy of many women against me. For what excellence of mind or body did not adorn thy youth? What woman who envied me then does not my calamity now compel to pity one deprived of such delights? What man or women, albeit an enemy at first, is not now softened by the compassion due to me?

And, though exceeding guilty, I am, as thou knowest, exceeding innocent. For it is not the deed but the intention that makes the crime. It is not what is done but the spirit in which it is done that equity considers. And in what state of mind I have ever been towards thee, only thou, who hast knowledge of it, canst judge. To thy consideration I commit all, I yield in all things to thy testimony. Tell me one thing only, if thou canst, why, after our conversion, which thou alone didst decree, I am fallen into such neglect and oblivion with thee that I am neither refreshed by thy speech and presence nor comforted by a letter in thine absence. Tell me, one thing only, if thou canst, or let me tell thee what I feel, nay what all suspect. Concupiscence joined thee to me rather than affection, the ardour of desire rather than love. When therefore what thou desiredst ceased, all that thou hadst exhibited at the same time failed. This, most beloved, is not mine only but the conjecture of all, not peculiar but common, not private but public. Would that it seemed thus to me only, and thy love found others to excuse it, by whom my grief might be a little quieted. Would that I could invent reasons by which in excusing thee I might cover in some measure my own vileness.

Give thy attention, I beseech thee, to what I demand; and thou wilt see this to be a small matter and most easy for thee. While I am cheated of thy presence, at least by written words, whereof thou hast an abundance, present to me the sweetness of thine image. In vain may I expect thee to be liberal in things if I must endure thee niggardly in words. Until now I believed that I deserved more from thee when I had done all things for thee, persevering still in obedience to thee. Who indeed as a girl was allured to the asperity of monastic conversation not by religious devotion but by thy command alone. Wherein if I deserve nought from thee, thou mayest judge my labour to have been vain. No reward for this may I expect from God, for the love of Whom it is well known that I did not anything. When thou hastenedst to God, I followed thee in the habit, nay preceded thee. For as though mindful of the wife of *Lot,* who looked back from behind him, thou deliveredst me first to the sacred garments and monastic profession before thou gavest thyself to God. And for that in this one thing thou shouldst have had little trust in me I vehemently grieved and was ashamed. For I (God wot) would without hesitation precede or follow thee to the Vulcanian fires according to thy word. For not with me was my heart, but with thee. But now, more than ever, if it be not with thee, it is nowhere. For without thee it cannot anywhere exist. But so act that it may be well with thee, I beseech thee. And well with thee will it be if it find thee propitious, if thou give love for love, little for much, words for deeds. Would that thy love, beloved, had less trust in me, that it might be more anxious! But the more confident I have made thee in the past, the more neglectful now I find thee. Remember, I beseech thee, what I have done, and pay heed to what thou owest me. While with thee I enjoyed carnal pleasures, many were uncertain whether I did so from love or from desire. But now the end shews in what spirit I began. I have forbidden myself all pleasures that I might obey thy will. I have reserved nothing for myself, save this, to be now entirely thine. Consider therefore how great is thine injustice, if to me who deserve more thou payest less, nay nothing at all, especially when it is a small thing that is demanded of thee, and right easy for thee to perform.

And so in His Name to whom thou hast offered thyself, before God I beseech thee that in whatsoever way thou canst thou restore to me thy presence, to wit by writing me some word of comfort. To this end alone that, thus refreshed, I may give myself with more alacrity to the service of God. When in time past thou soughtest me out for temporal pleasures, thou visitedst me with endless letters, and by frequent songs didst set thy *Heloise* on the lips of all men. With me every public place, each house resounded. How more rightly shouldst thou excite me now towards God, whom thou excitedst then to desire. Consider, I beseech thee, what thou owest me, pay heed to what I demand; and my long letter with a brief ending I conclude. Farewell, my all.

THE THIRD LETTER WHICH IS THE REPLY OF PETER TO HELOISE

Argument: Abelard *answers the last letter from* Heloise *and frankly excuses himself, protesting that his not having written to her for so long a time proceeded in no way from want of interest in her; on the contrary, he had such confidence in her prudence, learning, piety and devotion that he did not imagine that she required either exhortation or comfort. He bids her write again to him, saying what in the way of exhortation or divine comfort she wishes to have from him; and he himself will answer according to her desire. He asks her that both she and her community, the choir of holy virgins and widows, shall help him before God with their prayers, admirably expounding from the authority of the Scriptures what force prayer has with Him, and especially the prayers of wives for their husbands; and, reminding her of the prayers which are already being offered to God for him in that monastery by the holy women at each of the canonical Hours, prescribes others which may be said for his safety when he is absent. Furthermore he requires of her that, in whatsoever manner or place he may be destined to pass from this life, she will have his body brought to the Community of the Paraclete, and there buried.*

To Heloise his dearly beloved sister in Christ, Abelard her brother in the Same.

If since our conversion from the world to God I have not yet written thee any word of comfort or exhortation, it must be ascribed not to my negligence but to thy prudence, in which always I greatly trust. For I did not suppose it to be necessary to her on whom divine grace has abundantly bestowed all things needful, so that both by words and by examples thou art able to teach the erring, to comfort the weak, to exhort the lukewarm, as thou wert long since wont to do when under the Abbess thou didst obtain the priorship. Wherefore if now thou watch over thy daughters with as great diligence as then over thy sisters it is enough, we believe, that now we may consider any teaching or exhortation from us to be wholly superfluous. But if to thy humility it appear otherwise, and in those things also which pertain to God thou have need of our teaching and writings, write to me of what thou requirest, that I may write again to thee as God may be pleased to grant me. But thanks be to God Who, inspiring in your hearts solicitude for my most grave and assiduous perils, has made you partners in my affliction, and may divine mercy by the suffrage of your prayers protect me, and swiftly crush Satan beneath our feet. And to this end especially the Psalter which thou hast solicitously required of me, sister once dear in the world, now dearest in Christ, I have made haste to send thee. Whereon for our great and many excesses, and for the daily imminence of our perils, mayest thou offer a perpetual sacrifice of prayers to the Lord.

For of how great a place before God and His Saints the prayers of the faithful obtain, and especially the prayers of women for their dear ones and of wives for their husbands, many testimonies and examples occur to us. Which diligently observing, the Apostle bids us pray without ceasing. We read that the Lord said to *Moses:* "Let me alone that my wrath may wax hot." And to *Jeremy* He said: "Therefore pray not thou for this people, neither make intercession to me." By which words the Lord Himself manifestly professes that the prayers of the Saints are set as it were a bridle upon His wrath, whereby it may be checked, and He rage not against sinners to the fulness of their deserts. As a man whom justice leads almost spontaneously to vengeance the supplication of his friends may turn aside. So it is said to him who is praying or about to pray: "Let me alone, neither make intercession to me." The Lord ordains that prayer be not made to Him for the impious. The righteous man prays when the Lord forbids him, and obtains from Him what he demands and alters the sentence of the irate Judge. For thus it is added of *Moses:* "And the Lord repented of the evil which he thought to do unto his people." It is written elsewhere of the universal works of God: "He commanded, and they were created." But in this passage it is recorded also that He had said that the people had deserved affliction, and that prevented by the virtue of prayer He did not perform what He had said.

Take heed therefore how great is the virtue of prayer, if we pray as we are commanded, when that for which the Prophet had been fobidden by God to pray he nevertheless obtained by prayer, and turned Him aside from that which He had said. To Whom also another Prophet says: "In wrath remember mercy." Let them hear this and give heed, the Princes of the Earth who in the execution of the justice they have decreed and published are found obstinate rather than just, and blush to appear remiss should they be merciful, and untruthful if they alter their edict or do not execute what with little foresight they have decreed, or emend the words to fit the matter. Who indeed I might rightly say were comparable to *Jephthah* who, what he had foolishly vowed more foolishly performing, slew his only daughter. But whoso desires to be a member of Him, says with the Psalmist: "I will sing of mercy and judgment: unto Thee, O Lord, will I sing." "Mercy," as it is written, "exalteth judgment," according to what elsewhere the Scripture threatens: "He shall have judgment without mercy that hath shewed no mercy." Which the Psalmist himself diligently considering, at the supplication of the wife of *Nabal* the Carmelite, in mercy brake the oath which he had sworn in justice, to wit against her husband and for the destruction of his house. And so he set prayer above justice, and what the man had done amiss the supplication of the woman wiped clean.

Wherein for thee indeed, sister, is an example set, and assurance given; that if this woman's prayer obtained so much from a man thou be taught how much thy prayers for me may prevail before God. Inasmuch as God, Who is our Father, loves His children more than *David* loved a suppliant woman. And he indeed was reckoned pious and merciful, but Piety itself and Mercy is God. And this woman who then besought him was secular and lay, nor was she bound to the Lord by the profession of holy devotion. For if in thyself thou suffice not to secure it, the holy convent, as well of virgins as of widows, which is with thee will obtain what by thyself thou canst not. For when the Truth says to the Disciples: "Where two or three are gathered together in my name, there am I in the midst of them"; and again: "If two of you shall agree on earth as touching anything that they shall ask, it shall be done for them of my Father which is in Heaven"; who does not see how greatly the frequent prayer of a holy congregation prevails before God? If, as the Apostle asserts: "The effectual prayer of a righteous man availeth much," what is to be expected from the multitude of a holy congregation? Ye know, dearest sister, from the eight-and-twentieth Homily of Saint *Gregory* what aid the prayer of brethren speedily brought to an unwilling or resisting brother. Of whom, in the extremity to which he had been brought, in what an anxiety of peril his wretched soul was labouring, and with what desperation and weariness of life he recalled his brethren from their prayers, it is there diligently written and cannot have escaped thy wisdom.

And may that example invite thee and the convent of holy sisters to prayer, that it may keep me alive for you through Him from Whom, as *Paul* bears witness, women have received their dead raised to life again. For if thou turn the pages of the Old Testament and the New thou wilt find that the greatest miracles of resuscitation were displayed only or principally to women, and for them or in their persons were wrought. The Old Testament records two dead men who were raised to life at the supplication of their mothers, namely by *Elias* and by his disciple *Eliseus*. And the Gospel contains the resurrection of three dead men only, wrought by the Lord, which things being displayed to women strongly confirm by their example that Apostolic saying which we have quoted above: "Women received their dead raised to life again." It was to a widow at the gate of the city called Nain that He restored a son to life and gave him back to his mother, touched with compassion for her, and *Lazarus* also, His friend, at the entreaty of his sisters *Mary* and *Martha*, He raised from the dead. When He also accorded the same grace to the daughter of the ruler of the synagogue, paying heed to her father's petition, "women received their dead raised to life again." For she being raised to life received her own body again from death, as they the bodies of their dead. And with but few intercessions these resurrections were accomplished. So that the manifold prayers of your devotion will easily obtain the preservation of my life. The more the abstinence or the chastity of women consecrated to God is pleasing to Him, the more propitious will it find Him. And the better part of those who were raised from the dead were not of the faithful; thus we do not read that the widow aforesaid, to whom without her asking it the Lord restored her son, had lived in the faith. Whereas with us, not only does the integrity of our faith draw us together but our profession of the same vows unites us.

But, to leave now out of account the sacrosanct congregation of your college, in which the devotion of so many virgins and widows bears the yoke of the Lord, let me come now to thee alone, whose great sanctity I doubt not is effectual before the Lord, nor do I doubt that thou art bound to do all that thou canst for me above all men, especially when I am labouring in the toils of such great adversity. Remember therefore always in thy prayers him who is specially thine, and so much the more confidently watch in prayer as thou dost recognise it to be more righteous, and accordingly more acceptable to Him to whom prayer is made. Listen, I beseech thee, with the ear of thy heart to what thou hast heard so often with thy bodily ear. It is written in the Proverbs: "A virtuous woman is a crown to her husband." And again: "Whoso findeth a wife findeth a good thing, and obtaineth favour of the Lord." And another time: "Houses and riches are the inheritance of fathers: and a prudent wife is from the Lord." And in Ecclesiasticus: "Blessed is the man that hath a virtuous wife." And a little later: "A good wife is a good portion." And according to Apstolic authority: "The unbelieving husband is sanctified by the wife." An example whereof indeed in our own realm, that is France, divine grace has specially displayed, to wit when by the prayers of his wife rather than by the preaching of the saints *Clovis* the King being converted to the Faith of Christ placed his whole realm under the divine law, that the lesser folk might be encouraged by the example of the great to persevere in prayer. To which perseverance indeed the Lord's parable vehemently invites us, that if a man persevere in knocking: "I say unto you, Though he will not rise and give him, because he is his friend, yet because of his importunity he will rise and give him as many as he needeth." By which, to continue still of importunity in prayer, *Moses* relaxed the severity of divine justice and altered its sentence.

Thou knowest, beloved, what ardours of charity in my presence your convent was aforetime wont to exhibit in prayer. For every day at the conclusion of each of the Hours they used to offer this special supplication to the Lord for me, and, a proper response with its versicle having been first said and sung, added prayers to them and a collect as follows:

Response: Forsake me not, O Lord: O my God, be not far from me.

Versicle: Make haste, O God, to deliver me.

Prayer: Save thy servant, O my God: whose hope is in Thee. Lord, hear my prayer, and let my cry come unto Thee. (*Let us pray.*) God, Who through Thy servant hast been pleased to gather Thy handmaids together in Thy Name, we beseech Thee to grant that both he and ourselves may persevere in Thy Will. Through our Lord, *etc.*

But now, when I am absent, there is all the more need of your suffrage for me, in that I am fast bound by the anxiety of a greater peril. Beseeching you therefore I demand, and demanding beseech that I may find, now that I am absent, how far your true charity embraces the absent, by your adding this form of proper prayer at the conclusion of each Hour:

Response: O Lord, Father and Governor of all my whole life, leave me not to their counsels, and let me not fall by them.

Versicle: Take hold of shield and buckler, and stand up for my help. Leave me not.

Prayer: Save thy servant, O my God, whose hope is in Thee. Send him, Lord, help from Thy Sanctuary, and watch over him from Sion. Be unto him, O Lord, a tower of strength from the face of his enemy. Hear my prayer, O Lord, and let my cry come unto Thee. (*Let us pray.*) God, Who through Thy servant hast been pleased to gather Thy handmaids together in Thy Name, we beseech Thee that Thou wilt protect him from all adversity and restore him in safety to Thy handmaids. Through our Lord, *etc.*

And if the Lord should deliver me into the hands of mine enemies, so that they prevail over me and slay me, by whatsoever chance I may go the way of all flesh while absent from you, wheresoever, I beseech you, my body, either exposed or buried, may lie, have it brought to your cemetery, where our daughters, nay, sisters in Christ, seeing every day our sepulchre, may be encouraged to pour out prayer more fully for me to the Lord. For I deem no place to be safer or more salutary for a soul grieving for its sins and made desolate by transgression than that which to the true Paraclete, that is to the Comforter, is properly consecrated, and is specially distinguished by His Name. Nor do I think that there is a fitter place for Christian burial among any of the faithful than among women devoted to Christ. Women they were who, solicitous for the sepulchre of the Lord Jesus Christ, came to it with precious ointments, and went before and followed, diligently watching about His sepulchre and bewailing with tears the death of the Bridegroom, as it is written: "The women sitting over against the sepulchre and weeping lamented the Lord." And there before His Resurrection they were comforted by the apparition and speech of an angel, and thereafter were found worthy to taste the joy of His Resurrection, He appearing to them twice, and to touch Him with their hands. But this lastly above all things I demand of you, that whereas now ye labour in too great solicitude for the welfare of my body, then being solicitous especially for the salvation of my soul ye shew to the dead man how greatly ye loved the living, to wit by a special and proper suffrage of your prayers.

Live, prosper, and thy sisters too with thee.
Live, but in Christ be mindful, pray, of me.

THE FOURTH LETTER WHICH IS THE REPLY OF HELOISE TO PETER

Argument: *Filled with griefs and lamentations is this letter. For* Heloise *laments her own wretched plight, and that of the nuns her sisters, and* Abelard's *also, taking an occasion for her lamentations from the latter part of the preceding letter, in which* Abelard *reminds her that he must depart from this life. She makes use of many tender appeals, whereby she moves the reader to compassion for her own lot and for* Abelard, *so as haply to draw tears from his eyes. She deplores also the mutilation of* Abelard. *She complains greatly, too, of those burning carnal desires in the body, which aforetime she had known with* Abelard. *Then, not incongruously, she makes light of the outward and open form of her religion, and ascribes it to feint rather than to piety; she begs for the help of* Abelard's *prayers, and humbly rejects his praise of herself.*

To her all, after Christ, his all in Christ.

I marvel, my all, that, against the custom in writing letters, nay against the natural order of things, at the head of the greeting in thy letter thou hast made bold to set my name before thine, to wit the woman before the man, the wife before the husband, the handmaid before the master, the nun before the monk and priest, the deaconess before the Abbot. Right indeed is the order and honourable that they who write to their superiors or to their equals place the names of those to whom they are writing before their own. But if they write to their inferiors, those take precedence in the order of writing who take precedence in rank. This also we received with no little amazement, that whereas thou shouldst have brought us the remedy of comfort thou hast increased our desolation and hast provoked tears which thou shouldst have dried. For who among us could hear with dry eyes what thou hast put towards the end of thy letter, saying: "If the Lord should deliver me into the hands of mine enemies, so that they prevail over me and slay me," and the rest?

O, dearest, with what mind didst thou think that, with what lips couldst thou endure to say it? Never may God so forget His handmaids as to keep them to survive thee. Never may He concede that life to us which is harder to bear than any kind of death. It is for thee to celebrate our obsequies, for thee to commend our souls to God, and those whom thou hast gathered together for God to send first to him, that thou be no more disturbed by anxiety for them, and so much the more joyfully follow us the more assured thou already be of our salvation. Spare, I beseech thee, master, spare us words of this sort, whereby thou makest wretched women most wretched, and take not from us before our death that which is our life. "Sufficient unto the day is the evil thereof," and that day, wrapped about with every bitterness, will bring to all whom it shall find enough solicitude with itself. "For to what end," says *Seneca*, "anticipate evil, and before death lose one's life?" Thou askest us, my all, that, by whatsoever fate, if absent from us, thou mayest end this life, we shall have thy body brought to our cemetery, that there thou mayest gather a richer fruit of our prayers from our assiduous memory of thee. But how couldst thou suspect that thy memory could ever fail among us? Or what time will then be suitable for prayer when our extreme perturbation allows us no peace? When neither the soul retains the sense of reason nor the tongue the use of speech? When the maddened mind enraged, if I may so speak, against God Himself rather than appeased, will not so much placate him by prayer as anger him by complaints? Then there will be time only for the wretched to weep, pray they may not, and must hasten rather to follow than to bury thee, for we shall be more fit to be buried with thee than able to bury thee. Who, when in thee we shall have lost our life, will not at all be able to live with thee removed from us. Oh that we may not be able to live even until then! The very thought of thy death is as death to us.

But what will be the reality of that death if it find us living? Never, God grant, may we pay that debt to thee as thy survivors, may we yield thee that assistance which in the last hour we expect from thee. In this may we precede, not follow thee! Spare us, therefore, I beseech thee, spare at least her who is thine alone, namely by ceasing from the use of such words, wherewith as with swords of death thou piercest our souls, so that what comes before death is harder to bear than death itself. The heart overwhelmed by grief knows no rest, nor can the mind occupied by perturbations be given sincerely to God. Do not, I beseech thee, hinder that service of God to which especially thou didst devote us. Every inevitable thing which when it comes will bring with it the greatest grief we must desire to come suddenly, lest it torment us long beforehand with vain fears which no foresight can remedy. Which also the poet well considering, prays to God, saying:

> May whatsoe'er Thou hast in store
> Be swift and sudden. Let the human mind
> To future destiny be ever blind.
> Allow our fears to hope.

But with thee lost what hope remains to me? Or what reason for remaining in this pilgrimage when I may have no remedy save thee, nor aught else in thee save this that thou art alive, all other pleasure from thee being forbidden me to whom it is not allowed even to enjoy thy presence, that at times I might be restored to myself. O—if it be right to say so—cruel to me in all things God! O inclement clemency! O fortune unfortunate, which has already so spent all the arrows of its whole strength on me that it has none now wherewith to assail others; it has emptied its full quivers on me so that vainly do others now fear its onslaughts. Nor if any arrow still remained to it would it find in me a spot to wound. One thing amidst so many wounds it has feared, lest I end my torment by death. And albeit it does not cease to destroy me, it fears that destruction which it is bringing rapidly to pass.

Ah me, most wretched of the wretched! Unhappiest of the unhappy, who when I had been raised to so lofty a pinnacle, being preferred to all other women in thee, have now, fallen from thence, suffered as great a prostration in thee and in myself alike! For, the higher the step of advancement, the heavier is the fall. Whom among great and noble women did fortune ever set above or equal with me? Whom has it so cast down and crushed with grief? What glory did it give me in thee; what ruin has it brought me in thee! How vehement has it been to me in either direction, so as neither in good nor in evil to shew any mean. Which that it might make me the most wretched of all women first made me happier than any. That in thinking of how much I have lost the lamentations that consume me might be increased to equal the losses that have crushed me; that as great regret might follow for what I have forfeited as was previously my enjoyment of what I possessed, and that the supreme sadness of despair might terminate the joys of supreme pleasure.

And in order that from the injustice a greater indignation may arise, all the rights of equity are equally turned against me. For while anxiously we enjoyed the delights of love, and, to use a viler but more expressive word, abandoned ourselves to fornication, divine severity spared us. But when we corrected the unlawful with the lawful, and covered the vileness of fornication with the honesty of marriage, the wrath of the Lord vehemently increased the weight of His Hand upon us, nor did He allow an immaculate couch who had long endured one polluted. For men taken in the most flagrant adultery that would have been sufficient punishment which thou didst suffer. What others might merit by adultery thou didst incur by a marriage whereby thou thoughtest that thou hadst given satisfaction for all thy wrongdoing. What adulteresses bring to their lovers thine own wife brought to thee. And not while we were indulging still in our old pleasures, but when, already separated for a time, we were living chastely, thou indeed presiding over thy school in Paris, and I at thy command dwelling at Argenteuil among the nuns. When we were thus divided, that thou the more studiously mightest devote thyself to thy school, I the more freely to prayer or the meditation of holy books, while we were living thus, as in greater holiness so in greater chastity, thou alone didst pay in thy body the penalty for what we both alike had committed. Alone wert thou in the punishment, two were we in the fault; and thou who wert the less guilty hast borne all. For inasmuch as thou hadst given fuller satisfaction by humiliating thyself for me, and hadst exalted me and all my race alike, so thou hadst given less cause for punishment both to God and to those traitors.

Unhappy that I am, born to be the cause of so great a crime! O constant bane of women, greatest against the greatest men! Wherefore is it written in the Proverbs to beware of women: "Hearken unto me now therefore, O ye children, and attend to the words of my mouth. Let not thine heart decline to her ways, go not astray in her paths: for she hath cast down many wounded; yea, many strong men have been slain by her. Her house is the way to hell, going down to the chambers of death." And in Ecclesiastes: "All things have I seen in the days of my vanity . . . and I find more bitter than death the woman whose heart is snares and nets, and her hands as bands: whoso pleaseth God shall escape from her; but the sinner shall be taken by her." For the first woman drave the man from Paradise, and she who had been created for him by the Lord as a helpmeet was turned to his supreme destruction. That strongest Nazarite of the Lord, conceived by the message of an angel, *Delilah* alone overcame, and when he was betrayed to his foes and deprived of his eyes, grief at length carried him to such a pass that he brought down himself also in the overthrow of his enemies. The wisest of all men, *Solomon*, a woman alone whom he had taken to himself infatuated and drove him to such insanity that she plunged him, whom the Lord had chosen to build a Temple to Himself, after his father *David*, who was a righteous man, had been rejected for that task, in idolatry until the end of his days, abandoning that service of God which in his words as in his writings he preached and taught. *Job*, the most holy of men, endured the supreme and heaviest of blows from his wife, who urged him to curse God. And the most cunning tempter knew this well, for that he had often found it, to wit that the ruin of men was most easily effected through their wives. Who also into our time extending his wonted malice, him whom he could not bring down by fornication tried by marriage; and used a good thing ill who was not permitted to use an evil. Thanks be to God for this at least, that the tempter did not draw me into guilt by my consent, like the women aforesaid, albeit he turned me, from my affection, into a cause of the wickedness that was done.

But even though innocence may purge my heart, nor does consent incur me the guilt of the crime, yet many sins went before it which do not allow me to be altogether immune from the guilt of it. For indeed long before that time, ministering to the delights of carnal snares, I then deserved that which I now bewail, and the sequel is made a fitting punishment of my previous sins. Evil beginnings must lead to an untoward end. Oh, that I may have the strength to do fit penance for this fault, especially that I may be able in some measure to recompense by the long contrition of penitence that punishment of the wound inflicted on thee, and what thou to the present hour hast borne in my body may I all my life long, as is right, take upon my mind and in this way satisfy thee at least, if not God. For, if I am truly to set forth the infirmity of my most wretched heart, I find no penance wherewith I may appease God Whom always for that outrage I charge with the utmost cruelty, and, refractory to His dispensation, offend Him rather by my indignation than appease Him by my repentance. For what repentance of sins is that, however great the mortification of the body, when the mind still retains the same will to sin, and burns with its old desires? Easy is it indeed for anyone by confessing his sins to accuse himself, or even in outward satisfaction to mortify his body. But it is most difficult to tear away the heart from the desire of the greatest pleasures. Wherefore and with reason Holy *Job*, after first saying: "I will leave my complaint upon myself," that is, "I will let loose my tongue and will open my mouth in confession to accuse myself of my sins," straightway added: "I will speak in the bitterness of my soul." Which Saint *Gregory* expounding says: "Some there are who in open speech confess their faults, and yet in confession know not how to weep, and say lamentable things rejoicing. Wherefore if any detesting his faults speaks, it is necessary that he speak thus in the bitterness of his soul, and that this same bitterness punish whatsoever the tongue accuses by the judgment of the mind." But this bitterness indeed, how rare it is, Saint *Ambrose* diligently studying says: "They are easier to find who have kept innocence than they who have made repentance." So sweet to me were those delights of lovers which we enjoyed in common that they cannot either displease me nor hardly pass from my memory. Whithersoever I turn, always they bring themselves before my eyes with the desire for them. Nor even when I am asleep do they spare me their illusions. In the very solemnities of the Mass, when prayer ought to be more pure, the obscure phantoms of those delights so thoroughly captivate my wretched soul to themselves that I pay heed to their vileness rather than to my prayers. And when I ought to lament for what I have done I sigh rather for what I have had to forego. Not only the things that we did, but the places also and the times in which we did them are so fixed with thee in my mind that in the same times and places I re-enact them all with thee, nor even when I am asleep have I any rest from them. At times by the very motions of my body the thoughts of my mind are disclosed, nor can I restrain the utterance of unguarded words.

Oh, truly miserable I, and most worthy to utter that complaint of a stricken soul: "O wretched man that I am! Who shall deliver me from the body of this death?" Would that I might truthfully add also what follows: "I thank God through Jesus Christ our Lord." That grace, beloved, came to thee unsought, and by healing thee from these goads a single injury to thy body has cured many in thy soul, and in that wherein God is thought to be more adverse to thee, He is found to be more propitious. After the manner of a most faithful physician who does not spare pain that he may shew the way to health. But in me these goads of the flesh, these incentives of lust the very fervour of my youth and my experience of the sweetest pleasures greatly stimulate, and all the more oppress me with their assaults the weaker the nature is that they are assaulting. They preach that I am chaste who have not discovered the hypocrite in me. They make the purity of the flesh into a virtue, when it is a virtue not of the body but of the mind. Having some praise among men, I deserve none before God, Who tries out the heart and the reins and sees in the secret places. I am judged religious at this time, in which but a little part of religion is not hypocrisy, when he is extolled with the highest praise who does not offend the judgment of men. And this is peradventure in some measure praiseworthy, and seems in some measure acceptable to God, to wit if any by the example of his outward works, whatever his intention, is not a scandal of the Church, and if by his life the Name of God is not blasphemed among the infidels, nor the Order of his profession defamed among the carnal. And this also is a certain gift of divine grace, to wit one by the aid of which he comes not only to do good but to abstain from evil. But in vain does the former precede when the other follows not; as it is written: "Depart from evil, and do good." And in vain is either done, which is not done in the love of God.

But in the whole period of my life (God wot) I have ever feared to offend thee rather than God, I seek to please thee more than Him. Thy command brought me, not the love of God, to the habit of religion. See how unhappy a life I must lead, more wretched than all others, if I endure all these things here in vain having no hope of reward in the future. For a long time thou, like many others, hast been deceived by my simulation, so as to mistake hypocrisy for religion; and thus, strongly commending thyself to our prayers, what I expect from thee thou demandest from me. Do not, I beseech thee, presume so highly of me, nor cease by praying to assist me. Do not deem me healed, nor withdraw the grace of thy medicine. Do not believe me to be not in want, nor delay to succour my necessity. Do not think this strength, lest I fall before thou hold up the falling. False praise of themselves has injured many, and has taken away the support that they needed. Through *Esaias* the Lord cries: "O my people, they which lead thee cause thee to err, and destroy the way of thy paths." And through *Ezekiel* he says: "Woe to the women that sew pillows to all armholes, and make kerchiefs upon the head of every stature, to hunt souls!" Whereas by *Solomon* it is said: "The words of the wise are as goads, and as nails fastened by the masters of assemblies," nails, to wit, which cannot touch wounds softly but must pierce them. Cease, I beseech thee, from praise of me, lest thou incur the base mark of adulation and the charge of falsehood. Or, if thou suspect in me any good thing, the breath of vanity blow it away when it is praised. No one having skill in medicine judges an inward disease by inspection of the outward appearance. Nor do things obtain any merit before God which are common to the reprobate equally with the elect. And these things are they which are done outwardly, which none of the Saints so zealously performs as do hypocrites. "The heart is deceitful above all things, and desperately wicked: who can know it?" And "there is a way which seemeth right unto a man; but the end thereof are the ways of death." Rash is the judgment of man upon that which is reserved for divine scrutiny alone. Wherefore also it is written: "Judge none blessed before his death." To wit, praise not a man at that time when by praising him thou mayest make him no longer praiseworthy. And so much the more perilous is thy praise to me, the more pleasing it is: and so much the more am I taken and delighted by it, the more I study to please thee in all things.

Always, I beseech thee, be fearful for me rather than place thy trust in me, that I may ever be helped by thy solicitude. But now especially must thou fear, when no remedy is left in thee for my incontinence. I wish not that, exhorting me to virtue, and provoking me to fight, thou say: "Strength is made perfect in weakness"; and: "Yet he is not crowned, unless he strive lawfully." I seek not a crown of victory. It is enough for me to avoid danger. It is safer to avoid danger than to engage in battle. In whatsoever corner of heaven God may place me, He will do enough for me. For none there will envy any, since what he shall have will be sufficient for each. And indeed, that I may add the strength of authority also to this my counsel, let us hear Saint *Jerome*: "I confess my weakness, I wish not to fight in the hope of victory, lest peradventure I lose the victory." What need to abandon things certain, and to follow things uncertain?

THE FIFTH LETTER WHICH IS PETER'S REPLY TO HELOISE

Argument: *He divides the whole of* Heloise's *last letter into four heads, and replies clearly: he follows the reasoning of each, not so much to excuse himself as to teach, to exhort and to comfort* Heloise. *And first of all he gives the reason why in his last letter he set her name before his own. Secondly, if he made mention of his own perils and death, he explains that he had been adjured by her to do so. Thirdly, he approves her rejection of the praise that is given her: only she must do this sincerely and without any desire of praise. Fourthly, he pursues at length the occasion of their several conversion to the monastic life. The injury to a base part of his body, which she deplored, he thus extenuates, declaring it to be most salutary to them both, and a source of many good things in comparison with the lewd actions of the said shameful part: and on that account he extols the wisdom and clemency of God. Many other things also are included in the letter for the teaching and exhortation and comfort of* Heloise. *He includes also a short prayer wherewith the nuns of Paraclete may propitiate God towards* Abelard *and* Heloise.

To the Bride of Christ, the servant of the Same.

In four points, I observe, in which the body of thy last letter consists, thou hast expressed the commotion of they grief. And first of all thou complainest of this, that against the custom in letters, nay against the natural order of things even, our letter to thee placed thy name before mine in the greeting. Secondly, that when I ought rather to have offered thee a remedy for thy comfort, I increased thy desolation and provoked the tears that I should have stayed, by adding in that letter: "If the Lord should deliver me into the hands of mine enemies, so that they prevail over me and slay me," etc. And thirdly thou hast added thine old and assiduous complaint against God, of the manner of our conversion to God and of the cruelty of that betrayal which was practised upon me. Lastly, thou hast made an accusation of thyself against our praise of thee, with no mean supplication that henceforth I presume not so. And each of these points I have decided severally to answer, not so much in excuse of myself as for thine instruction or exhortation, that thou mayest more readily assent to our petitions when thou hast understood that they are based upon reason, and may give ear to me more fully in thine own case when thou findest me less reprehensible in mine, and be the more reluctant to despise me the less deserving thou seest me to be of reproach.

Of the unnatural (as thou sayest) order of our greeting, that was done, if thou examine it closely, according to thine opinion also. For it is common knowledge, as thyself hast shewn, that when any writes to his superiors their names are put first. And thou must understand that thou didst become my superior from that day on which thou becamest to me my lady, becoming the bride of my Lord, according to the words of Saint *Jerome*, writing thus to *Eustochium*: "For this reason I write 'my lady,' *Eustochium*.

For I must call her my lady who is the bride of my Lord." Right happy is such an exchange of wedlock; that being formerly the wife of a wretched man thou art now exalted to the bed of the King of Kings. Nor, by the privilege of this honour art thou set over thy former husband only, but over all and sundry the servants of that King. Marvel not therefore if both alive and dead I commend myself especially to thy prayers, since it is established by the common law that with Lords their wives can more prevail by intercession than the rest of their households, ladies rather than slaves. As a type whereof that Queen and Bride of the King of Kings is diligently described, where it is said in the Psalm: "Upon thy right hand did stand the Queen." As though, to speak openly, she being joined to his side adheres most intimately to her spouse and goes by his side, all the rest standing apart or following. Of the excellence of this prerogative the bride in the Canticles, exulting, that Ethiopian, so to speak, whom *Moses* took to wife, says: "I am black, but comely, O ye daughters of Jerusalem. The King hath brought me into his chambers." And again: "Look not upon me because I am black, because the sun hath looked upon me." In which words, albeit generally the contemplative soul is described which is called especially the Bride of Christ, yet that they more expressly pertain to you your outward habit shews. For that outward cult of black or coarse garments, in the likeness of the mournful vesture of good widows lamenting the husbands whom they loved, shows you in this world, according to the Apostle, to be widows indeed and desolate, such as are to be relieved at the charge of the Church. The grief of which widows for their spouse that was slain the Scripture commemorates, saying: "The women sitting over against the sepulchre and weeping lamented the Lord."

The Ethiopian woman also has an outward blackness in the flesh, and in so far as pertains to outward things appears less comely than other women; whereas she is not unlike them inwardly, but in many things is more comely and more white, as in her bones or her teeth The whiteness of which teeth is commended in the husband himself where it is said: "His teeth shall be white with milk." And so she is black in outward things, but in inward things comely; because in this life afflicted in the body by frequent tribulations of adversities, she darkens outwardly in the flesh, as is said by the Apostle: "Yea and all that will live godly in Christ shall suffer persecution." For as by white prosperity, so not incongruously by black is indicated adversity. But inwardly, as in the bones, she is white, because her soul is rich in virtues, as it is written: "The King's daughter is all glorious within." For the bones, which are within, surrounded by the outward flesh, and of that flesh which they bear or sustain are the strength and fortitude, fitly express the soul which gives life to the flesh itself, within which it is, sustains it, moves it, governs it, and ministers to it all wellbeing. Whereof the whiteness or the comeliness are those virtues wherewith it is adorned.

And she is black also in outward things because, while she is still an exile in this pilgrimage, she keeps herself vile and abject in this life, that in the other she may be made sublime, which is hidden with Christ in God, entering then into her inheritance. So indeed the true sun changes her colour, because the heavenly love of the bridegroom so humiliates her or torments her with tribulations, lest prosperity puff her up. He changes her colour thus, that is, he makes her unlike the rest of women who pant for earthly things and seek the glory of the world, that she may truly be made a lily of the valley by her humility: not indeed a lily of the mountains, like those foolish virgins who from purity of the flesh or from outward abstinence growing puffed up in themselves, are become parched by the fire of temptation. And rightly, in addressing the daughters of Jerusalem, that is the more imperfect of the faithful who deserve rather to be called daughters than sons, she says: "Look not upon me, because I am black, because the sun hath looked upon me." As who should say more openly: "If I thus humiliate myself or endure adversities in so manly a wise, it is not by my virtue but by His grace, whom I serve." Not thus is the use of heretics or hypocrites, who looking to the sight of men, in the hope of earthly glory, vehemently humiliate themselves or endure many evils to no good end. Whose abjection or tribulation of this sort, which they endure, is greatly to be marvelled at, since they are more wretched than all men, who enjoy the good things neither of this present life nor of the life to come. This also the bride diligently considering says: "Marvel not that I do so." But we must marvel at them who, vainly burning with the desire of earthly praise, deprive themselves of earthly riches, impoverishing themselves here as in the world to come. Which indeed is the continence of the foolish virgins, who are shut out from the door.

Rightly also does she say that because she is black, as we have said, and comely, she is beloved and taken into the chamber of the King, that is into the secret place or quiet of contemplation and to that bed whereof she says elsewhere: "By night on my bed I sought him whom my soul loveth." For the uncomeliness of her colour chooses the hidden rather than the open, and the secret rather than the public. And whoso is such a wife desires the secret enjoyment of a husband rather than the open, and will more readily be felt in bed than seen at table. And it often happens that as the flesh of black women is more uncomely, so is it softer to the touch, and so the enjoyment of them is greater and comes more easily in secret pleasures than in public, and their husbands, to enjoy them, take them in rather to their chambers than out before the world. According to which metaphor this spiritual bride fitly, when she said: "I am black but comely," straightway added, "therefore the King hath loved me and hath brought me into his chambers," relating each to each, namely that because she is comely he has loved her, and because she is black he has brought her into his chambers. Comely, as I have said, with inward virtues, which the bridegroom has loved; black outwardly from the adversity of bodily tribulations. Which blackness indeed, that to wit of bodily tribulations, easily turns away the minds of the faithful from the love of things earthly, and attaches them to the longing for life eternal, and often leads them from the tumultuous life of the world to the secret places of contemplation.

Thus Saint *Jerome* writes that in *Paul* was wrought the beginning of our, that is of the monastic, life. This abjectness also of coarse garments seeks retirement rather than publicity, and is eminently in keeping with the humility and the more secret place which befits our profession. For that nothing more provokes us to display in public than a costly garment, which is sought by none save for vainglory and the pomp of the world, Saint *Gregory* proves to us in these words: "For none adorns himself thus in secret but where he may be seen." As for the aforesaid chamber of the bride, it is that to which the Bridegroom himself in the Gospel invites whoso prays, saying: "But thou, when thou prayest, enter into thy closet, and when thou hast shut the door pray to thy Father which is in secret." As who should say: "Not in the streets and public places like the hypocrites." And so His chamber He calls a place that is secret from the tumults and from the sight of the world, where one may pray more quietly and more purely. Such are surely the secret places of monastic solitudes where we are bidden to close the door, that is to stop up every approach, lest the purity of prayer be any way obstructed, and our eye ravish the unhappy soul. And many of our habit, scorners of this counsel, nay this divine precept, we still find it hard to endure, who when they celebrate the divine offices, opening their cloisters or their quires, shamelessly comport themselves in the public view of women and men alike, and then especially when on solemn feasts they have decked themselves with precious ornaments, are made like unto those to whom they display themselves, profane men. In whose judgment a feast is the better celebrated, the richer it is in outward ornaments and more abundant in offerings. Of whose most wretched blindness, wholly contrary to the religion of Christ, which is of the poor, it is the more honourable to keep silence, the more scandalous it is to speak. Who utterly Judaizing, follow their own custom in place of a rule, and have made God's commandment vain by their tradition attending not to what they ought but to what is their wont. When, as Saint *Augustine* also reminds us, the Lord has said: "I am the Truth," not, "I am the custom." To the prayers of these, which to wit are made with an open door, let him commend himself who will. But ye who in the Chamber of the Heavenly King, led thither by Himself and resting in His embrace, with the door ever shut give yourselves up wholly to Him, the more intimately are joined to Him, according to the words of the Apostle: "He that is joined unto the Lord is one spirit," so much the purer and the more efficacious we believe you to be in prayer, and therefore the more vehemently we demand your aid. Which prayers also we believe are to be made the more devoutly for me, the more closely we are bound by a tie of mutual charity.

But if by the mention of the perils in which I labour, or of the death which I fear, I have distressed you, it was done at thine exhortation, nay adjuration. For so the first letter which thou didst address to me, contains in a certain passage the words: "And so in His Name Who still protects thee in a certain measure for Himself, in the Name of Christ, as His handmaids and thine, we beseech thee to deign to inform us by frequent letters of those shipwrecks in which thou still art tossed, that thou mayest have us at least, who alone have remained to thee, as partners in thy grief or joy. For they are wont to bring some comfort to a grieving man who grieve with him, and any burden that is laid on several is borne more easily, or transferred." Why therefore dost thou complain that I have made you partners in my anxiety, when thou didst by adjuration compel me? Did it behove thee, in so great a desperation of life, whereby I am tormented, to rejoice? Partners not in grief but in joy only do ye wish to be; nor to weep with them that weep but to rejoice with them that do rejoice? For there is no greater difference between true friends and false than that the former associate themselves with adversity, the latter with prosperity. Cease, I beseech thee, from saying such things, and forbear from complaints of this sort, which are worlds apart from the bowels of charity! Or if thou art still offended in this respect, it behoves me nevertheless, being placed in such a nick of peril, and in daily despair of life, to be solicitous for the welfare of my soul, and to provide for it while I may.

Nor wilt thou, if thou truly love me, find this provision odious. Nay rather, if thou hadst any hope of divine mercy towards me, so much the more wouldst thou wish me to be set free from the hardships of this life as thou seest them to be more intolerable. Thou at least knowest that whoso may deliver me from this life will snatch me from the greatest torments. What I shall hereafter incur is uncertain, but from what I shall be absolved is in no question. Every wretched life has a happy ending, and whoso truly feel compassion for the anxieties of others, and grieve for them, desire that they may be ended; and to their own hurt, even, if those whom they see to be anxious they truly love, and look not so much to their own advantage as to their friends'. Thus when a son has long been lying sick his mother desires his sickness to end even in death, a sickness which she herself cannot endure, and bears more easily to be robbed of him than to have him as a fellow-sufferer. And whosoever most delights in the presence of a friend yet prefers that his absence should be happy than his presence wretched. For hardships which he is unable to remedy he cannot endure. But to thee it is not given to enjoy our presence, wretched as it may be. Nor can I see why, when thou mightest provide anything in me for thine own advantage, thou shouldst prefer me to live most wretched rather than more happily to die. For if thou desirest to prolong our miseries for thine own advantage, thou art proved an enemy rather than a friend. If thou art reluctant so to appear, cease, I beseech thee, as I have said before, from these complaints.

But I approve thy reproval of praise; because in this thou shewest thyself to be the more praiseworthy. For it is written: "He that is first in his own accusation is just"; and: "He that humbleth himself shall be exalted." May it be so in thy heart as in thy writing! If it be so, thine is true humility, nor will it vanish away at our words. But see, I beseech thee, lest in this very matter thou be seeking praise when thou seemest to be fleeing it, and reprove that with thy mouth which thou desirest in thy heart. Whereof to *Eustochium* the virgin thus among other things writes Saint *Jerome:* "We are led by our natural evil. We give ear willingly to our flatterers, and albeit we reply that we are unworthy and a cunning blush suffuse our cheeks, yet inwardly the soul rejoices in its own praise." Such cunning also in the wanton *Galathea Virgil* describes, who what she desired drew after her by flight, and by the feint of a repulse incited her lover more hotly towards her: "And she flies to the willows," he says, "and wishes first to be seen." Before she hides herself she wishes to be seen, in that by that very flight whereby she seems to repulse the company of the youth, she may the more certainly obtain it. Thus it is that, when we seem to be shunning the praise of men, we excite it more warmly towards ourselves, and when we pretend that we wish to hide, lest any forsooth should discover what there is in us to praise, we excite more hotly to our praise the imprudent, because we seem more worthy of that praise. And this we say because it often occurs, not because we suspect such things of thee, being in no doubt as to thy humility. But from these words also we wish thee to refrain, lest thou appear to those who know thee less, as *Jerome* says, to be seeking fame by shunning it. Never will my praise puff thee up, but it will provoke thee to better things, and thou wilt embrace all the more zealously those things that I shall have praised, the more anxious thou art to please me. Our praise is not to thee a testimony to thy piety wherefrom thou mayest derive any pride. Nor ought we to believe our friends in their praise of anything, as we ought not to believe our enemies in their vituperation.

It now remains for us to come to that old, as we have said, and assiduous complaint on thy part, that namely wherein thou rather presumest to accuse God for the manner of our conversion than seekest to glorify Him as is fitting. I had thought that this bitterness of thy heart at so manifest an act of divine mercy had long since vanished. Which bitterness, the more perilous it is to thee, wearing out thy body and soul alike, is so much the more miserable and grievous to me. Since thou seekest to please me in all things, as thou professest, in this one thing at least, that thou mayest not torment me, nay that thou mayest supremely please me, lay aside this bitterness. Wherewith neither canst thou please me nor attain with me to blessedness. Wilt thou endure my proceeding thither without thee, I whom thou dost profess thy willingness to follow to the Vulcanian fires? In this one thing at least seek piety, lest thou sunder thyself from me whom am hastening, as thou believest, to God; and all the more readily, the more blessed is the goal to which we shall come, that our fellowship may be the more pleasant the more happy it also is. Remember what thou hast said. Call to mind what thou hast written, to wit that in this manner of our conversion, wherein God is believed to have been more thoroughly against me, He shewed Himself to be, as is manifest, more propitious to me. In this one thing at least let His disposition be pleasing to thee, that it is most salutary to me, nay to thee and me alike, if the force of grief admit reason. Neither grieve that thou art the cause of so great a good, for which thou needst not doubt that thou wert principally created by God. Neither lament that I have borne this loss, save when the blessings of the passions of the martyrs and of the death of Our Lord Himself shall make thee sad. Had it befallen me justly, wouldst thou have borne it any more easily, or would it offend thee less? Of a surety, if it were so, the consequence would be that it would be more ignominious for me and more praiseworthy for mine enemies, since justice would acquire praise for them and transgression contempt for me. Neither would any now reproach what has been done, so that he might be moved to compassion for me.

Yet, that in this way we may mitigate the bitterness of this grief, we shall shew that it befell us as justly as profitably, and that God was avenged more righteously upon the wedded than upon the fornicators. Thou knowest that after the pact of our marriage, when thou didst retire to Argenteuil with the nuns in cloister, I on a certain day did come to thee privily to visit thee, and what the intemperance of my desire then wrought with thee, even in a certain part of the refectory itself, since we had no place else whereto we might repair. Thou knowest, I say, how shamelessly we then acted in so hallowed a place, and one consecrated to the Most Holy Virgin. Which, all other shameful acts apart, must be a token of a far more dire punishment. Need I recall our earlier fornications and most shameful pollutions which preceded our marriage? Or shall I then recall my supreme betrayal whereby I turned away from thee thine uncle, with whom I was living constantly in his own house? Who would not consider that I was justly betrayed by him whom so shamelessly I myself had first betrayed? Dost thou think that the momentary pain of that wound suffices for the punishment of such crimes? Nay, for such wrongdoing is such a payment fitting? What wound dost thou imagine to satisfy the justice of God for so great a contamination, as we have said, of the most consecrated abode of His Mother? Of a surety, unless I am greatly in error, it was not that most wholesome wound that was turned to a punishment of those crimes, but the wounds which daily without ceasing I now endure. Thou knowest also how, when I carried thee pregnant to mine own country, thou didst put on the sacred habit and feign thyself to be a nun, and by such a pretence irreverently cozen the religion which now thou holdest. Wherefore consider how fitly to that religion divine justice, nay grace has led thee against thy will, which thou wert not afraid to cozen; wishing thee to expiate in the same habit the profanation that thou hadst made of it, and that the truth of the event should furnish a remedy for the lie of thy pretence, and correct the falsehood. And if thou wilt add to the divine justice wrought upon thee the thought of our own interest, thou wilt be able to call what God then did to us not so much His justice as His grace.

Take heed, therefore, take heed, beloved, with what drawnets of His mercy, from the depths of this so perilous sea the Lord has fished us up, and from the gullet of what a Charybdis He has saved our ship-wrecked albeit unwilling souls, so that each of us may fitly break out in that cry: *"Yet the Lord thinketh upon me."* Think, and think again in what dangers we were placed, and from what dangers the Lord plucked us out; and repeat always with the utmost thanksgiving what things the Lord has done for our soul; and comfort by our example any unrighteous who may despair of God's bounty, that they all may know what things are given to those that supplicate and pray, when such benefits are conferred upon the sinful and reluctant. Perpend the supreme designs of divine piety towards us, and how mercifully the Lord has turned His judgment into regeneration, and how prudently He has made use of the evil also, and piously deposed impiety, that the most just injury to one part of my body might heal two souls. Compare the danger and the manner of deliverance. Compare the sickness and the medicine. Examine the cause—our deserts, and marvel at the effect—His mercy.

Thou knowest to what great infamies my immoderate lust had sacrificed our bodies, until no reverence for honour, nor for God even, for the days of Our Lord's Passion or of any solemnity soever could recall me from wallowing in that filth. And thee also unwilling and to the utmost of thy power resisting and dissuading me, being weaker by nature, often with threats and blows I drew to consent. For with such ardour of concupiscence I was attached to thee that those wretched and most obscene pleasures which even to name confounds us, I preferred both to God and to myself; nor could divine clemency seemingly decide otherwise than by forbidding me those pleasures utterly, without any hope. Wherefore most justly and most clemently, albeit with the supreme treachery of thine uncle, that I might grow in many things, of that part of my body have I been diminished wherein was the seat of lust, and the whole cause of his concupiscence consisted, that rightly that member might mourn which had committed all in us, and might expiate in suffering what it had misdone in enjoyment, and might cut me off from those filthinesses wherein as in the mire I had immersed myself wholly, circumcising me in mind as in body; and so make me more fit to approach the holy altar, in that no contagion of carnal pollutions might ever again call me thence. With what clemency also did He wish me to suffer so greatly in that member, the privation of which would both aid the salvation of my soul and not degrade my body, nor prevent me in any ministration of mine office. Nay, it would make me so much more prompt to all things that are honourably done, the more wholly it set me free from the heavy yoke of concupiscence.

When therefore of these vilest members which from their practice of the utmost filthiness are called shameful, nor bear their proper name, divine grace cleansed me rather than deprived me, what else did it do than, to preserve the purity of cleanness, remove the sordid and vicious? This purity of cleanness indeed we have heard that sundry wise men most vehemently desiring have laid hands also upon themselves, that they might remove utterly from themselves this disgrace of concupiscence. For the removal of which thorn in the flesh the Apostle also is recorded to have besought the Lord, and not to have been heard. An example is that great philosopher of the Christians, *Origen*, who, that he might wholly extinguish this fire in himself, was not afraid to lay hands upon himself; as if he understood in the letter that they were truly blessed who for the Kingdom of Heaven's sake made themselves eunuchs, and believed such to be truthfully fulfilling what the Lord enjoins about the members by which offence cometh, that we should cut them off and cast them from us, and as if he interpreted that prophecy of *Esaias* as history rather than as mystery, wherein the Lord prefers eunuchs to the rest of the faithful, saying: "The eunuchs that keep my sabbaths, and choose the things that please me, and take hold of my covenant; even unto them will I give in mine house and within my walls a place and a name better than of sons and of daughters: I will give them an everlasting name, that shall not be cut off." And yet *Origen* incurs no small blame when in the punishment of his body he seeks a remedy for his fault. Having zeal, doubtless, for God, but not according to knowledge, he incurs the guilt of homicide, by laying a hand upon himself. By the suggestion of the devil or by the greatest of errors, plainly he wrought this upon himself, which through the mercy of God was perpetrated upon me by another. I escape blame, I incur it not. I deserve death, and I obtain life. I am called, and I hold back. The Apostle prays, and is not heard. He persists in prayer, and prevails not. Truly the Lord thinketh upon me. I will go and declare what the Lord hath done for my soul.

Approach then also, my inseparable comrade, in a common thanksgiving, who hast been made a partner both in the fault and in the grace. For of thy salvation also the Lord is not unmindful, nay He is most mindful of thee, Who, by a sort of holy presage of His Name, marked thee down to be especially His, to wit when he called thee *Heloise,* after His Own Name which is *Elohim;* He, I say, in His clemency has resolved to aid two in one, which two the devil strove in one to extinguish. For, but a little while before this befell us, He had bound us mutually by the indissoluble law of the nuptial sacrament, when I desired to retain thee, beloved beyond measure, for myself for all time, nay when He Himself was already preparing to convert us both to Himself by these means. For if thou hadst not been joined to me already in matrimony, easily on my withdrawal from the world, either at the suggestion of thy kindred or in thy relish for carnal pleasures, thou mightest have clung to the world. See, therefore, how solicitous the Lord was for us, as though He were reserving us for some great ends, and as though He were indignant, or grieved, that those talents of literary knowledge which He had entrusted to us both should not be dispensed to the glory of His Name; or as though, even, He feared for His most incontinent servant what is written in the Scripture: "that women make even the wise to fall away." As it is known of the wisest of men, namely *Solomon.*

But the talent of thy prudence, what usury it returns daily to the Lord, thou who hast already borne many spiritual daughters to the Lord, while I remain utterly barren, and labour in vain among the sons of perdition! Oh, how detestable a loss, how lamentable a misfortune, if, given over to the filthiness of carnal pleasures, thou were to bring forth a few children with pain for the world who now art delivered of a numerous progeny with exultation for heaven! Nor wouldst thou then be more than a woman, who now transcendest men even, and hast turned the curse of *Eve* to the blessing of *Mary*. Oh, how indecently would those holy hands, which now turn the pages of sacred books, serve the obscenities of womanly cares! He Himself has deigned to raise us up from the contagion of this filth, from the pleasures of this mire, and to draw us to Himself by force, wherewith He chose by striking him to convert Saint *Paul*, and by this example, haply, wrought in us, to deter others, skilled also in letters, from similar presumption. Let not this, therefore, distress thee, sister, I beseech thee, neither trouble thou the Father Who paternally corrects us; but pay heed to what is written: "Whom the Lord loveth He chasteneth, and scourgeth every son whom He receiveth." And elsewhere: "He that spareth his rod hateth his son." This punishment is momentary, not eternal; one of purgation, not of damnation. Hear the prophet, and take courage: "What do ye imagine against the Lord? He will make an utter end; affliction shall not rise up the second time." Hearken to that supreme and mighty exhortation of the Truth: "In your patience possess ye your souls." Wherefore also *Solomon:* "He that is slow to anger is better than the mighty; and he that ruleth his spirit than he that taketh a city." Does He not move thee to tears or to compunction, the Only-begotten Son of God, innocent, for thee and for all mankind taken by the hands of most impious men, led, beaten, and with veiled face mocked and buffeted, spat upon, crowned with thorns, and finally on what was then so ignominious a gibbet, the Cross, hung between thieves, and by that then horrible and execrable form of death slain? Hold Him ever, sister, as thy true Spouse, and the Spouse of all the Church before thine eyes, bear him in thy mind. Behold Him going out to be crucified for thee, and Himself bearing the Cross. Be of the people, of the women who wept and wailed for Him, as *Luke* relates in these words: "And there followed Him a great company of people, and of women, which also bewailed and lamented him." To whom indeed graciously turning, with clemency He foretold the destruction that was to come in vengeance of His death, which indeed, if they were wise, they might avoid by following this counsel: "Daughters of Jerusalem," He said, "weep not for Me, but weep for yourselves, and for your children. For, behold, the days are coming, in the which they shall say, Blessed are the barren, and the wombs that never bare, and the paps which never gave suck. Then shall they begin to say to the mountains, Fall on us; and to the hills, Cover us. For if they do these things in a green tree, what shall be done in the dry?"

Have compassion upon Him Who suffered willingly for thy redemption, and look with compunction upon Him who was crucified for thee. Be present ever in thy mind as His Sepulchre, and with the faithful women bewail and lament. Of whom also, as I have said, it is written: "The women seated over against the sepulchre lamented the Lord." Prepare with them the ointments for His burial, but better ointments, spiritual indeed not corporeal; for he requires the former fragrance who did not accept the latter. Be compunctious over these duties with the whole force of thy devotion. To which compunction of compassion indeed Himself also, through *Jeremy*, exhorts the faithful, saying: "Is it nothing to you, all ye that pass by? behold, and see if there be any sorrow like unto my sorrow, which is done unto me." That is, if there be any suffering for whom ye ought to grieve in compassion when I alone, for no fault, pay the penalty for the wrongdoing of others. He Himself is the Way whereby the faithful out of exile pass into the promised land. Who also raised up the Cross, wherefrom He thus cries, as a ladder for us to that end. Here for thee is slain the Only-begotten Son of God, as a free-will offering. Over Him alone grieve with compassion, be compassionate with grief. And that which was prophesied by *Zachary* the Prophet of devout souls, do thou fulfil: "They shall mourn for him, as one mourneth for his only son, and shall be in bitterness for him, as one that is in bitterness for his first-born."

See, sister, what a lamentation arises among those who love the King, over the death of his first-born and only-begotten son. Consider with what lamentation the household, with what sorrow the whole court is consumed; and when thou comest to the bride of the only-begotten who is dead, thou shalt not endure her intolerable wailings. This lamentation, sister, be thine; this wailing be thine, who hast given thyself in happy matrimony to the Bridegroom. He bought thee not with His wealth but with Himself. With His own Blood He bought thee and redeemed thee. What right He has over thee see, and behold how precious thou art. This price, indeed, which was paid for him the Apostle considering, and perpending how small a part of this price he was worth for whom it was paid, and attaching what return he should make for such a grace, says: "God forbid that I should glory save in the Cross of our Lord Jesus Christ, by whom the world is crucified unto me, and I unto the world." Thou art greater than the heaven, thou art greater than the world; of whom the Creator of the world is Himself become the price. What, I ask, has He, Who lacketh nothing, seen in thee, that to purchase thee He should strive even unto the agony of so horrid and ignominious a death? What, I say, does He seek in thee save thyself? He is a true friend who desires thyself, not what is thine. He is a true friend who when about to die for thee said: "Greater love hath no man than this, that a man lay down his life for his friends."

He truly loved thee, and not I. My love, which involved each of us in sin, is to be called concupiscence, not love. I satisfied my wretched desires in thee, and this was all that I loved. For thee, thou sayest, I have suffered, and peradventure that is true; but rather through thee, and that unwillingly. Not from love of thee but by compulsion of myself. Neither for thy salvation, but for thy grief. But He for thy salvation, He for thee of His own Will suffered, Who by His suffering heals all sickness, takes away all suffering. In Him, I beseech thee, not in me, be thy whole devotion, thy whole compassion, thy whole compunction. Grieve for the iniquity of such cruelty perpetrated upon One so innocent, not for the just punishment in righteousness of me, nay the supreme grace, as has been said, given to us both. For thou art unrighteous, if thou lovest not righteousness; and most unrighteous, if thou knowingly art adverse to the will, nay to the so great grace of God. Weep for thy Saviour, not for thy seducer; for thy Redeemer, not for thy defiler; for the Lord dead for thee, not the servant living, nay now for the first time truly freed from death. Beware, I beseech thee, lest what *Pompey* said to the mourning *Cornelia* be most basely applied to thee:

> After the combat still the Hero lives:
> His fortune perishes; thy tears are shed
> For that which thou didst love.

Pay heed, I pray thee, to this, and blush, lest what thou hast in mind be our former most shameless filthiness. Accept, therefore, sister, accept, I beg of thee, with patience such things as mercifully have befallen us. This is the rod of the father, not the sword of the persecutor. The father strikes that he may correct, lest the enemy wound that he may kill. With a wound He prevents death, He deals it not; he trusts in the steel that he may cut off the disease. He wounds the body, and heals the soul. He should have slain, and He makes to live. He withers up the uncleanness, that He may make clean. He punishes once that He may not punish always, one suffers by the wound that two may be spared from death. Two were in the fault, one in the punishment. This also is granted by the divine commiseration to the infirmity of thy nature, and in a measure justly. For inasmuch as naturally thou wert the weaker in sex and the stronger in continence, thou wert less liable to punishment. I give thanks to the Lord for this, Who thee then both set free from punishment, and preserved for a crown, and together with me, by the suffering of my body, cooled once and always from all the heat of this concupiscence, in which I had been wholly absorbed by my unbounded incontinence, lest I be destroyed; many passions of the heart, too strong for thy youth, from the assiduous suggestion of the flesh, He has reserved for the crown of martyrdom. Which albeit it may weary thee to hear, and thou forbid me to say, yet the truth is manifest. For to whom there is ever the strife, remains the crown; for he shall not be crowned, except he strive lawfully. But for me no crown remains, since there remains no cause for strife. The matter for the strife is lacking in him from whom is plucked out the thorn of concupiscence.

Yet I esteem it to be something if, though I may hereafter receive no crown, I may nevertheless escape some punishment, and by the pain of one momentary punishment may haply be forgiven many and eternal. For it is written of the men, nay the beasts, of this most wretched life: "The beasts have rotted in their dung." Also I complain less that my merit is diminished, while I doubt not that thine increases. For we are one in Christ, one flesh by the law of matrimony. Whatsoever is thine cannot, I consider, but be mine also. But thine is Christ, for thou art become His Bride. And now, as I have said, thou hast me for thy servant, whom formerly thou knewest as thy lord; yet more joined to thee now by spiritual love than subjected by fear. Wherefore also in thy patronage of us before Him we greatly trust, that I may obtain that by thy prayer which I cannot by mine own. And now especially, when the daily pressure of perils or perturbations allows me neither to live nor to find leisure for prayer. Nor to imitate that most blessed eunuch in authority under *Candace* Queen of the Ethiopians, who had the charge of all her treasure, and had come from so far to Jerusalem for to worship. To whom as he was returning there was sent by an angel *Philip* the Apostle, that he might convert him to the faith: Which he had merited already by his prayer or assiduity in holy reading. Whereby indeed, that not even then upon his journey might he be idle, albeit very rich and a Gentile, it befell by a great benefit of divine dispensation that the passage in the Scripture was before him which should furnish to the Apostle a most opportune occasion for his conversion. But that nothing may prevent this our petition, nor delay its fulfilment, I have studied to compose a prayer also, which ye may repeat as suppliants for me to the Lord, and to send it to thee.

GOD, Who from the first beginning of the human creation, with woman formed from the rib of man didst sanctify the great sacrament of the nuptial bond, and Who hast raised marriage to the greatest honour, as well by being born of a Virgin given in marriage, as by the first of Thy miracles, and for the incontinence of my frailty, when it pleased Thee, hast aforetime granted this remedy, despise not the prayer of Thine handmaid, which for mine own excesses and for those of my beloved in the sight of Thy Majesty I pour forth in supplication. Pardon, O most bountiful, nay bounty itself: pardon our so great offences, and may the ineffable immensity of Thy Mercy make trial of the multitude of our faults. Punish, I beseech Thee, in this world the guilty, that Thou mayest spare them in the world to come. Punish for the time, punish not in eternity. Take to Thy servants the rod of correction, not the sword of wrath. Afflict our flesh, that Thou mayest preserve our souls. Be a purifier, not an avenger; bountiful rather than just; the Merciful Father, not the Austere Lord. Prove us, O Lord, and try us, as the Prophet asks Thee of himself, as though to say: First examine my strength, and according thereto moderate the burden of temptations. Which also Saint *Paul* promising to Thy faithful, says: "God is faithful, Who will not suffer you to be tempted above that ye are able; but will with the temptation also make a way to escape, that ye may be able to bear it." Thou hast joined us together, O Lord, and Thou hast put us asunder when it pleased Thee and in the manner that pleased Thee. Now, O Lord, what Thou hast mercifully begun most mercifully finish. And these whom Thou hast divided one from another once upon earth join perennially to Thyself in heaven. Our hope, our portion, our expectation, our comfort, Lord Who art Blessed, world without end. AMEN.

Farewell in Christ, Bride of Christ, in Christ fare well, and in Christ dwell. AMEN.

THE SIXTH LETTER WHICH IS FROM THE SAID HELOISE TO THE SAID PETER

Argument: *Two things chiefly in this letter* Heloise *prays that* Abelard *will write back to her and her nuns: of which one is, that he will instruct them from whence the order of nuns has its origin. The other is that he will write some Rule for them, and prescribe a certain way of life, which shall apply to women only, this never having been attempted hitherto by any of the Holy Fathers. She seems to have been impelled to ask this by certain articles of the Benedictine Rule, which by women can scarcely or not at all without the greatest danger be obeyed: whereof she discourses so learnedly that she may seem to carry conviction that the Rule itself was written by the Holy Founder for men only, and not for women. Wherefore she judges that it is unbefitting that as heavy burdens be laid upon the weaker female sex as on the stronger male. She adds also her own opinion, wherefore the Holy Fathers did not prescribe rules for women, asserting that it suffices for women if they be not inferior to clerks and secular churchmen, or the monks who are called Canons Regular, in continence and abstinence. She discusses at length the moderate dispensation and discreet consideration of Saint* Benedict, *wherewith he tempered his Rule, and the actual observance of the Rule: especially the forbidden eating of meat and and the conceded use of wine. She treats fully also of outward works, and makes little of them, preferring inward. Lastly she urges* Abelard *that he will temper all things, whether of fasting or of holy practices, with such discretion as the weakness of the female sex requires. And here thou canst observe the erudition of the woman, and a bosom filled with all good doctrine. For what thing of great price wilt thou not find in so rich a store, whether thou seek philosophy or theology or even eloquence? Oh happy age, to behold such a woman in whom thou art left in doubt at what first, at what last, to marvel!*

To her Lord, who is specially his, singularly.

Lest haply thou shouldst find cause to blame me in anything for disobedience, upon the words of my unbounded grief is set the bridle of thine injunction, that in writing at least I may moderate those expressions which in speech it is not difficult so much as impossible to avoid. For nothing is less in our power than the heart, which we are forced rather to obey than able to command. Wherefore also when its motions excite us, there is none who may so repel their sudden promptings that they shall not readily break out, and flow forth the more easily in words, which are the ever ready language of the heart's passions. According as it is written: "Out of the abundance of the heart the mouth speaketh." I will hold back my hand therefore from writing what I cannot restrain my tongue from speaking. Would that the heart of the mourner were as ready to obey as the hand of the writer. And yet some remedy for my grief it is in thy power to confer, albeit thou mayest not altogether remove it. For as one nail drives out another, so a new thought expels an old, when the mind intent in another direction is obliged to dismiss altogether or to lay aside for a time the remembrance of what is past. But the more wholly any thought occupies the mind, and draws it away from other things, the more honourable we esteem that of which we think, and the more necessary the direction in which we turn our mind.

And so all we handmaids of Christ, and in Christ thy daughters demand with supplication two things of thy fatherhood which we foresee to be right necessary for ourselves. Whereof the former is that thou wilt instruct us by what origin the order of nuns began and what is the authority for our profession. And the other is that thou wilt institute some rule for us and set it forth in writing, which shall be proper for women and shall definitely describe the state and habit of our conversation; which we do not find to have been at any time done by the holy Fathers. Through the default and indigence whereof it now arises that to the profession of the same Rule men and women alike are received into monasteries, and the same yoke of monastic institution is imposed on the feeble sex equally with the strong. Inasmuch as at present the one Rule of Saint *Benedict*, among the Latins, women profess equally with men, which as it was clearly written for men alone, so by men alone can be obeyed in full, whether they be subordinates or superiors. Not to speak here of the other articles of the Rule, what is it to women that is written there touching cowls, femorals and scapulars? What is it to them touching tunics or woollen garments for the flesh, since the monthly purgations of their superfluous humours utterly shun these things. How also does it touch them, that is laid down concerning the Abbot, that he himself shall read the Gospel, and thereafter intone the hymn? What of the Abbot's table, set apart for him with the pilgrims and the guests? Does it in any way become our religion either that an Abbess should ever give hospitality to men, or that she should eat with those men whom she has taken in? Oh how easy a step to the destruction of the souls of men and women is their dwelling together in one place! But especially at table, where gluttony prevails and drunkenness, and wine is drunk with enjoyment, wherein is luxury. Whereof also Saint *Jerome* forewarning us, writing to a mother and daughter, reminds them, saying: "Hard is it to preserve modesty at table." And the poet himself also, the teacher of luxury and uncleanness, in his book entitled Of the Art of Loving, studiously sets forth what an occasion of fornication banquets especially furnish, saying:

> When wine has sprinkled Cupid's thirsty wings
> He droops, and where he has alighted stays . . .
> Then laughter comes; the poor exalts his head:
> Fly grief and care, and wrinkles leave the brow . . .

There often girls have snared the hearts of youths,
And Venus in their veins, fire burns in fire.

And even if they admitted the women only, to whom they had given hospitality, to their table, is there no hidden danger there? Certes, to the seduction of a woman nothing so easily conduces as womanly flattery. Nor does a woman communicate the foulness of a corrupted mind to any so easily as to another woman. Wherefore also the aforesaid *Jerome* greatly exhorts the women of a sacred profession to shun the approach of women of the world. Finally, if excluding men from our hospitality we admit only women, is it not evident that we must offend and exasperate the men whose services monasteries of the weaker sex require, especially if upon them from whom we receive most we appear to bestow but little gratitude or none? And if the tenor of the aforesaid Rule cannot be observed by us, I fear lest those words of the Apostle *James* be said for our damnation also: "Whosoever shall keep the whole law, and yet offend in one point, he is guilty of all." Which is to say: In this he is pronounced guilty who performs many things, that he does not fulfil all. And he is made a transgressor of the law by one thing, whereof he was not the fulfiller unless he observed all its precepts. Which straightway diligently expounding, the Apostle has added: "For he that said, Do not commit adultery, said also, Do not kill. Now if thou commit no adultery, yet if thou kill, thou art become a transgressor of the law." As who should say openly: Therefore he becomes guilty by the transgression of any one precept soever, because the same Lord Who ordains one ordains also the other. And whatsoever precept of the law be violated, He is contemned Who established the law not in one commandment but in all the commandments alike.

But, to pass over the institutes of this Rule, which we cannot altogether, or may not without danger observe: where has it ever been the custom for convents of nuns to go out to gather the harvest, or to undertake the work of the fields? Or can we in a single year make probation of the constancy of the women we receive, or, by three readings of the Rule, as is therein ordered, instruct them? Nay, what could be more foolish than to enter upon an unknown path, not yet explored? What more presumptuous than to choose and profess a life of which thou knowest nothing, or to make a vow which thou canst not fulfil? And inasmuch as discretion is the mother of all virtues, and reason is the mediator of all good, who will consider that to be either a virtue or good which is seen to disagree with both reason and discretion? For those virtues which exceed bounds and measure, as *Jerome* asserts, are to be reckoned in the tale of vices. But who does not see it to be disjoined from all reason and discretion if, in imposing burdens, the strength of those upon whom they are to be imposed be not first considered, that human industry may follow the natural constitution. Who lays such burdens upon an ass as he deems fitted for an elephant? Who enjoins the same things upon children or upon the aged as upon men? That is, the same for the weak as for the strong, for the sick as for the whole, for women as for men? For the weaker sex, forsooth, as for the stronger? Whereto the Pope Saint *Gregory* diligently attending, in the fourteenth chapter of his Pastoral, has thus distinguished, both touching admonition and touching precepts: "In one way therefore are men to be admonished and in another way women, for heavy burdens are to be laid upon the former, but on the latter things lighter: and let great things exercise the one, but light things correct the other gently."

Certain it is that they who wrote the rules for monks not only were silent altogether concerning women, but also laid down things which they knew to be in no way suitable to them, and let it be seen plainly enough that by no means were the necks of bull and heifer to be brought under the same yoke of a common rule, since those whom nature created unequal it is not fitting to make equal in labour. And of this discretion Saint *Benedict* not unmindful, as though filled with the spirit of all the the righteous, to the quality of men or of the times so moderates all things in the Rule, that all things may be done within measure. Thus first of all, beginning with the Abbot, he orders that he shall so preside over his subordinates, that according to the quality (he says) or intelligence of each he may so conform and adapt himself that not only he may not suffer any detriment of the flock committed to him, but may rejoice in the increase of a good flock, and may ever be suspicious of his own frailty and remember that the bruised reed he shall not break. He must also discern the times, bearing in mind the discretion of Holy *Jacob* when he said: "The children are tender, and the flocks and herds with young are with me; and if men should overdrive them, in one day all the flock will die." Taking therefore these and other testimonies of discretion, the mother of virtues, let him temper all things, that they may be what the strong desire and the weak shun not.

To this moderation of dispensation indeed pertains the indulgence given to children, the aged and the weak generally, the feeding of the lector or septimanarius in the kitchen before the rest, and in the convent itself the provision of the quality or quantity of the food according to the diversity of the man. Of each of which matters is it diligently written there. The statutory times of fasting also he thus relaxes according to the quality of the season or the quantity of the labour, as natural infirmity demands. What, I ask, when he who thus moderates all things to the quality of men and seasons, that those things may be done by all without murmuring which are instituted; what, I say, would he provide for women were he to institute a Rule for them also, as for men? For if in certain things he is obliged to temper the rigour of the Rule to the young, the old and the infirm according to the weakness or infirmity of their nature, what would he provide for the weaker sex whose feeble and infirm nature is known to all? Perpend therefore how far it departs from all discretion of reason that women and men alike should be bound by the profession of a common Rule, and the weak laden with the same burden as the strong. I deem that it is sufficient for our infirmity that the virtue as well of continence as of abstinence should make us equal to the rulers of the Church themselves, and to the clergy, who are confirmed in holy orders. Especially since the Truth saith: "Every one that is perfect shall be as his master." In which also it would be reputed a great thing, if we could equal the religious laity. For what we think to be of little account in the strong, in the weak we admire. In the words of the Apostle: "Strength is made perfect in weakness." But, lest the religion of the laity be considered a small thing, what was the religion of *Abraham*, of *David*, of *Job*, albeit they had wives, *Chrysostom* in his Seventh Sermon upon the Epistle to the Hebrews reminds us, where he says: "Many are the things in which a man may labour, to charm that beast. What are they? Labours, readings, vigils. 'But what are those to us, who are not monks?—dost thou ask me? Ask *Paul* rather, when he says: 'Patient in all tribulation, continuing instant in prayer'; and when he says: 'Make not provision for the flesh, to fulfil the lusts thereof.' For he wrote these things not to monks only, but to all that were in the cities. For the secular man ought not to have anything more than the monk, save only that he may lie with a wife. For in this he has licence, but in other things not at all, but ought to do all things similarly to the monks. For the Beatitudes also, which are the words of Christ, were spoken not to monks only. Otherwise the whole world must perish, and He has enclosed in a narrow space those things that are of virtue. And how can marriage be honourable, which is so great an hindrance to us?"

From which words, it is plainly perceived that whoso adds the virtue of continence to the evangelical precepts, will fulfil monastic perfection. And would to God that our Religion could rise to that level, that it should fulfil the Gospel, not overpass it, lest we desire to be more than Christians. For this reason surely, if I be not mistaken, the Holy Fathers have decided not to set up for us, as for men, any general Rule, as it were a new law, nor to burden our weakness with a magnitude of vows, paying heed to the words of the Apostle: "Because the law worketh wrath: for where no law is, there is no transgression." And again: "Moreover the law entered, that the offence might abound." The same great preacher of continence also, greatly considering our infirmities, and as though urging the younger widows to a second marriage, says: "I will therefore that the younger women marry, dear children, guide the house, give none occasion to the adversary to speak reproachfully." Which also Saint *Jerome* considering to be most salutary, advises *Eustochium* of the rash vows taken by women, in these words: "But if they that be virgins, yet on account of other faults be not saved, what shall become of those that have prostituted the members of Christ, and have turned the Temple of the Holy Ghost into a brothel? Better were it for a man to undergo matrimony, to have trodden the level ground, than, straining after the heights, to fall into the depths of hell. Whose rash profession Saint *Augustine* also considering, in his book, Of Widowly Continence, writes to *Julian* in these words: "Let her who has not begun deliberate; let her who has attempted persevere. Be no occasion given to the adversary, no oblation taken from Christ."

Wherefore also the Canons, considering our weakness, have decreed that deaconesses ought not to be ordained before forty years, and then after diligent probation, whereas deacons may be promoted from twenty. And there are those in monasteries who are called Canons Regular of Saint *Augustine*, professing as they say a certain rule, who deem themselves in no way inferior to monks, albeit we see them eat flesh and wear linen garments. Whose virtues if our weakness can equal, surely it is not to be considered a little thing. And that in all matters of food we should be given a safer and milder indulgence nature itself also provides, which has furnished our sex with a greater virtue of sobriety. For it is evident that women can be maintained at a far more sparing cost and with less nourishment than men, nor does physic teach us that they are so easily inebriated. Whereof also *Macrobius Theodosius*, in the seventh book of the Saturnalia, reminds us in these words: "*Aristotle* says that women are rarely inebriated, old men often. The woman is of an extremely humid body. This we learn from the lightness and brilliancy of her skin. We learn it especially from the regular purgations, relieving the body of its superfluous humours. When therefore wine that has been drunk falls into so general an humour, it loses its strength; nor does it easily strike the seat of the brain, its strength being extinguished." Likewise: "The woman's body is cleansed by frequent purgations, it is pierced with many holes, that it may open channels and provide a way for the humours flowing into the issue of egestion. By these holes the vapour of wine is speedily released. Whereas in old men the body is dry, as is proved by the roughness and dulness of their skin." And so, considering these things, perpend how much more safely and rightly to our nature and infirmity any food and drink may be allowed, whose hearts cannot easily be burdened with gluttony and drunkenness, since from the former our parsimony in food, from the latter the quality of the female body, as I have said, protects us. It should be enough for our infirmity and should be reckoned a great thing if, living continently and without possessions, and wholly occupied with the service of God, we equal the leaders of the Church themselves, or the religious laity in our way of living, those in fine who are called Canons Regular and profess that they especially follow the Apostolic life.

Lastly, it is a great mark of providence in those who bind themselves to God by a vow that they should vow less and perform more, and ever add something gratuitous to the payment of what they owe. For thus, with His Own mouth, the Truth says: "When ye shall have done all those things which are commanded you, say, We are unprofitable servants: we have done that which was our duty to do." As who should say openly: Therefore are we unprofitable and good for nothing, and to be deemed of no merit, because contented with the mere payment of what was our duty we have given nothing freely in addition. Of which things indeed, to be freely added, the Lord Himself also elsewhere, speaking in a parable, says: "And whatsoever thou spendest more, when

I come again I will repay thee." Whereunto indeed if in these days many rash professors of monastic religion were more diligently to give heed, and were to consider what profession they were swearing, and were carefully to study the actual tenour of the Rule, they would offend less through ignorance and sin less through neglect. But now indiscriminately all alike hastening to the monastic life, and being inordinately received, more inordinately live, and, with the same facility wherewith they profess an unknown Rule, scorning that Rule, set up the customs they prefer as a law. We must take heed therefore that we presume not to lay that burden upon the woman, under which we see well-nigh all men totter, nay succumb. We see that the world has now grown old, and that men themselves, with all other creatures which are of the world, have lost the pristine vigour of their nature, and, in the words of the Truth, the love not of many but of well-nigh all has waxed cold. So that, in accordance with the quality of men, it is necessary either to change or to temper those Rules that were written for men.

Of which discretion indeed Saint *Benedict* being not unmindful avows that he has so tempered the rigour of the monastic life that he regards the Rule written by himself, when compared with former institutes, as no more than an institution of honest living, and some beginning of godly conversation, saying: "We have written this Rule, that observing it we may shew ourselves to have in a certain measure be it honesty of conduct or a beginning of conversation. For the rest, for whoso hastens to the perfection of conversation, there are the teachings of the Holy Fathers, the observation whereof may lead men to the pinnacle of perfection." Likewise: "Whosoever thou art, therefore, that hastenest to the heavenly kingdom, practise, Christ helping thee, this least Rule of a beginning, and then finally thou shalt come, God protecting thee, to the higher pinnacles of doctrine and virtues." Who, as he himself says, whereas we read that of old the Holy Fathers were wont to complete the whole Psalter in a day, so tempered psalmody to the lukewarm that, in his distribution of the Psalms over the week, monks may be content with a lesser number of them than the secular clergy. What moreover is so contrary to monastic religion as that which most foments luxury and excites tumults, and wipes out that image of God Himself in us, whereby we are exalted above the rest of creation, namely reason? But that thing is wine, which above all things else pertaining to nourishment the Scripture asserts to be harmful, warning us to beware thereof. Of which also that wisest of the wise reminds us in the Proverbs, saying: "Wine is a mocker, strong drink is raging; and whosoever is deceived thereby is not wise. Who hath woe? who hath sorrow? who hath contentions? who hath babbling? who hath wounds without cause? who hath redness of eyes? They that tarry long at the wine; they that go to seek mixed wine. Look not thou upon the wine when it is red, when it giveth his colour in the cup, when it moveth itself aright: at the last it biteth like a serpent, and stingeth like an adder. Thine eyes shall behold strange women, and thine heart shall utter perverse things: yea, thou shalt be as he that lieth down in the midst of the sea, or as he that lieth upon the top of a mast. They have stricken me, shalt thou say, and I was not sick; they have beaten me, and I felt it not: when shall I awake? I will seek it yet again." Likewise: "It is not for kings, O *Lemuel*, it is not for kings to drink wine, nor for princes strong drink; lest they drink, and forget the law, and pervert the judgment of any of the afflicted." And in Ecclesiasticus it is written: "Wine and women make the wise to fall away." *Jerome*, also, writing to *Nepotian* of the life of the clergy and seeming greatly indignant that the priests of the Law, abstaining from all that might make them drunken, should in this abstinence surpass our priests, says: "Never smell of wine, lest thou hear said of thee those words of the philosopher: This is not offering a kiss, but proffering a cup." Priests given to wine the Apostle also condemns, and the Old Law forbids: "Do not drink wine nor strong drink, when ye go into the tabernacle of the congregation." By strong drink in the Hebrew tongue is understood every potion that may inebriate, whether that which is produced by fermentation; or from the juice of apples, or of the hive, is decocted into sweetness, and potions of herbs, or when the fruit of the palm is pressed into liquor, or water enriched with boiled grain. Whatsoever inebriates and upsets the balance of the mind, shun thou as it were wine. Lo, what is forbidden for the enjoyment of kings is to priests utterly denied, and is clearly more perilous than any food.

And yet that so spiritual man, Saint *Benedict*, is constrained by a certain dispensation of the times to allow it to monks. "Albeit," he says, "we read that wine is not for monks, yet because in our times it is wholly impossible to persuade monks of this," and so forth. He had read, if I be not mistaken, what is written in the Lives of the Fathers in these words: "Certain persons told the Abbot Pastor of a certain monk that he did not drink wine, and he said to them that wine was not for monks." And again: "Once upon a time there was a celebration of masses on the Mount of *Anthony* the Abbot, and there was found there a jar of wine. And one of the elders taking up a small vessel bore the cup to the Abbot *Sisoi* and gave it to him. And he drank once; and a second time, and he took it and drank. He brought it to him also a third time, but he took it not, saying: Peace, brother, knowest thou not that it is Satan?" And furthermore of the Abbot *Sisoi* "*Abraham* says therefore to his disciples: If it come to pass on the Sabbath and the Lord's Day at church, and he shall drink three cupfuls, is it overmuch? And the old man said: If it were not Satan it would not be overmuch." Where, I ask, is flesh meat ever condemned by God or forbidden to monks? Look, I beseech thee, and give heed by what necessity he tempers the Rule in this thing even which is more perilous to monks and which he knew to be not for them. Since forsooth in his day it was not possible to persuade monks to abstinence of this kind. Would that the same dispensation in these days also might be used, that in those things which, being means between good and evil, are called indifferent there might be such tempering, that what now cannot be enforced by persuasion the profession should not exact, and all mean things being conceded without scandal it should suffice to forbid only things sinful: and so also dispensation might be given in food as in raiment, that what can be more cheaply purchased might serve, and in all things necessity and not superfluity be considered.

For no great care need be given to those things which do not prepare us for the Kingdom of God, or which commend us least to God. And these are all such things as are worn outwardly and are common alike to the reprobate and to the penitent, to the hypocrites and to the religious. For nothing so distinguishes Jews from Christians as the discrimination of outward and inward actions, especially since between the children of God and of the devil love alone discriminates, which the Apostle calls the fulfilling of the law and the end of the precept. Wherefore also the same, diminishing this boasting of works that he may set above it the righteousness of faith, addressing Jewry, says: "Where is boasting then? It is excluded. By what law? of works? Nay; but by the law of faith. Therefore we conclude that a man is justified by faith without the deeds of the law." And again: "For if *Abraham* were justified by works, he hath whereof to glory; but not before God. For what saith the scripture? *Abraham* believed God, and it was counted unto him for righteousness." And yet again: "But to him that worketh not, but believeth on him that justifieth the ungodly, his faith is counted for righteousness." The same also allowing Christians the use of all manner of meat and from such things distinguishing those that justify, says: "For the kingdom of God is not meat and drink; but righteousness, and peace, and joy in the Holy Ghost." All things indeed are clean, but the evil is in the man who eateth to offend. It is good not to eat meat and not to drink wine, nor to do aught whereby thy brother may be offended or scandalised or weakened. For in this place there is not any eating of meat forbidden, but the offence of eating, whereby certain of the converted Jews were scandalised, when they saw those things also eaten which the law had forbidden. Which scandal indeed the Apostle *Peter* seeking also to avoid was gravely reprimanded by him and wholesomely corrected. As *Paul* himself, writing to the Galatians, records. And again, writing to the Corinthians: "But meat commendeth us not to God." And again: "Whatsoever is sold in the shambles, that eat. For the earth is the Lord's, and the fulness thereof." And to the Colossians: "Let no man therefore judge you in meat or in drink." And a little later: "If ye be dead with Christ from the rudiments of the world, why, as though living in the world, are ye subject to ordinances (Touch not; taste not; handle not; which all are to perish with the using;) after the commandments and doctrines of men?" The rudiments of the world he calls the first elements of the law touching carnal observances; in the doctrine whereof as in the learning of the rudiments of letters the world at first, that is a people still carnal, was practised. From these rudiments indeed, that is from carnal observances, they are dead who are Christ's or are of His Own, for they owe them nothing, dwelling now not in the world, that is among carnal men paying heed to forms, and discerning, that is distinguishing certain meats or things whatsoever from others and so saying: Touch not these or those. Which things, forsooth, being touched or tasted or handled, says the Apostle, are for the destruction of the soul by that very use wherewith we use them, even for some purpose of humility, according I say to the precept and doctrine of men (that is of carnal persons, and I understanding the law carnally,) rather than of Christ or of His Own.

For He, when he destined His Apostles to the service of preaching, where more than ever all scandals were to be avoided, yet so allowed them the eating of all meats that, by whomsoever they might hospitably be taken in, they should live as those lived, to wit eating and drinking such things as might be set before them. And assuredly Saint *Paul* foresaw already by the Holy Spirit that they would fall away from this, the Lord's teaching and his own.

Whereof he writes to *Timothy*, saying: "Now the Spirit speaketh expressly, that in the latter times some shall depart from the faith, giving heed to seducing spirits, and doctrines of devils; speaking lies in hypocrisy; having their conscience seared with a hot iron; forbidding to marry, and commanding to abstain from meats, which God hath created to be received with thanksgiving of them which believe and know the truth. For every creature of God is good, and nothing to be refused, if it be received with thanksgiving: for it is sanctified by the word of God and prayer. If thou put the brethren in remembrance of these things, thou shalt be a good minister of Jesus Christ, nourished up in the words of faith and of good doctrine, whereunto thou hast attained." Who moreover would not prefer *John* and his disciples wasting themselves with overmuch fasting to Christ Himself and His Disciples in religion, if he turned his bodily eye to the exhibition of outward abstinence? Whereof also the said disciples of *John*, murmuring against Christ and His Disciples, as though still Judaizing in outward things, questioned the Lord Himself, saying: "Why do the disciples of *John* and of the Pharisees fast, but thy disciples fast not?" Which Saint *Augustine* diligently examining, and seeking out what difference there is between virtue and the exhibition of virtue, thinks thus of things that are done outwardly, that works add nothing to merit. For so he says in his book, Of Conjugal Welfare: "Continence is a virtue not of the body but of the soul. But the virtues of the heart are made manifest now in the body, now in the natural habit, as the virtue of martyrs has been apparent in the endurance of suffering." Likewise: "For patience was already in *Job*, which the Lord knew and bore testimony thereto, but it was made known to men by the proof of temptation." Likewise: "In truth, that it may be more openly understood how virtue may be in natural habit, although not in works, I will quote an example whereof no Catholic is in doubt. That the Lord Jesus in the verity of the flesh was anhungered, and athirst, and did eat and drink, none doubteth of those who are faithful to His

Gospel. Was there not then in Him a virtue of continence in meat and drink, as great as in *John* the Baptist? For *John* came neither eating nor drinking, and they said: He hath a devil. The Son of man came eating and drinking, and they said: Behold a man gluttonous, and a wine-bibber, a friend of publicans and sinners." Likewise: "Thereafter He added, when He had said these things touching *John* and Himself: *But Wisdom is justified of her children,* who see that the virtue of continence ought always to subsist in natural habit, but in works to be made manifest according to the opportunity of things and seasons, as the virtue of patience to the Holy Martyrs. Wherefore, as the merit of patience is not unequal in *Peter,* who suffered, and in *John* who suffered not, so is the merit of continence not unequal in *John* who knew not marriage and in *Abraham* who begat sons and daughters. And the celibacy of the one and the marriage of the other, according to the difference of the times, fought for Christ. But *John* had continence in works also, *Abraham* in habit only. And so at that time when the Law also, after the days of the Patriarchs, declared him accursed who should not raise up seed in Israel; and he who could not did not come forth, nevertheless he had it. But after that the fulness of the time came, that it might be said: He that is able to receive it, let him receive it; he that has, let him work; he that will not work, let him not say, falsely, that he has.

From these words it is clearly gathered that virtues alone acquire merit before God; and whoso are equal in virtue, howsoever they may differ in works, deserve equally of Him. Wherefore whosoever are truly Christians are thus wholly occupied with the inner man, that they may adorn him with virtues and cleanse him of vices, that for the outer man they may assume no charge, or but a little. Wherefore also we read that the Apostles themselves behaved themselves thus rustically and almost shamelessly in the company even of the Lord, so that as though forgetful of all reverence and honesty when they passed through the cornfields, they were not ashamed to pluck the ears, to strip and to eat them, in the manner of children. Nor were they heedful even of the washing of their hands when they were about to sit down to meat. Who when they were rebuked by divers persons, as though for uncleanness, the Lord excusing them said: "To eat with unwashen hands defileth not a man." When also He added generally that by no outward things is a man defiled; but from those things only which proceed out of the heart, which are, He says, "evil thoughts, murders, adulteries," and the rest. For unless the spirit be first corrupted by evil intention, it cannot be a sin whatsoever is done outwardly in the body. Wherefore also He well says that adultery or murder proceed out of the heart, which are perpetrated without bodily contact, according to the texts: "Whosoever looketh on a woman to lust after her hath committed adultery with her already in his heart." And: "Whosoever hateth his brother is a murderer." And even with contact or injury to the body these things are not committed, when for instance a woman is ravished by violence or a judge compelled by justice to kill a man. "For no murderer," as it is written, "hath eternal life." It is not, therefore, what things are done, but in what state of mind they are done that we must consider, if we seek to please Him who trieth the heart and the reins and seeth in the hidden places, who will judge the secrets of men, says *Paul*, "according to my Gospel"; that is, according to the doctrine of my preaching. Wherefore also the modest offering of the widow, that was two mites which make a farthing, was preferred to the copious offerings of all the rich by Him to Whom it is said: "My goodness extendeth not to Thee," to Whom the offering is made pleasing rather by the offerer than the offerer by the offering, as it is written: "The Lord had respect unto *Abel* and to his offering." That is to say, He looked first at the devotion of the offerer and thereafter was pleased with the gift offered. Which devotion indeed of the heart is so much the more valued by God as we trust less in those things which are done outwardly. Wherefore also the Apostle, after the general indulgence in matters of food, whereof as we have said above he writes to *Timothy*, has added touching the exercise of the body also: "Exercise thyself rather unto godliness. For bodily exercise profiteth little; but godliness is profitable unto all things, having promise of the life that now is, and of that which is to come." Inasmuch as the pious devotion of the mind to God, both in this life earns things needful from Him, and in that which is to come things eternal.

By which lessons indeed what else are we taught than to know Christ, and with *Jacob* to provide a refection for our Father of the domestic animals? Not with *Esau* to go to the field to hunt for venison, and in outward things play the Jew. Hence cometh also that verse of the Psalmist: "Thy vows are upon me, O God; I will render praises unto thee." Whereto add also that line of the poet: "Seek nothing for thyself without." Many and beyond number are the testimonies of the learned, both secular and ecclesiastic, wherein for those things that are without and are called indifferent, we are taught not greatly to care. Otherwise the works of the Law, and the insupportable yoke of its slavery, as *Peter* says, would be preferable to the freedom of the Gospel and the pleasant yoke of Christ and His light burden. To which pleasant yoke and light burden Christ of Himself inviting us says: "Come unto me, all ye that labour and are heavy laden." Wherefore also the Apostle aforesaid, vehemently rebuking certain persons already converted to Christ but thinking still to retain the works of the Law, as it is written in the Acts of the Apostles, says: "Men and brethren, why tempt ye God, to put a yoke upon the neck of the disciples, which neither our fathers nor we were able to bear? But we believe that through the grace of the Lord Jesus Christ we shall be saved, even as they." And do thou, I beg of thee, an imitator not of Christ only but of this Apostle, in discretion as in name do thou so moderate the precepts of works as shall suit our weak nature, and that we may be set free above all for the offices of divine praise. Which oblation indeed, refusing all outward sacrifices, the Lord commending says: "If I were hungry, I would not tell thee; for the world is mine, and the fulness thereof. Will I eat the flesh of bulls, or drink the blood of goats? Offer unto God thanksgiving; and pay thy vows unto the Most High: and call upon me in the day of trouble; I will deliver thee, and thou shalt glorify me."

Nor indeed do we say this rejecting the labour of corporal works, when necessity may have demanded them; but lest we think those things great which serve the body and obstruct the celebration of the divine office, especially when on apostolic authority it is allowed especially to devout women that they may be sustained by the provision of others rather than by the fruits of their own labour. Wherefore *Paul* to *Timothy:* "If any man or woman that believeth have widows, let them relieve them, and let not the church be charged; that it may relieve them that are widows indeed." Widows indeed he calls those whomsoever devoted to Christ, to whom not only is He dead but the world also is crucified, and they to the world. Who, it is fitting, should be relieved at the charge of the Church, as from the private fortune of their proper husband. Wherefore also the Lord Himself provided for His Mother as procurator an Apostle rather than her own husband, and the Apostles instituted seven Deacons, that is Ministers of the Church, who should minister unto devout women. We know indeed that the Apostle writing to the Thessalonians so restrained certain idle or curious livers that he ordered that if any would not work neither should he eat. And Saint *Benedict* enjoined the work of the hands principally for the avoidance of idleness. But did not *Mary* sit idle that she might hear the words of Christ; while *Martha* toiled as well for her as for the Lord, and murmured as though in jealousy at her sister's repose, as who should bear alone the burden of the day and the heat? Wherefore also to-day we see those frequently murmur who labour in outward things, when they minister earthly things to those who are occupied with divine offices. And often of those things which tyrants seize from them they complain less than of those which they are compelled to pay to the lazy, as they say, and idle. Whom nevertheless they observe not merely to be hearing the words of Christ but also to be assiduously occupied in the reading and singing of those words. Nor do they heed that it is not a great matter, as the Apostle says, if they communicate carnal things to them from whom they look for things spiritual. Nor is it unbecoming that they who pay heed to earthly things should serve those who are occupied with spiritual things. Hence also to the Ministers of the Church by the sanction of the Law itself was this wholesome liberty of leisure conceded, that the Tribe of *Levi* should receive no earthly inheritance, whereby they might the more expeditiously serve the Lord, but from the labour of others should take tithes and oblations.

Touching the abstinence also of fasts, which Christians regard as abstinence from vices rather than from food, thou must consider whether thou shouldst decree aught to be added to the institution of the Church, and must institute what is fitting for us. But chiefly touching the ecclesiastical offices and the order of the Psalms must provision be made, that in this, at least, if it please thee, thou mayest exonerate our infirmity. Let it not be necessary, when we complete the Psalter in the week, to repeat the same Psalms; which week also when Saint *Benedict* had distributed it according to his view, his admonition left it within the competence of others, that if it should seem better to any he might order the Psalms otherwise. Expecting, forsooth, that with the lapse of time the ceremonies of the Church would become more ornate, and that what had at first received a rough foundation would afterwards enjoy the splendour of the building. But this before all things we wish thee to define, what is to be done by us touching the reading of the Gospel in the night watches. For it seems perilous that at such times priests or deacons (by whom this reading might be intoned) should be admitted among us, whom it behoves to be segregated especially from every approach and from the sight of men; both that we may be able to devote ourselves more sincerely to God and also that we may be safer from temptation. On thee now, Master, while thou livest, it falls to institute for us what is to be followed by us in perpetuity. For thou art, after God, the founder of this place, thou, through God, art the planter of this congregation, thou, with God, shalt be the institutor of our religion. A second preceptor after thee haply we shall have, and one who shall build something upon another's foundation. And so, we fear, less solicitous for us, or less readily heard by us, and one who in fine albeit equally willing, may not be equally able. Speak thou to us and we will hear. Farewell.

THE SEVENTH LETTER WHICH IS THE REPLY OF PETER TO HELOISE. TOUCHING THE ORIGIN OF NUNS

Argument: Abelard, *asked by* Heloise *in the last letter to write to her and her companions of the origin of the order of nuns, in this letter most amply responds to her and their desire; and deduces that order from the primitive Church, nay from the Sacred College of the Lord and Saviour, and relates what* Philo *the Jew, what the Tripartite History record of the first ascetics. And the female sex at each stage of the letter he extols with remarkable praise, and not only among Christian or Jewish but among gentile or pagan women widely descants on the praises of virginity. In short, the whole letter contains nothing almost, but the most elegant eulogy of the female sex. Yet principally it takes up the praise of virginity, whereof even among the pagans marvellous examples may be found.*

To thy charity, dearest sister, raising the question whence began the order of thy profession, for thine own instruction and for that of thy spiritual daughters in a few words, if I may, and succinctly I will respond. From our Lord Jesus Christ the order whether of monks or of nuns fully adopted the form of its religion. Albeit even before the Incarnation some beginning of this matter had preexisted as well among men as among women. Wherefore also *Jerome*, writing to *Eustochium*, speaks of the "Sons of the Prophets, of whom we read, as of monks, in the Old Testament," and so forth. *Anna* also, a widow, the Evangelist records as assiduous in the Temple and in divine worship, who equally with *Simeon* merited to receive the Lord in the Temple and to be filled with the spirit of prophecy. And so Christ, the end of justice, and the consummation of all good, coming in the fulness of time that He might make perfect the good things that had been begun, or reveal things hidden; as He had come to call either sex and to redeem them, so thought fit to unite both sexes in the true monkhood of His congregation, that thereafter authority for this profession might be given both to men and to women, and the perfect way of life might be laid before all, which they should imitate. For there with His Apostles and the rest of the disciples we read of an assembly of holy women with His Mother: who renouncing the world and abandoning all possessions, that they might possess only Christ, as it is written: "The Lord is the portion of mine inheritance," devoutly performed that office whereby all, according to the rule given by the Lord, converted from the world are initiated into the community of this life: "Whosoever he be of you that forsaketh not all that he hath, he cannot be my disciple."

And how devoutly these most holy women and true nuns followed Christ, and what thanks and honour both Christ Himself and afterwards the Apostles paid to their devotion the Sacred Scriptures diligently record. We read in the Gospel that a Pharisee murmured who had taken the Lord into his house, and was rebuked by Him, and that the service of the woman which was a sinner was set far above his hospitality. We read also that when *Lazarus*, after he was restored to life, sat down with the rest, his sister *Martha* alone served the tables, and *Mary* poured a pound of precious ointment over the Lord's feet, and wiped them with her hair, and that the house was filled with the odour of this precious ointment, and by the price thereof, because it seemed to be so vainly consumed, *Judas* was led to concupiscence, and the disciples were indignant. And so *Martha* being busy with the food, *Mary* dispensed the ointment; and Him whom the one inwardly restored the other in His weariness refreshed outwardly. Nor does the text of the Gospel record that any but women ministered to the Lord; which moreover had dedicated their own possessions to His daily nourishment, and chiefly procured for Him the necessities of this life. He Himself to the disciples at table, He Himself in the washing of feet shewed Himself a most humble servant. But from none of the disciples, nor indeed from any man do we learn that He accepted this service; but that women alone, as we have said, performed the ministry of these or the other services of humanity. And as in one thing *Martha*, so we know that in the other *Mary* rendered service. Who indeed in the exhibition of this was as much more devout as she had been aforetime more sinful. The Lord with water poured into a basin performed the office of that ablution. But she exhibited it to Him with the intimate tears of compunction, not with water from without. The feet of the disciples, when they were washed, the Lord dried with a linen towel. She, in place of linen, used her hair. The application of ointment she added over and above, which we nowhere read that the Lord employed.

And who does not know that a woman so far presumed upon His favour that she anointed His head also with ointment? Which ointment indeed was not poured forth from the alabaster box but is said to have been spilled when the alabaster was broken, that the vehement desire of extreme devotion might be expressed, which considered that this vessel should be kept for no further use which she had employed in such a service. Wherein also she displays by her very deed that effect of unction which aforetime *Daniel* had prophesied that it should come to pass, to wit after the Most Holy had been anointed. For behold, a woman anoints the Most Holy, and by her deed proclaims Him at once to be Him in Whom she believes, and Whom the Prophet had foretold in words. What, I ask, is this bounty of the Lord, or what the dignity of women, that He should allow both His head and His feet to be anointed by women only? What, I demand, is this prerogative of the weaker sex that the supreme Christ, anointed from His very conception with all the unguents of the Holy Spirit, a woman also should anoint and, as though with bodily sacraments consecrating Him to be King and Priest, make Him in body the Christ, that is to say the anointed?

We know that first of all a stone was anointed by the Patriarch *Jacob* as a type of the Lord. And afterwards it was permitted to men only to celebrate the anointing of priests or kings, or whatsoever sacraments of unction. Albeit as times women may presume to baptise. Aforetime the Patriarch sanctified a stone for the temple, now also the pontiff sanctifies the altar with oil. And so men imprint the sacraments by figures. But the woman wrought in very truth, as the Word Himself attesteth, saying: "She hath wrought a good work on me." Christ Himself by a woman, Christians by men are anointed. To wit, the Head by a woman, the members by men. And the woman is recorded to have well poured forth the ointment, not dropped it on his head. According to what the bride sings of Him in the Canticles, saying: "Thy name is as ointment poured forth." The abundance also of that ointment, by the fact that it ran down from the head to the hem of the garment, the Psalmist mystically prefigures, saying: "It is like the precious ointment upon the head, that ran down upon the beard, even *Aaron's* beard; that went down to the skirts of his garments." A threefold unction, as Saint *Jerome* also comments on the twenty-fifth Psalm, we read that *David* received, and so Christ or the Christians. For the feet of the Lord, or His head, received the unction of a woman. But after He was dead *Joseph* of Arimathea and *Nicodemus*, as *John* relates, buried Him with spices. Christians also are sanctified by a threefold unction: whereof one is given in baptism, one in confirmation, and the third is the anointing of the sick. Perpend therefore the dignity of woman, from whom when He was alive Christ, being twice anointed, to wit both on the head and on the feet, received the sacraments of Kingship and Priesthood. But the ointment of myrrh and aloes which is used to preserve the bodies of the dead, prefigured the future incorruptibility of the Lord's Body, which also the elect shall enjoy in the resurrection. But the former anointings by the woman shew forth His special dignity both as King and as Priest. The anointing of the head the higher, that of the feet the lower dignity. And lo, He receives the sacrament of Kingship also from a woman, Who nevertheless rejected the Kingdom that was offered to Him by men, and fled from those who would have taken Him by force to make Him a King. Of the heavenly, not of the earthly King the woman performs the sacrament; of Him, I say, who, touching Himself, said afterwards: "My kingdom is not of this world."

Bishops glory when with the applause of the populace they anoint earthly kings, when they consecrate mortal priests, adorned with splendid and golden vestments. And often they bless those whom the Lord curses. The humble woman, with no change of garment, with no prepared rite, with the Apostles themselves even enangered, performs these sacraments before Christ, not by the office of prelation but by the zeal of devotion. O great constancy of faith, O inestimable ardour of charity, which believeth all things, hopeth all things, endureth all things. The Pharisee murmurs when by the woman which was a sinner the feet of the Lord are anointed; the Apostles are openly indignant, because the woman has presumed also to touch His head. The faith of the woman remains on each occasion unmoved, trusting in the bounty of the Lord, nor does the advocacy of the Lord's commendation fail her on either. Whose ointment indeed, how acceptable, how pleasing the Lord found it He Himself professes when, demanding that it be kept for Him, He says to the indignant *Judas:* "Let her alone; against the day of my burial she has done this." As who should say: Turn not away this her service from the living, lest thou take from the dead the exhibition of her devotion in this matter. One thing certain is, that holy women prepared spices for the Lord's burial. Which this woman would then have been less concerned to do, had she before been put to shame by a rejection. He, however, while the disciples were indignant at such presumption on the part of the woman, and, as *Mark* records, murmured against her, after He had turned away their wrath by soft answers, so greatly extolled this offering that He wished it to be inserted in the Gospel, that it might be preached with the Gospel wheresoever that should be preached, for a memorial, to wit, and in praise of the woman who had done this thing, in doing which she was charged with no mean presumption. And nowhere do we read of the services of any other person whatsoever, that such commendation was given by the Lord or such sanction. Who also, preferring the poor widow's charity to all the offerings of the Temple, diligently shews how acceptable to Him is the devotion of women. *Peter* indeed made bold to boast that he and his fellow Apostles had left all things for Christ. And *Zacchaeus*, having received the Lord at His coming for which he longed, gave the half of his goods to the poor, and if he had taken anything falsely restored it four-fold. And many others incurred greater expense in Christ, or for Christ, or brought things far more precious to sacrifice to God, or left them.

And yet they did not so win the praise of the Lord's commendation, as did the women. Whose devotion, how great it had ever been towards Him, the end of the Lord's life plainly shews. For these, when the Prince of the Apostles himself denied Him, and when the Apostle beloved of the Lord fled, and the rest were scattered, stayed fearless, nor could any fear or any desperation part them from Christ, either in His Passion or in His Death. So that to them specially that saying of the Apostle may seem to apply: "Who shall separate us from the love of Christ? Shall tribulation or distress?" Wherefore *Matthew*, when he had related of himself and of the rest: "Then all the disciples forsook him, and fled," added thereto the perseverance of the women, who remained by the Crucified as long as it was permitted them. "And many women," he says, "were there beholding afar off, which followed Jesus from Galilee, ministering unto him." Whom moreover remaining unmoved by His sepulchre the same Evangelist diligently describes, saying: "And there was *Mary Magdalene*, and the other *Mary*, sitting over against the sepulchre." Which women Saint *Mark* also commemorating, says: "There were also women looking on afar off: among whom was *Mary Magdalene*, and *Mary* the mother of *James* the less and of *Joses*, and *Salome* (Who also, when he was in Galilee, followed him, and ministered unto him;) and many other women which came up with him into Jerusalem." And *John* relates that he himself stood by the Cross, and remained with the Crucified, who before had fled; but he sets first the perseverance of the women, as though by their example he had been animated and called back: "Now there stood by the cross of Jesus his mother, and his mother's sister, *Mary* the wife of *Cleophas*, and *Mary Magdalene*. When Jesus therefore saw his mother, and the disciple standing by," and so forth.

But this constancy of the holy women, and this failure of the disciples, Holy *Job* had long before prophesied in the person of the Lord, saying: "My bone cleaveth to my skin and to my flesh, and I am escaped with the skin of my teeth." For in the bone, which sustains and carries flesh and the skin, is the strength of the body. In Christ's body therefore, which is the Church, His bone is called the stable foundation of the Christian Faith, or that fervour of love, whereof it is sung: "Many waters cannot quench love, neither can the floods drown it." Whereof also the Apostle: "Beareth all things, believeth all things, hopeth all things, endureth all things." The flesh is in the body the inward part, and the skin the outward. The Apostles, therefore, occupied with preaching the inward food of the soul and the women procuring things needful for the body are compared to the flesh and the skin. And so, when the flesh was consumed, the bone of Christ clave to the skin, since, when the Apostles were offended by the Lord's Passion, and in despair at His Death, the devotion of the holy women remained unshaken, and in no way departed from the bone of Christ, because in faith, or in hope, or in charity it retained such constancy that not from the Dead even would they be separated in mind or in body. And men are naturally, both in mind and in body, stronger than women. Wherefore rightly is the manly nature indicated by the flesh, which is nearer to the bone; womanly weakness by the skin. The Apostles themselves also, whose office it is to bite by rebuking the backslidings of others, are called the Teeth of the Lord. To Whom only the lips, that is words rather than deeds, remained when, already in despair, they spoke rather of Christ than wrought anything for Christ.

Such indeed were the disciples to whom, as they were journeying to the town of Emmaus, and talking the while of all these things that had happened, He appeared and rebuked their despair. What had *Peter* or the other disciples then save words only, when it had come to the Lord's Passion, and the Lord Himself had foretold that they would be offended because of His Passion. And "though all men," said *Peter*, "shall be offended because of thee, yet will I never be offended." And again: "Though I should die with thee, yet will I not deny thee." They said, I repeat, and acted not. For he, the first and greatest of the Apostles, who had had such constancy in words that he could say to the Lord: "I am ready to go with thee, both into prison, and to death," and to whom the Lord then specially committing His Church, had said: "and when thou art converted, strengthen thy brethren," at the voice of one maidservant is not ashamed to deny Him. And not once only does he do this, but a third time, while He still lives, denies Him, and from Him living all the disciples similarly at one moment of time scatter in flight, whereas not even after His Death are the women separated from Him either in mind or in body. Among whom that blessed sinner, seeking Him after His Death and confessing her Lord, says: "They have taken away the Lord out of the sepulchre." And again: "If thou have borne him hence, tell me where thou hast laid him, and I will take him away." The rams flee, yea and the shepherds of the Lord's flock; the ewes remain unafraid. The former the Lord rebukes as weak flesh, because in the very moment of His Passion they could not watch with Him one hour. Passing a sleepless night by His sepulchre, the women first deserved to see the glory of the Risen Lord. To whom, by their faithfulness after His Death, they shewed not so much by words as by deeds how greatly they had loved Him in His Life.

And by that same solicitude which they had felt over His Passion and Death, they first were rejoiced by His Resurrection into life. For when, according to *John*, *Joseph* of Arimathea and *Nicodemus*, winding the Lord's Body in linen clothes, with spices, buried Him, *Mark* relates, touching the zeal of these women, that *Mary Magdalene*, and *Mary* the mother of *Joses* beheld where He was laid. Of them also *Luke* makes record, saying: "And the women also, which came with him from Galilee, followed after, and beheld the sepulchre, and how his body was laid. And they returned, and prepared spices and ointments." Evidently regarding the spices of *Nicodemus* as insufficient, unless they added their own. And on the Sabbath day indeed they rested, according to the commandment. But (says *Mark*) when the Sabbath was past, *Mary Magdalene*, and *Mary* the mother of *James*, and *Salome*, very early in the morning, on the day of the Resurrection itself, came unto the sepulchre at the rising of the sun. Now, as we have shewn their devotion, let us proceed to shew what honour they merited. First of all by an angelic vision they were comforted concerning the Lord's Resurrection, now accomplished, then the Lord Himself they first saw and touched. And first indeed *Mary Magdalene*, who was more fervent than the rest. Afterwards she, and with her the others, of whom it is written that after the angelic vision, "they departed from the sepulchre, and did run to bring his disciples word. And behold, Jesus met them, saying, All hail! And they came and held him by the feet, and worshipped him. Then said Jesus unto them, Go tell my brethren that they go into Galilee, and there shall they see me." Whereof *Luke* also treating says: "It was *Mary Magdalene*, and *Joanna*, and *Mary* the mother of *James*, and other women that were with them, which told these things unto the apostles."

That these also were first sent by the angel to tell the news to His disciples *Mark* hides not, where it is written that the angel speaking to the women said: "He is risen; he is not here. But go your way, tell his disciples and *Peter* that he goeth before you into Galilee." The Lord Himself also, appearing first to *Mary Magdalene*, says to her: "Go to my brethren, and say unto them, I ascend unto my father." From which we gather that these holy women were constituted as it were female Apostles over the Apostles. Since sent to the Apostles either by the Lord or by angels they announced that great joy of the Resurrection, for which all were waiting, that by them the Apostles might first learn what presently they were to preach to the whole world. Whom also after the Resurrection, the Lord meeting them, the Evangelist records to have been greeted by Him, that both by His meeting and by His greeting them He might shew how solicitous and how grateful He was to them. For we do not read of His having saluted others with that special form of words, to wit, "All hail;" nay, we read rather that He had already forbidden the Apostles that salutation, when He said to them: "Salute no man by the way." As though He would reserve the privilege thenceforward for devout women, which in His Own Person He shewed to them when He had already acquired the glory of immortality.

The Acts of the Apostles also, when they relate that shortly after the Lord's Ascension the Apostles returned from the Mount of Olives to Jerusalem, and diligently describe the religion of that Sacred College, do not omit either the continuance in devotion of the holy women, where it is said: "These all continued with one accord in prayer and supplication, with the women, and *Mary* the mother of Jesus." But not to speak of the Hebrew women who, being first converted to the Faith when the Lord was still living in the Flesh, and preaching, initiated the form of this religion, let us consider the widows of the Greeks, who thereafter were received by the Apostles; with what diligence, with what care these too were treated by the Apostles, when for their service that most glorious standard-bearer of the Christian Host, *Stephen* the First Martyr, with certain other spiritual men was set apart by the Apostles themselves. Wherefore in the said Acts of the Apostles it is written: "When the number of the disciples was multiplied, there arose a murmuring of the Grecians against the Hebrews, because their widows were neglected in the daily ministration. Then the twelve called the multitude of the disciples unto them, and said, It is not reason that we should leave the word of God, and serve tables. Wherefore, brethren, look ye out among you seven men of honest report, full of the Holy Ghost and wisdom, whom we may appoint over this business. But we will give ourselves continually to prayer, and to the ministry of the word. And the saying pleased the whole multitude: and they chose *Stephen*, a man full of faith and of the Holy Ghost, and *Philip*, and *Prochorus*, and *Nicanor*, and *Timon*, and *Parmenas*, and *Nicolas* a proselyte of Antioch: whom they set before the Apostles; and when they had prayed, they laid their hands on them." Wherefore the continence of *Stephen* is greatly commended, because he was deputed to the ministry and service of holy women. And the ministration of his service how excellent it was and acceptable as well to the Lord as to the Apostles, they both by their own prayer and by the laying on of hands did declare, as though adjuring them whom they were setting apart for this service, that they should act faithfully, and both by their benediction and by their prayer helping them so far as they were able. Which administration also Saint *Paul* claiming for himself for the completion of his own Apostolate says: "Have we not power to lead about a sister, a wife, as well as other Apostles?" As who should say openly: Is it not permitted to us both to have assemblies of holy women and to lead them about with us in our preaching, as it has been to the rest of the Apostles, to wit that they might minister things needful to them in their preaching of their proper substance? Wherefore *Augustine*, in his book, Of the Work of Monks, says: "To this end faithful women also having earthly substance went with them and ministered to them of their substance, that they might lack none of those things that pertain to the substance of this life." Likewise: "Whoso does not believe that it was the practice of the Apostles that with them women of holy conversation went about wheresoever they preached the Gospel, let him hear the Gospel and recognise how they did this, following the example of the Lord Himself." For in the Gospel it is written: "And it came to pass afterward, that he went throughout every city and village, preaching and shewing the glad tidings of the kingdom of God; and the twelve were with him. And certain women, which had been healed of evil spirits and infirmities, *Mary* called *Magdalene*, out of whom went seven devils, and *Joanna* the wife of *Chusa*, *Herod*'s steward, and *Susanna*, and many others, which ministered unto him of their substance."

So that from this it is evident that the Lord also, when He went forth preaching, was sustained in bodily things by the ministration of women, and that they like the Apostles clave to Him as inseparable companions. But in time the religion of this profession being multiplied in women as in men, in the very beginning of the infant Church, equally with men, so women also possessed habitations of monasteries proper to themselves. Wherefore too the Ecclesiastical History thus, among other matters, in the second book and sixteenth chapter, records the praise which *Philo,* a most learned Jew, not only uttered but also magnificently wrote of the Church of Alexandria under *Mark*, saying: "In many parts of the world are there men of this kind." And a little later: "There is in sundry places a house consecrated to prayer, which is called Senivor, or monastery." Likewise thereafter: "And so not only do they understand the hymns of the learned elders, but they themselves make new hymns to God, chanting them in all tones and numbers with a right honest and pleasing harmony." Likewise, to omit certain matters touching abstinence and the offices of divine worship, it adds: "But with the men of whom we have spoken are also women, among whom are several virgins already of great age, who have preserved the chastity and integrity of the body not from any necessity but from devotion, while in the study of wisdom they labour to consecrate themselves not in soul only but in body, deeming it unworthy to give over to lust the vessel prepared for the receipt of wisdom, and to bring to bed of a mortal birth those bodies of which a sacred and immortal cohabitation with the Divine Word is required, whereby a posterity may be left in no way subject to the corruption of mortality." And in the same passage also, of *Philo:* "He writes also touching their convents, that men and women are severally congregated in the same places, and that they keep vigils, as the custom is among us."

Whence comes that saying in praise of Christian philosophy, that is of the monastic prerogative, which the Tripartite History records as having been seized upon no less by women than by men. For it says as follows, in the eleventh chapter of the first book: "Of this most elegant philosophy the founder was, as some say, *Elias* the Prophet, or *John* the Baptist." And *Philo* the Pythagorean relates that in his time the best of the Hebrews, coming from all parts, used to philosophise on a piece of land by the Lake Maria, situated upon a hill. And he mentions their habitation and their food and their conversation, such as we now see to exist among the monks of the Egyptians. He writes that until sunset they did not taste food, that they ever abstained from wine, and from things containing blood, that their meat was bread and salt and hyssop, and their drink water. Women dwelt among them, virgins of riper years, for the love of philosophy abstaining of their own free will from marriage. Whence comes that passage of *Jerome*, in the book, Of Illustrious Men, in the eighth chapter, touching the praise of *Mark* and of his Church, writing thus: "The first to announce Christ in Alexandria, he established a Church of so great learning, and continence of life as to compel all followers of Christ to his example." Lastly *Philo*, the most eloquent of the Jews, seeing that the first Church of Alexandria was still Judaizing, wrote in praise of his own people a book treating of their conversion, and just as *Luke* narrates that in Jerusalem the faithful had all things in common, so he hands down to posterity what he saw done in Alexandria under the doctorate of *Mark*. Likewise in the eleventh chapter: "*Philo* the Jew, an Alexandrian by birth, of a family of priests, for this reason is included by us among ecclesiastical writers because in writing a book of the first Church of *Mark* the Evangelist in Alexandria he takes up the praise of our people, recording their existence not only there but in many provinces besides, and calling their habitations monasteries."

Whence it appears that the first Church of the believers in Christ was such as monks now imitate and desire to follow, to wit that nothing be the property of any, none among them be rich nor any poor, that their patrimonies be divided among the needy, that they devote themselves to prayer and psalms, to learning also and to continence. As *Luke* also reports the Christians at first to have been in Jerusalem. And if we turn to the old histories we shall find there that women, in those things which pertain to God, or to any singularity of religion, were not separated from men. Who also, the sacred Histories tell us, like men not only sang but even composed divine hymns. Indeed the first hymn of the liberation of the Children of Israel not men only but also women descanted to the Lord; thence straightway they acquired authority for the celebration of the divine offices in the Church. According as it is written: "And *Miriam* the prophetess, the sister of *Aaron*, took a timbrel in her hand; and all the women went out after her with timbrels and with dances. And *Miriam* answered them, Sing ye to the Lord, for He hath triumphed gloriously." Nor indeed is the Prophet *Moses* there mentioned, nor is he said to have answered them, like *Miriam*, nor are the men reported to have had timbrels or dances like the women. And so when *Miriam*, answering them, is called a prophetess, it appears that it was not so much in dictating or reciting as in prophesying that she uttered that song. When moreover she is described as answering the others, it is shewn how orderly or harmoniously they chanted. But the fact that not with the voice alone, but with timbrels and dances they sang not merely suggests their extreme devotion but also diligently expresses in a mystical manner the form of the spiritual song in monastic congregations. Whereunto also the Psalmist exhorts us, saying: "Praise him with the timbrel and dance," that is with the mortification of the flesh, and that concord of charity whereof it is written: "And the multitude of them that believed were of one heart and of one soul." Nor is mystery lacking in what they are reported to have done in their singing, wherein are figured the joys of the contemplative soul. Which while it attaches itself to heavenly things deserts as it were the tabernacle of its earthly habitation, and, of the intimate delights of its contemplation, fashions a spiritual hymn to the Lord with the utmost exaltation. We find there also the hymns of *Deborah* and of *Hannah*, not to speak of the widow *Judith*, as we find in the Gospel the hymn of *Mary* the Mother of the Lord. Which *Hannah*, for example, offering *Samuel* her infant son in the tabernacle of the Lord, gave authority for the taking of children into monasteries. Wherefore *Isidore* says to the brethren established in the Honorian convent: "Whosoever has been left by his own parents in a monastery, let him know that he is to remain there for ever. For *Hannah* offered her son *Samuel* to God. Who also in the service of the Temple, to which he had been destined by his mother, remained, and, where he was established, there served."

It is clear also that the daughters of *Aaron* equally with their brothers so pertained to the sanctuary and the hereditary office of *Levi*, that from this source the Lord instituted alimony for them, as it is written in the Book of Numbers, where he speaks thus to *Aaron:* "All the heave offerings of the holy things, which the children of Israel offer unto the Lord, have I given thee, and thy sons and thy daughters with thee, by a statute for ever." Whence it appears that the religion of women was not disjoined from the order of clerics. Which women also were clearly joined with the men in name, since we speak both of deaconesses and of deacons. As though in these we recognise severally the Tribe of *Levi* and female Levites. We have also in the same book that solemn vow and consecration of the Nazarites of the Lord, established equally for women as for men, the Lord Himself speaking thus to *Moses:* "Speak unto the children of Israel, and say unto them, When either man or woman shall separate themselves to vow a vow of a Nazarite, to separate themselves unto the Lord; he shall separate himself from wine and strong drink, and shall drink no vinegar of wine, or vinegar of strong drink, neither shall he drink any liquor of grapes nor eat moist grapes, or dried. All the days of his separation shall he eat nothing that is made of the vine tree, from the kernels even to the husk."

Of this religion indeed I consider those women to have been who assembled at the door of the tabernacle, of whose looking-glasses *Moses* made the laver in which *Aaron* and his sons should wash themselves, as it is written: "And he made the laver of brass, of the looking-glasses of the women assembling, which assembled at the door of the tabernacle of the congregation." Diligently is the fervour described of their great devotion, who when the tabernacle was closed staying by the door of it kept the watches of holy vigils, passing the nights in prayer, and not ceasing from divine worship while the men slept. But that the tabernacle was closed to them fitly indicates the life of the penitent, who that they may more severely afflict themselves with the lamentations of penance are segregated from the rest. Which life is specially shewn to be that of the monastic profession, the order of which is said to be nothing else than a milder form of penance. But by the tabernacle, at the door of which they assembled, is to be mystically apprehended that whereof the Apostle writes to the Hebrews: "We have an altar, whereof they have no right to eat which serve the tabernacle," that is, in which they are not worthy to participate who to the body, in which they minister here as in a camp, offer pleasurable service. But the door of the tabernacle is the end of this present life, when the soul goes hence from the body and enters upon the life to come. At this door assemble those who are anxious concerning the going out from this life and the entering upon the future life, and by repentance so dispose their going out from hence that they may be worthy of the entering in thither.

Touching which daily entering in and going out of the holy Church is that prayer of the Psalmist: "The Lord shall preserve thy coming in, and thy going out." For then does he guard at once our coming in and our going out, when on our going out from hence, and being already purged by repentance, he straightway introduces us thither. And rightly did he name the coming in before the going out, paying heed not to the order but to the dignity, since this going out from mortal life is in pain, but that coming in to life eternal is supreme exaltation. And their looking-glasses are outward works, whereby the brightness or foulness of the soul is judged, as from a material looking-glass the condition of the human face. From these looking-glasses the laver is made in which *Aaron* and his sons may wash themselves, when the works of holy women and the so great constancy of the weaker sex to God vehemently rebuke the negligence of bishops and priests, and especially move them to tears of compunction. And if, as becomes them, they take care for these women, the works of the women prepare pardon for their sins, whereby they may be absolved. From these looking-glasses Saint *Gregory* prepared a laver of compunction for himself when, marvelling at the virtue of holy women and at the victory of the weaker sex in martyrdom, and lamenting he asked: "What will savage men say when delicate girls bear such things for Christ, and the weaker sex triumphs with so great agony that frequently we know them to have won the twofold crown of virginity and martyrdom?" To these indeed who, as has been said, assemble at the door of the tabernacle, and had already, like Nazarites of the Lord, consecrated to Him their widowhood, I have no doubt that that Holy *Anna* belonged who equally with Holy *Simeon* was found worthy to receive the special Nazarite of the Lord, the Lord Jesus Christ, in the Temple, and that she might be more a prophet recognised Him at the same instant as *Simeon*, by the Holy Spirit, and revealed His Presence and publicly proclaimed Him. Whose praises indeed the Evangelist diligently pursuing says: "And there was one *Anna*, a prophetess, the daughter of *Phanuel*, of the tribe of *Aser;* she was of a great age, and had lived with an husband seven years from her virginity. And she was a widow of about fourscore and four years, which departed not from the temple, but served God with fastings and prayers night and day. And she coming in that instant gave thanks likewise unto the Lord, and spake of him to all them that looked for redemption in Jerusalem." Note each thing that is said, and perpend how zealous in the praise of this widow was the Evangelist and with what eulogy he has extolled her excellence. Of which prophetess indeed the grace which she had been wont to enjoy, and her paternity, and her Tribe, and, after seven years which she had lived with her husband, the long period of holy widowhood in which she had devoted herself to God, and her assiduity in the Temple, and her instance in fasting and prayer, her confession of praise, the thanks which she gave to the Lord and her public preaching of Him, touching the promise and birth of the Saviour, he has diligently expressed: and *Simeon* indeed the Evangelist had previously commended for his righteousness, not for his prophecy, nor does he record that there was in him so great a virtue of continence or abstinence, nor such solicitude for divine worship, nor has he added aught touching his preaching to others.

Of this profession and religion also are those widows indeed, of whom, writing to *Timothy*, the Apostle says: "Honour widows that are widows indeed." Likewise: "Now she that is a widow indeed, and desolate, trusteth in God, and continueth in supplications and prayers night and day. And these things give in charge that they may be blameless." And again: "If any man or woman that believeth have widows, let them relieve them, and let not the church be charged; that it may relieve them that are widows indeed." Now widows indeed he calls them who have not disgraced their widowhood with a second marriage, or who from devotion rather than from necessity so persevering have dedicated themselves unto the Lord. Desolate he calls them who thus renounce all things, so that they retain no subsidy of earthly solace, or who have none that shall care for them. Whom indeed he further ordains are to be honoured, and considers that they should be supported at the charge of the Church, as though from the property of their Husband Christ. Among whom also such as are to be elected to the ministry of the diaconate he diligently describes, saying: "Let not a widow be taken into the number under threescore years old, having been the wife of one man. Well reported of for good works; if she have brought up children, if she have lodged strangers, if she have washed the saints' feet, if she have relieved the afflicted, if she have diligently followed every good work. But the younger widows refuse." Which indeed Saint *Jerome* expounding says: "Beware in the ministry of the diaconate, lest a bad example be furnished in place of a good, to wit if the younger widows are chosen for this ministry who are more prone to temptation and lighter by nature: and not being made prudent by the experience of a long life furnish a bad example to those to whom they ought especially to set a good." Against which example indeed in the younger widows, because the Apostle had already learned it from certain experience, he openly professes, and in addition offers counsel. For after he had first said: "But the younger widows refuse," he straightway added the reason of this warning and the medicine of his counsel, saying: "For when they have begun to wax wanton against Christ, they will marry; having damnation, because they have cast off their first faith. And withal they learn to be idle, wandering about from house to house, and not only idle, but tattlers also and busybodies, speaking things which they ought not. I will therefore that the younger widows marry, bear children, guide the house, give none occasion to the adversary to speak reproachfully. For some are already turned aside after Satan."

And this provision of the Apostle, touching the election of deaconesses, Saint *Gregory* following, writes to *Maximus*, Bishop of Syracuse, in these words: "Youthful abbesses we do most vehemently forbid. Let thy brotherhood, therefore allow no Bishop to give the veil except to a virgin of threescore years, whose life and morals they shall have proved." And what we now call abbesses anciently they named deaconesses, that is ministers rather than mothers. For *deacon* is by interpretation *minister*, and they considered that deaconesses should be named rather from their ministry than from their prelacy, according to what the Lord Himself instituted both by His example and in words, saying: "But he that is greatest among you shall be your servant." And again: "For whether is greater, he that sitteth at meat, or he that serveth? Is not he that sitteth at meat? But I am among you as he that serveth." And elsewhere: "Even as the Son of man came not to be ministered unto but to minister." Wherefore also *Jerome* this very name of abbot, in which he knew that many already gloried, on the Lord's Own authority ventured not a little to refute. Who expounding that passage where it is written in the Epistle to the Galatians: "Crying Abba, Father," says: "*Abba* is a Hebrew word signifying the same as *Father*. And inasmuch as *Abba* means *Father* in the Hebrew and Syriac tongues, and the Lord in the Gospel ordains that no man is to be called Father except God, I know not by what licence in the monasteries we either call others by this name or allow ourselves to be so called. And verily He commanded this Who had said that we must not swear. If we do not swear let us not call any man Father. If we interpret the word Father otherwise, we shall be forced also to think differently about swearing." Of the number of these deaconesses assuredly that *Phebe* was one, of whom the Apostle, diligently commending her to the Romans, and beseeching them for her, says: "I commend unto you *Phebe* our sister, which is a servant of the church which is at Cenchrea: that ye receive her in the Lord, as becometh saints, and that ye assist her in whatsoever business she hath need of you: for she hath been a succourer of many, and of myself also." Which passage indeed *Cassiodorus* and *Claudius* alike expounding profess that she was a deaconess of that Church. "It means," says *Cassiodorus*, "that she was a deaconess of the mother Church. Which in the parts of the Grecians to this day is still carried out, as it were a training in arms. To whom also the use of baptism in the Church is not denied." *Claudius* says: "This passage teaches on Apostolic authority that women also may be ordained in the service of the Church, in which office *Phebe* established with the Church which is at Cenchrea the Apostle greatly praises and commends."

Which women also the same Apostle writing to *Timothy* includes among the deacons themselves, and regulates their life with a like moral instruction. For there ordering the grades of ecclesiastical ministries, having descended from the bishop to the deacon, he says: "Likewise must the deacons be grave, not double tongued, not given to much wine, not greedy of filthy lucre; holding the mystery of the faith in a pure conscience. And let these also first be proved; then let them use the office of a deacon, being found blameless. Even so must their wives be grave, not slanderers, sober, faithful in all things. Let the deacons be the husbands of one wife, ruling their children and their own houses well. For they that have used the office of a deacon well purchase to themselves a good degree, and great boldness in the faith which is in Christ Jesus." Thus what he had in the former place said of the deacons, "not double tongued," he here says of the deaconesses, "not slanderers." As there, "not given to much wine," so here, he says, "sober." But touching the other things which there follow, here he briefly concludes, "faithful in all things." Who also as he forbids the bishops and deacons to be the husbands of two wives, so also he has instituted that the deaconesses shall be the wives of one husband, as we have already recorded: "Let not a widow," he says, "be taken into the number under threescore years old, having been the wife of one man, well reported of for good works; if she have brought up children, if she have lodged strangers, if she have washed the saints' feet, if she have diligently followed every good work. But the younger widows refuse."

In which description indeed or instruction of deaconesses it is easy to see how much more diligent was the Apostle than in the aforementioned institution as well as bishops as of deacons. For what he says of them, "well reported of for good works," or, "if she have lodged strangers," he has nowhere said of the deacons. And as to what he added, "if she have washed the saints' feet, if she have relieved the afflicted," and the rest, there is no mention made touching either bishops or deacons. And of bishops indeed and deacons he says "being found blameless." But the women he not only orders to be blameless but says that they shall have followed every good work. Prudently also he provides for the maturity of their age, that they may have authority in all things, saying: "not under threescore years old," and that not only to their lives but also to their great age, proved in many things, may reverence be paid. Wherefore also the Lord, albeit He loved *John* the most, yet set *Peter*, as being the elder, as well over him as over the others. For all men are less vexed when an elder than when a younger man is set over them; and more willingly do we obey an elder, to whom not only his own life but the law of nature also and the order of time have given precedence. Hence also *Jerome*, in his first book Against Jovinian, where he treats of the prelacy of *Peter*, says: "One is chosen, that a head being set up all occasion of schism may be removed. But wherefore was not *John* chosen? Deference was paid to age, because *Peter* was the elder, lest one who was still a youth, and almost a boy, should be preferred to men of advanced age, and the Good Master, Who was bound to remove all occasion of quarrelling from the disciples, might seem to furnish a cause for jealousy of the young man whom He had loved." This point that abbot diligently considered who, as it is written in the Lives of the Fathers, withdrew the priorship from a younger brother, who had come first to conversion, and gave it to an elder; for this sole reason, that he was his senior in age. For he feared lest that brother after the flesh might bear ill the setting of a younger man over himself. He remembered that the Apostles themselves had been angered concerning two of their number, when their mother interceding with Christ seemed to have obtained some privilege, especially since it was one of those two who was younger than the other Apostles. To wit *John* himself, of whom we spoke just now.

Nor in the institution of deaconesses only was the care of the Apostle most watchful, but in general it is clear how zealous he was with regard to widows of holy profession, that he might cut off all occasion of temptation. For after he had first said: "Honour widows that are widows indeed," he straightway added: "but if any widow have children or nephews, let them learn first to show piety at home, and to requite their parents." And a little later: "But if any provide not for his own, and specially for those of his own house, he hath denied the faith, and is worse than an infidel." In which words indeed he provides at once for the needs of humanity and for the religious profession. Lest haply under the pretence of religion poor orphans be abandoned, and carnal compassion towards the needy perturb the holy profession of the widow, and force her to look backward, and at times even lead her to sacrilege, and to provide somewhat for her own whereof she defrauds the community. Wherefore the necessity of the advice is evident that whoso are involved in the care of household matters, before, passing to true widowhood, they devote themselves wholly to the divine service, should in this way requite their parents, and as by their care they themselves were brought up so provide by the same rule for their own posterity. Who also enlarging the religion of widows orders them to continue in supplications and prayers night and day. Of whose needs also being greatly solicitous, he says: "If any man or woman that believeth have widows, let them relieve them, and let not the church be charged; that it may relieve them that are widows indeed." As who should say openly: If there be any widow who has such kinsfolk that are able to minister things needful to her from their own resources, let them provide for her in this matter, that the public funds of the Church may be sufficient for the support of the rest. Which injunction indeed openly shews that if any be obdurate towards their own widows in this matter, they are to be constrained to the payment of this debt by Apostolic authority. Who not for their needs alone but also providing for their honour says: "Honour widows that are widows indeed."

Such we believe those to have been one of whom he himself calls mother, and the other *John* the Evangelist calls his lady, out of reverence for their holy profession. "Salute," says *Paul*, "*Rufus* chosen in the Lord, and his mother and mine." But *John*, in the Second Epistle which he writes, says: "The elder unto the elect lady and her children." By whom also demanding that he be loved he has added later: "And now I beseech thee, lady, that we love one another." On whose authority also *Jerome* relying, in writing to the virgin of your profession *Eustochium*, was not ashamed to call her lady: nay wherefore he should do so he straightway added, saying: "For this reason write 'my lady,' *Eustochium*. For I must call her my lady who is the Bride of Our Lord."

Who also later in the same epistle, setting the privilege of this holy profession above every boast of earthly happiness, says: "I will not that thou consort with matrons, I will not that thou approach the houses of nobles, I will not that thou frequently look upon that which despising thou hast willed to be a virgin. If the ambition of courtiers gather around the wife of the Emperor, wherefore dost thou an injury to thine husband? To the wife of man wherefore dost thou, the Bride of God, hasten? Learn in this matter holy pride. Know that thou art better than they." Who also writing to a virgin dedicated to God of the virgins consecrated to God, what blessedness in heaven and what dignity they enjoy on earth, thus beginning says: "How great blessedness holy virginity shall enjoy in heavenly things, apart from the testimony of Holy Scripture, we are taught also by the custom of the Church, wherefrom we learn that a special merit subsists in those who are spiritually consecrated. For whereas each and all of the multitude of the faithful receive equal gifts of grace, and all alike glory in the same sacramental blessings, these have something special beyond the rest, when out of that holy and spotless flock of the Church, as holier and purer victims by the merits of their intention, they are both chosen by the Holy Spirit and are offered by the High Priest on the Altar of God." Likewise: "Virginity therefore possesses what the others have not, since it both obtains a special grace and rejoices, if I may say so, in a proper privilege of consecration. For the consecration of virgins, unless in the imminent peril of death, may not be celebrated at any other season save the Epiphany and the Paschal White Sunday, and on the Nativities of the Apostles. Nor except by the High Priest, that is the Bishop, are either they or the veils that are to be laid upon their sacred heads to be blessed." Whereas to monks, albeit they are of the same profession, or order, and of a worthier sex than are the virgins, it is permitted to receive benediction upon any day whatsoever, and from the Abbot, both for themselves and for their garments, that is to say their cowls. Priests also and the other inferior grades of the clergy can always be ordained on the fasts of the Four Seasons, and Bishops be consecrated upon any Sunday. But the consecration of virgins, being more precious and so rarer, has reserved for itself the exultation of the chief festivals. In whose marvellous virtue the whole Church greatly rejoices, as the Psalmist also foretold, in these words: "The virgins her companions that follow her shall be brought unto thee." And again: "With gladness and rejoicing shall they be brought: they shall enter into the King's palace." Which consecration also *Matthew*, being at once an Apostle and an Evangelist, is said to have composed or dictated, as we read in his Passion, where he too is recorded as having fallen a martyr for their consecration or in defence of the virginal calling. But no benediction either of clergy or of monks have the Apostles left to us in writing. And their religion alone is called by the name of sanctity, since they from *sanctimony*, that is from *sanctity*, have been styled *sanctimoniales*.

And just as the sex of women is feebler, so is their virtue more pleasing to God and more perfect, according to the testimony of the Lord Himself, wherein exhorting the weakness of the Apostles to the crown of strife He says: "My grace is sufficient for thee; for my strength is made perfect in weakness." Who likewise, speaking of the Members of His Own Body, which is the Church, through the same Apostle, as though He would specially commend the honour of such weak members, added in the same Epistle, namely the First to the Corinthians: "Nay, much more those members of the body, which seem to be more feeble, are necessary: and those members of the body, which we think to be less honourable, upon these we bestow more abundant honour; and our uncomely parts have more abundant comeliness. For our comely parts have no need: but God hath tempered the body together, having given more abundant honour to that part which lacked: that there should be no schism in the body; but that the members should have the same care one for another."

But who would say that there was so complete a fulfilment by the dispensation of the divine grace in any as in the very infirmity of the womanly sex, which both sin and nature had made contemptible? Examine the different states in this sex, not only virgins and widows, or wives, but also the abominations of harlots, and thou wilt see the grace of Christ to be fuller in them, so that according to the words of the Lord and the Apostle: "The last shall be first, and the first last:" and, "Where sin abounded, grace did much more abound." The benefits of which divine grace, or the honours shewn to women, if we seek for them from the first beginning of the world, we shall straightway find that the creation of woman excelled by a certain dignity, inasmuch as she indeed was created in Paradise, but man without. So that women are warned especially to pay heed to this, that Paradise is their native country, and how much more it becomes them to pursue the celibate life of Paradise. Wherefore *Ambrose* in the book, Of Paradise, says: "And God took the man whom He had made, and set him in Paradise. Thou seest how he who already existed is taken. In Paradise He placed him. Note that the man was made without Paradise, and the woman within. In the inferior place man is found the better and she that was made in the better place is considered inferior."

The Lord also first restored *Eve*, the root of all evil, in *Mary* before He repaired *Adam* in Christ. And as from woman sin, so from woman begins grace, and the privilege of virginity has flowered again. And already in *Anna* and *Mary* the form of their holy profession is shewn to widows and virgins before in *John* or the Apostles the examples of monastic religion are set before men. And if, after *Eve*, we consider the virtue of *Deborah*, of *Judith*, of *Esther*, surely we shall blush not a little for the strength of the male sex. For *Deborah*, a Judge of the Lord's people, when the men failed, gave battle, and, their enemies overthrown, and the Lord's people set free, powerfully triumphed. *Judith*, unarmed, with her *Abra*, approached a terrible host, and with his own sword cut off the head of one *Holofernes*, she alone destroyed the whole might of her enemies, and set free a people that was in despair. *Esther*, by the secret suggestion of the Spirit, against even the decree of the law, joined herself in marriage with the gentile king, forestalled the counsel of the most impious *Haman*, and the king's cruel edict, and turned the uttered sentence of the royal deliberation, almost in a moment of time, against the adversary. It is ascribed to great virtue that *David* with a sling and a stone attacked *Goliath* and overthrew him. *Judith*, a widow, proceeded against the hostile army without sling and stone, with no armament soever, to do battle. *Esther* by her word alone set her people free, and the sentence being turned against her enemies they rushed into the snare which they had spread. The memory of which famous deed has earned yearly among the Jews the tribute of a solemn rejoicing. Which no deeds of men, howsoever splendid, have obtained.

Who does not marvel at the incomparable constancy of the mother of seven sons, which, together with their mother, being taken, as the History of the Maccabees relates, the most impious king *Antiochus* vainly endeavoured to compel to eat the flesh of swine against the Law? Which mother, forgetting her own nature and heedless of human affection, nor having any but the Lord before her eyes, for as many sons as with her sacred exhortations she sent before her to the Crown, so herself triumphed in as many martyrdoms, consummated lastly by her own. If we search through the whole sequence of the Old Testament, what can we compare to the constancy of this woman? That vehement tempter to the last of Holy *Job*, considering the impotency of human nature to resist death, says: "Skin for skin, yea, all that a man hath will he give for his life." For so do we naturally shrink from all the straits of death that often in defence of one member we offer the other, and in the preservation of this life fear no discomforts. But this woman endured the loss not only of all that she had but of her own and her sons' lives, rather than incur a single offence against the Law. What is this transgression, I ask, to which she was driven? Was she ever forced to renounce God, or to offer incense to idols? Nothing, I say, was exacted of them, save that they should eat meat which the Law forbade them.

O brethren and fellow monks, who so shamelessly day by day against the institution of the Rule and our profession yearn after meat, what have ye to say to the constancy of this woman? Are ye so unashamed that when ye hear these things ye blush not nor are confounded? Know, brethren, that the reproach which the Lord utters to the unbelieving touching the queen of the south, saying: "The queen of the south shall rise up in the judgment with this generation and shall condemn it;" is far more to be urged against you touching the constancy of this woman, who did things far greater, and ye by the vow of your profession are more strictly bound to religion. Whose virtue indeed, being proved by so great an agony, has deserved to obtain this privilege in the Church, that her martyrdom has solemn lessons and a mass, which privilege has been conceded to none of the saints of old, to wit those who in their death preceded the Coming of the Lord, albeit in the same History of the Maccabees that venerable elder *Eleazar*, one of the chiefs of the Scribes, is said to have been already crowned with martyrdom for the same cause. But because, as we have said, inasmuch as the female sex is naturally weaker, so is its virtue more acceptable to God and more worthy of honour; that martyrdom has not deserved any memory in our feasts, in which a woman bore no part, as though it were not held a great matter if the stronger sex should endure stronger things. Wherefore also in praise of the aforesaid woman the Scripture breaking forth more fully says: "But the mother was marvellous above all, and worthy of honourable memory; for when she saw her seven sons slain within the space of one day she bare it with a good courage, because of the hope she had in the Lord. Yea, she exhorted every one of them in her own language, filled with courageous spirits, and stirring up her womanish thoughts with a manly stomach." Who would not consider that daughter of *Jephthah* to be a vine to be gathered in the praise of virgins? Who, lest her father be held to account for his vow, albeit a rash vow, and lest the benefit of divine grace be cheated of the promised victim, urged her victorious father against her own throat. What would she, I ask, have done in the agony of the martyrs, if haply she had been forced by the infidels to fall away by denying God? Would she, when asked concerning Christ, with him who was already the Prince of the Apostles, have said: "I know him not"? Sent away by her father for two months in freedom, at the end of that time she returns to her father to be slain. Freely she betakes herself to death, and provokes rather than fears it. Her father's foolish vow is punished, and she redeems her father's promise, a great lover of the Truth. How would she abhor this failure in herself which in her father she cannot endure? How great is this fervour of the virgin as well towards her carnal as towards her heavenly father? Who at the same time by her death determined both to set one free from perjury and to preserve for the other what had been promised Him. Wherefore deservedly this fortitude of a girl's courage by a special privilege was entitled to obtain this, that the daughters of Israel yearly assemble together to celebrate the obsequies of this virgin with certain solemn hymns, and compassionately deplore her suffering with pious tears.

To pass over all other examples, what has been so necessary to our redemption, and to the salvation of the whole world as the female sex which brought forth for us the Saviour Himself? The singularity of which honour the woman who first ventured to intrude upon Saint *Hilarion* opposed to his marvelling, saying: "Wherefore turn away thine eyes? Wherefore shun mine entreaty? Look not upon me as a woman but as one that is wretched. This sex gave birth to the Saviour." What glory can be compared to this, which that sex won in the Mother of the Lord? The Redeemer might, had he wished, have assumed His Body from a man, as He chose to form the first woman from a man. But this singular grace of His humility He transferred to the honour of the weaker sex. He could also have been born of another and a more worthy part of the woman's body than are the rest of men, who are born of that same vilest portion wherein they are conceived. But, to the incomparable honour of the weaker body, He far more highly consecrated its genitals by His Birth than He had done those of the male by circumcision.

And, to pass over for the present the singular honour given to virgins, we must turn our pen to the rest of women as we proposed. Consider therefore what grace the Advent of Christ straightway shewed to *Elisabeth* the wife, and what to *Anna* the widow. The husband of *Elisabeth*, *Zacharias*, a great priest of the Lord, the diffidence of unbelief still kept dumb, while at the coming and salutation of *Mary*, *Elisabeth* herself presently filled with the Holy Ghost both felt the babe leap in her womb and first uttering prophecy concerning *Mary's* Conception, which was already fulfilled, revealed herself more than a prophet. For straightway she announced the Virgin's Conception in Her presence, and encouraged the Mother of the Lord to magnify Him therefor. And the gift of prophecy is seen to be more excellently fulfilled in *Elisabeth*, who straightway recognised the Son of God Conceived, than in *John* who made Him manifest when He was already long since born. As therefore we call *Mary Magdalene* the Apostle of the Apostles, so let us not hesitate to call her the Prophet of the Prophets, or that holy widow *Anna*, of whom we have written more fully above. And if we extend the grace of prophecy among the Gentiles also, let the Sibyl come forth into the midst and profess those things which were revealed to her concerning Christ. With whom if we compare all the Prophets, *Esaias* himself even, who, as *Jerome* states, is to be called not so much Prophet as Evangelist, we shall see that in this grace also the woman far excels the men. Of whom *Augustine*, offering testimony against heresies, says: "Let us hear what the Sibyl also, their Prophetess, says concerning the same: The Lord, she says, has given another to be worshipped by men of faith." Likewise: "Know Him to be Thy Lord, the Son of God. In another place she calls the Son of God *Symbolum,* that is *Counsellor.* And the Prophet says His Name shall be called Wonderful, Counsellor." Of whom again that same Father, *Augustine,* in the eighteenth book Of the City of God, says: "At that time some maintain that the Erechthean Sibyl prophesied, whom others believe rather to have been her of Cumae. And there are seven and twenty verses of her prophecy; which, as one has interpreted them in Latin verses, contain the following: *In token of Judgment the earth shall be moist with sweat. From Heaven a King shall come that shall be throughout the ages, present in the flesh that he may judge the world.* The first letters of which verses being joined together in the Greek make the following: Jesus Christ Son of God Saviour."

Lactantius also cites certain prophecies of the Sibyl concerning Christ. "Afterwards," she says, "He shall fall into the hands of ungodly men. They shall give to God buffets with their unclean hands, and from an impure mouth spit forth envenomed spittle. But He shall offer His Holy Back meekly to their blows, and receiving their buffets shall keep silence, lest any hear and know His Word, or speak in the Hell from which he shall come again, and He shall be crowned with a crown of thorns. For food they shall give Him gall, and vinegar for His thirst. In their hospitality this table shall they furnish. For, foolish race, thou hast not understood that Thy God is to be praised by the minds of mortals, but hast crowned Him with thorns, hast mixed gall for Him. The veil of the Temple shall be rent, and in the middle of the day there shall be night for three hours, and He shall die, and for three days shall be fallen asleep, and then returning from Hell shall come to the light, being first made manifest as a beginning of the Resurrection."

This prophecy of the Sibyl surely, if I be not mistaken, that greatest of our poets, *Virgil,* had heard and had paid heed to it when in the fourth Eclogue he foretold the miraculous birth that was shortly to befall under *Augustus Caesar,* in the time of *Pollio*'s Consulate, of a certain child to be sent down from heaven upon earth, which also should take away the sins of the world, and should miraculously establish as it were a new age in the world, taught, as he himself says, by the prophecy of the Cumaean song, that is of the Sibyl, who is called Cumaean. For he speaks thus, as though exhorting all men to rejoice among themselves and to sing or write of this so great child which is to be born, in comparison wherewith he deems all other matters lowly and base, saying:

> Sicilian Muse, begin a loftier strain!
>
> . . . . . .
>
> The last great age, foretold by sacred rhymes,
> Renews its finish'd course; Saturnian times
> Roll round again, and mighty years, begun
> From their first orb, in radiant circles run.
> The base degenerate iron offspring ends;
> A golden progeny from heav'n descends.

Examine everything that is said by the Sibyl, and see how completely and openly she embraces the sum of the Christian Faith concerning Christ. Who, in prophesying or writing, has omitted neither His Divinity nor His Humanity, nor either His First or His Second Coming, nor either Judgment. To wit, the First Judgment, wherein He was unjustly judged in His Passion, and the Second, wherein He is justly to judge the world in Majesty. And in that she omits neither His Descent into Hell nor the glory of His Resurrection, she is seen to surpass not the Prophets only but even the Evangelists themselves, who wrote but little touching that Descent.

Who is there that does not marvel also at that so familiar and prolonged colloquy wherein He Himself, alone with her, deigned so diligently to instruct that Gentile, a Samaritan woman, whereat the Apostles themselves were greatly astonished? Water also of an unbeliever and one whom He had rebuked for the number of her husbands He chose to ask, to drink, He Whom we know to have sought no other sustenance from any. The Apostles come to Him, and offer Him the meat that they have bought, saying: "Master, eat." Yet do we not find that their offerings were accepted, but that He pleaded, as though in excuse of Himself: "I have meat to eat that ye know not of." He asks drink of the woman. From which favour she excusing herself says: "How is it that thou, being a Jew, askest drink of me, which am a woman of Samaria? For the Jews have no dealings with the Samaritans." And again: "Sir, thou hast nothing to draw with, and the well is deep." And so He seeks drink from an unbelieving woman, and when she refuses it, Who heeds not the meat offered Him by the Apostles. What is this grace, I ask, which he manifests to the weaker sex, namely that He should ask water from the woman Who gives life to all men? What, I say, save that He may openly suggest that the virtue of women is so much the more pleasing to Him, the weaker their nature is known to be, and that He thirsts so much the more keenly with longing for their salvation, the more admirable is known to be their virtue? And so, when He asks that drink of the woman, He suggests that he wishes to quench this His thirst principally for the salvation of women. Which drink also calling meat, he says: "I have meat to eat that ye know not of." Which meat afterwards explaining, He adds: "My meat is to do the will of my Father." Implying this to be as it were the special will of His Father, where the salvation of the weaker sex is concerned.

We read also that the Lord held a familiar colloquy with *Nicodemus*, that ruler of the Jews, which *Nicodemus* also, coming secretly to Him, He instructed concerning his salvation; but that this colloquy was not immediately followed by such fruit. For we know both that this Samaritan woman was filled with the spirit of prophecy in that same hour, wherein she professed that Christ was already come to the Jews and would come also to the Gentiles, when she said: "I know that Messias cometh, which is called Christ: when he is come, he will tell us all things;" and that many from that city came unto Christ for the saying of the woman, and believed on Him and made Him tarry among them for two days, albeit He says elsewhere to His disciples: "Go not into the way of the Gentiles, and into any city of the Samaritans enter ye not." The same *John* relates elsewhere that certain of the Gentiles, who had come up to Jerusalem that they might worship at the feast, sent word to Christ through *Philip* and *Andrew*, that they wished to see Him. Yet does he not relate that they were admitted, nor that such abundance of Christ was granted to their request as to this Samaritan woman who in no wise sought it. With whom His preaching among the Gentiles is seen to have been begun, whom not alone did He convert, but through her, as has been said, won over many. Straightway lightened by the star and converted to Christ, the Wise Men are said to have brought many to Him by their exhortation or doctrine, but to have gone to Him alone. Wherefrom also it is clear what great grace the woman procured from Christ among the Gentiles, who running before and announcing His Coming to her city, and preaching those things that she had heard, in so short a time herself gained many of her people.

And if we turn over the pages of the Old Testament and of the Gospels, we shall see that those supreme benefits of the raising of the dead divine grace principally bestowed upon women, and that such miracles were not performed save for them or in their persons. For first through *Elias* and *Eliseus*, at the intercession of mothers, we read that their sons were raised to life. And the Lord Himself raising to life the son of a certain widow, and the daughter of the ruler of the Synagogue, and at the prayer of his sisters *Lazarus*, bestowed the benefit of this vast miracle especially upon women. Wherefore is that saying of the Apostle writing to the Hebrews: "Women received their dead raised to life again." For both the maid who was raised to life received her dead body, and the other women for their own comfort received those whom they were lamenting as dead restored to them. From which also it is clear what grace He has always shewn to women, whom first rejoicing by raising both themselves and their men to life, finally also by His Own Resurrection He greatly exalted those women to whom, as has been said, He first appeared. And indeed this sex since it was moved, amid a people that persecuted Him, by a certain natural compassion towards the Lord, appears to have acquired merit. For, as *Luke* records, when the men were leading Him to be crucified, their women followed bewailing Him and lamenting. To whom He, turning round, and as though compassionately rewarding this devotion in the very hour of His Passion, foretells to them, that they may be able to escape it, the coming destruction: "Daughters of Jerusalem, weep not for me, but weep for yourselves, and for your children. For behold, the days are coming, in the which they shall say, Blessed are the barren, and the wombs that never bare." For His release also *Matthew* records the wife of His most unjust judge as having aforetime faithfully worked, saying: "When he was set down on the judgment seat, his wife sent unto him, saying, Have thou nothing to do with that just man: for I have suffered many things this day in a dream because of him." And while He was preaching we read that a woman only of the whole crowd lifted up her voice in such praise of Him that she said that blessed was the womb that bare Him and the paps that gave Him suck. Whereby she was straightway privileged to hear the pious correction of her confession, albeit that was most true, He Himself at once answering her: "Yea rather, blessed are they that hear the word of God, and keep it."

John alone among Christ's Apostles obtained this privilege of love, that he should be called the Beloved of the Lord. But of *Martha* and *Mary John* himself writes: "Now Jesus loved *Martha*, and her sister, and *Lazarus*." This same Apostle, who by the privilege, as has been said, of love, records that he alone was loved by the Lord, has distinguished the women with that same privilege which he has ascribed to none other of the Apostles. In which honour, moreover, if he associated their brother with them, yet he placed them before him, believing them to come first in love.

We must lastly, to return to Christian women, proclaim with marvelling, and marvel to proclaim the respect paid by divine mercy to the very abjectness of common harlots. What could be more abject than *Mary Magdalene*, or *Mary* the Egyptian according to the state of their former life. Whom nevertheless afterwards, by honour or by merit, divine grace raised to a great sublimity. The former indeed remaining permanently in the Apostolic community, as we have already related, and the other, as it is written, striving beyond the bonds of human virtue in the agony of the anchorites, that the virtue of holy women might be pre-eminent among the monks of either kind, and that those words which the Lord says to the unbelieving: "The harlots go into the kingdom of God before you," might be seen to apply to them also, the men of faith, and that according to the difference of sex or of life the last should be first and the first last. Who, lastly, does not know that women embraced the exhortation of Christ and the counsel of the Apostles with so great zeal of chastity that, to preserve the integrity of flesh and mind alike they offered themselves as a holocaust to God in martyrdom, and triumphant in the twofold crown, sought to follow the Lamb, the Bridegroom of Virgins, whithersoever He should go?

Which perfection indeed of virtue we know to be rare in men but frequent in women. Some of whom, moreover, we read to have had so great zeal for this privilege of the flesh that they did not hesitate to lay hands on themselves, lest they should forfeit the incorruption which they had vowed to God, and that they might come as virgins to their Virgin Spouse. Who also has shewn the devotion of holy virgins to be so pleasing to Himself that a multitude of a Gentile people hastening to seek the protection of Saint *Agatha*, spreading out her veil against the terrible fire of boiling Etna, He saved from the loss both of body and of soul. Nor do we know any monk's cowl to have obtained the grace of so great a benefit. We read indeed that at the touch of the mantle of *Elias* Jordan was divided hither and thither, so that he and *Eliseus* went over on dry ground; but by the veil of a virgin a vast multitude of a people until then unbelieving were saved both in mind and in body, and unto them converted the way to heaven lay open. This also not a little commends the dignity of holy women, that they consecrated themselves by their own words, saying: "With His Ring He hath espoused me: I am betrothed to Him." For these are the words of Saint *Agnes*, whereby the virgins who make her profession are betrothed to Christ. And if any seek to know the form and dignity of your religion among the Gentiles, and to derive therefrom certain examples for your exhortation, he will readily understand that among them also a certain institution of this calling had pre-existed, saving such things as pertain to the tenor of the Faith, and that many things pre-existed among them as among the Jews, which collected from either source the Church has retained, but has changed for the better. Who does not know that all the orders of the clergy, from the doorkeeper to the bishop, and the very use of the ecclesiastical tonsure, whereby they become clerks, and the fasts of the Four Seasons, and the sacrifice of unleavened bread, not to say the ornaments of the sacerdotal vestments themselves, and certain ceremonies of dedication or other sacraments, were taken by the Church from the Synagogue? Who does not know moreover that she has not only retained, by a most profitable dispensation, the grades of secular dignities in kings and the other princes, and certain decrees of the laws, or teachings of philosophical doctrines among the converted nations; but has also taken from them certain grades of ecclesiastical dignities, likewise the form of continence and the religion of bodily purity?

For it is evident that our Bishops or Archbishops now preside, where of old they had flamens or archflamens: and that what were then temples erected to demons were afterwards consecrated to the Lord and dedicated in memory of the Saints. We know too that among the Gentiles the privilege of virginity most brightly shone when the curse of the Law coerced the Jews into marriage, and that so highly among the Gentiles was this virtue or purity of the flesh valued that in their temples great convents of women dedicated themselves to the celibate life. Wherefore *Jerome* upon the Epistle to the Galatians (in the third book) says: "What does it behove us to do, in whose condemnation Juno has her *onewomen* and Vesta her *univirgins*, and other idols their continent?" And he says *onewomen* and *univirgins*, meaning *onewoman* nuns, who had known men, and *univirgin* nuns, who were virgins. For *monos*, whence we have *monk*, that is *solitary*, means *one*. Who also, in his first book Against Jovinian, after citing many examples of the chastity or continence of Gentile women, says: "I know that I have multiplied the catalogue of women, that whoso despise the faith of Christian modesty may from the heathen at least learn chastity." Who in the same book had already so commended that virtue of chastity that it would seem that the Lord had especially approved this purity of the flesh in every people, and exalted several even of the unbelieving either by the conferring of merits or by the manifestation of miracles. "What am I to say," he asks, "of the Erichthrean Sibyl and the Cumaean, and of the other eight? For *Varro* declares that there were ten, whose distinction is virginity, and the reward of virginity divination." Likewise: "*Claudia*, a Vestal Virgin, when she had come under the suspicion of fornication, is said to have drawn a vessel by her girdle, which thousands of men were unable to move." And *Synodius*, Bishop of Clermont, in the preface to his book, speaks thus:

> Such as was neither *Tanaquil*, nor she
> Whom thou, *Tricipitinus*, didst engender,
> Nor she, to Phrygian Vesta dedicated,
> Who, gainst the foaming tide of Albula,
> Did draw a vessel by her virgin hair.

Augustine, in the twenty-second book Of the City of God, says: "If now we come to their miracles, which, wrought by their gods, they set against our martyrs, will they not also be found to work for us, and wholly to profit us? For among the great miracles of their gods that one surely is great of which *Varro* relates that a Vestal Virgin when she was in jeopardy from a false suspicion of fornication filled a sieve with water from the Tiber and carried it to her judges, spilling never a drop from any part of it. Who bore the weight of the water when so many holes gaped? Cannot Almighty God so take away the heavy weight of a terrestrial body that the said body may dwell quickened in that same element wherein the quickening Spirit has willed?" Nor is it to be marvelled at if in these or other miracles God has exalted the chastity of the unbelievers also, or has allowed it to be exalted by the agency of demons, that the believers might now be the more animated thereunto, the more they know it to have been exalted among the unbelievers also. We know too that grace was conferred on the prelacy, not on the person of *Caiaphas*, and that false apostles also occasionally shone in miracles; and that these were granted not to their persons but to their office. What wonder, then, if the Lord have given this concession not to the persons of unbelieving women but to the virtue of their continence, that the innocence of the virgin might at least be set free, and the false accusation against her probity be brought to nought? For it is clear that the love of continence is a good thing even among unbelievers, as also the observance of the conjugal pact is a gift of God among all peoples.

And so it need seem no marvel if God should honour His gifts, not the error of unbelief, by signs which are shewn to the unbelieving and not to the believing; especially when by these, as has been said, innocence is set free, and the malice checked of perverse men, and to this good, which is thus magnified, men are the more strongly urged, in that so much the less do the unbelieving sin the more they abstain from the pleasures of the flesh. Which now also with many other things against the aforesaid incontinent heretic Saint *Jerome* has not unfairly concluded, that what he does not marvel at in Christians he may blush to find in the heathen. Who moreover would deny to be gifts of God the power even of unbelieving princes, albeit they may use it perversely, or their love of justice or the clemency which they shew, taught by natural law, or the other things which become princes? Who would gainsay that they were good, because they are mixed with evil? Especially when, as Saint *Augustine* adds, and as reason manifestly attests, things cannot be evil except in a good nature? Who does not approve that which is contained in the poet's maxim: "From love of virtue the good hate to sin." Who does not rather approve than reject the miracle of *Vespasian*, when he was not yet Emperor, which *Suetonius* relates, to wit of the blind man and the lame man healed by him, that princes may more strongly desire to emulate his example? Or what Saint *Gregory* is reported to have done, touching the soul of *Trajan?* Men know how to find a pearl in the mire, and to discern the grain from the straw. And God cannot be ignorant of His gifts when conjoined with unbelief, nor can He hate any of those things that He has made. Which, the more brightly they shine by signs, the more fully He shews to be His, nor can what is His be corrupted by the depravity of men; and He shews also how He is to be regarded by the believing Who so reveals Himself to the unbelieving. And how great dignity among the unbelieving that modesty dedicated to the temples acquired the punishment of violation indicates. Which punishment, to wit, *Juvenal* recording in his Fourth Satire, against *Crispinus*, speaks of it thus:

> With whom but lately in defilement lay
> A priestess who beneath the ground to-day,
> Her blood still warm, must pass.

Wherefore also *Augustine*, in the third book Of the City of God, says: "For the ancient Romans themselves used to bury alive the priestesses of Vesta who were taken in fornication. But adulterous wives, albeit to some punishment, yet they never condemned to death." So much the more strictly did they sanction what they thought to be a divine sanctuary than the human marriage-bed. And with us the care of Christian princes provides so much the more for our chastity the more sacred it undoubtedly is. Wherefore *Justinian Augustus* says: "If any shall dare, I do not say to ravish, but to attempt merely with a view to matrimony the holy virgins, he shall be punished with death." The sanction also of ecclesiastical discipline, which seeks the remedy of penitence, not the punishment of death, with how severe a sentence it prevents your lapses is not in doubt. Whence these words of Pope *Innocent* to *Victricius*, Bishop of Rouen: "They who spiritually wed Christ, and are veiled by the priest, if afterwards they either publicly marry or are secretly corrupted, they are not to be admitted to the doing of penance, unless he to whom they have joined themselves have departed this life." But they who, not yet covered by the holy veil, yet have always pretended to remain in the virginal state, albeit they have not been veiled, by them penance is to be done for a certain time; because their bridal vow was held by the Lord. For if among men it is the common rule that contracts made in good faith may for no reason be broken, how much the less can this pact which they have made with God be broken without punishment? For if the Apostle *Paul* said that they have damnation who have departed from the state of widowhood, because they have cast off their first faith, how much the more virgins who have not at all preserved the faith of their former state? Wherefore also the famous *Pelagius* says to the daughter of *Mauritius*: "An adulteress against Christ is more guilty than one against her husband. Wherefore fittingly did the Roman Church lately decree so severe a sentence for such an offence, that it hardly deems them fit for penance who have violated the body consecrated to God with a lustful pollution." And if we choose to examine what care, what diligence, what charity the Holy Doctors, inspired by the examples of the Lord Himself and of the Apostles, have always shewn to devout women, we shall find them to have embraced, and cherished these women's devotion with the utmost zeal of affection, and with manifold study of doctrine or of exhortation to have steadfastly instructed and increased their religion.

And, to omit the rest, let me produce the principal Doctors of the Church, namely *Origen*, *Ambrose* and *Jerome*. The first of whom indeed, to wit that greatest philosopher of the Christians, embraced the religion of women with so great zeal that he laid hands upon himself, as the Ecclesiastical History relates, lest any suspicion might lead him away from the teaching or exhortation of women. Who, moreover, does not know what a harvest of divine books, at the bidding of *Paula* and *Eustochium*, Saint *Jerome* left to the Church? To whom among other things writing a sermon upon the Assumption of the Lord's Mother, according to their petition, he professes the same, saying: "But inasmuch as I cannot refuse whatever ye enjoin, being bound by your too great love, I shall attempt what ye exhort me to do." We know however that several of the greatest Doctors, men sublime by the dignity both of their order and of their life, writing to him from afar off begged for some brief script from him and did not obtain it. Wherefore also is that passage of Saint *Augustine* in the second book of the Retractations: "I wrote also two books to the presbyter *Jerome* dwelling at Bethlehem, one of the origin of the soul, the other of the intention of the Apostle *James* when he says: For whosoever shall keep the whole law, and yet offend in one point, he is guilty of all; consulting him upon each. And in the former, the question which I set forth I myself did not solve. In the latter, what appeared to me to be the solution I did not withhold. But I would know whether he approved of this, and consulted him. And he answered, praising me for the said consultation, but said that he had not the leisure to reply. And I, so long as he was in the body, was unwilling to make these books public, lest haply he might at some time reply, and that they might rather be published with his reply. But he being dead, I have published them." Behold so great a man for so long a time to have awaited a short and little answer from the aforesaid *Jerome*, and to have had it not. Whom on the other hand, at the petition of the said women, we know to have toiled over either the transcription or the dictation of so many and great volumes, displaying far more reverence in this matter for them than for a Bishop. Whose virtue peradventure he embraces with so much the greater zeal, nor can he bear to cause them sorrow, the frailer he considers their nature to be. Wherefore also at times the zeal of his charity towards women of this kind is found to be so great, that in their praise he appears to go some way beyond the bounds of truth, as though he had experience of that in himself which elsewhere recording he says: "Charity has no measure." Who at the very outset of his Life of Saint *Paula*, as though seeking to direct the reader's attention to himself, says: "If all the members of my body were turned to tongues, and every joint sounded with the human voice, I could say nothing worthy of the holy and venerable *Paula*."

Yet he has described sundry venerable lives, and lives shining with miracles, of the Holy Fathers, wherein the things are far more marvellous that are reported. Yet none of them is he found to have extolled with such a wealth of words as he used to commend this widow. Who also, writing to the virgin *Demetrias*, has marked the forefront of that letter with so great praise of her that he appears to fall into immoderate adulation. "Among all the matters," he says, "which from my childhood unto this age I have written whether with mine own hand or by the hand of scribes, nothing has been more difficult than the present work. For in writing to *Demetrias*, the virgin of Christ, who moreover is first in nobility and in riches in the City of Rome, if I say all the things that befit her virtues, I shall be deemed a flatterer." For it had been most pleasant to the holy man by whatsoever art of words to move a frail nature to the arduous study of virtue. But that works may furnish us in this matter with more certain arguments than words, with so great charity did he cultivate women of this sort that his immense sanctify imprinted a blot upon his own reputation. Which also he himself indeed, writing to *Asella* of feigned friends and of his detractors, records, among other things, saying: "And albeit some think me a reprobate, and covered with every ignominy, yet thou doest well in that, of thine own conscience, thou deemest even evil men to be good. For it is dangerous for a man to judge his neighbour's servant, and it is not a light fault to have spoken evil of the righteous. Certain men have kissed my hands and with the tongues of vipers have slandered me. They grieved with their lips, in their hearts they rejoiced. Let them say what they have ever detected in me other than what became a Christian? No fault is found in me save my sex, nor in that would fault ever be found save when *Paula* comes to Jerusalem." Likewise: "Before I knew the house of the holy *Paula,* my praises were sounded throughout the city, in the judgment of well-nigh all I was deemed worthy of the supreme Pontificate. But after I began to venerate, to worship, to take her upon my charge for the merit of her sanctity, all my virtues straightway departed from me." And a little later, "Salute," he says, "*Paula* and *Eustochium,* whether they will or no, mine in Christ."

We read also that the Lord Himself displayed such familiarity to the blessed harlot that the Pharisee who had invited Him began thereupon inwardly to doubt Him, saying to himself: "This man, if he were a prophet, would have known who and what manner of woman this is that toucheth him." What wonder, therefore, if for the gain of such souls the members of Christ themselves, incited by His example, do not shun the detriment of their own reputation? Which indeed *Origen,* as has been said, when he sought to avoid, endured to inflict a more grievous detriment upon his body. Nor in the doctrine or exhortation of women only has the wonderful charity of the Holy Fathers been revealed, but also in their comforting them it has at times so vehemently shone that, to soothe women's grief, their compassion appears to promise certain things contrary to the Faith. Such indeed is that comfort of Saint *Ambrose* which on the death of the Emperor *Valentinian* he ventured to write to his sisters, and to promise them his salvation who had died a catechumen. Which is seen to dissent widely from the Catholic Faith and from the truth of the Gospel. Wherefore also, whereas we see innumerable virgins follow the Mother of the Lord in the pattern of this excellence, we know of few men who have obtained the grace of this virtue; whereby, whithersoever He should go, they might be able to follow the Lamb Himself. In the zeal of which virtue, when certain women laid hands upon themselves that they might preserve that integrity of the flesh which they had vowed to God, not only is this not blameworthy in them, but these their martyrdoms have won them many dedications of churches. Betrothed virgins also, if before they have mingled carnally with their husbands they have decided to choose the monastic life, and rejecting man to make God their Husband, have freedom of action in this matter which we nowhere read to have been granted to men. Many of whom also have been inflamed with such zeal for chastity that not only against the decree of the law, for the preservation of chastity, have they put on male attire, but even among monks they have excelled by such great virtues that they have merited to become abbots. As we read of Saint *Eugenia,* who with the knowledge, nay at the behest of Saint *Helenus* her Bishop, assumed the male habit and, baptised by him, was taken into a college of monks.

And now to the former of thy latest petitions, dearest sister in Christ, I deem that I have sufficiently replied, to wit touching the authority for your Order, and moreover of the commendation of its proper dignity, that so much the more zealously ye may embrace the calling of your profession, the more fully ye are aware of its excellence. Now that the second also, God willing, I may accomplish, let me obtain by your merits and by your prayers. Farewell.

THE EIGHTH LETTER WHICH IS FROM THE SAME PETER TO HELOISE: AN INSTITUTE OR RULE OF NUNS

Argument: Abelard, *having been asked two things by* Heloise, *has answered the former of them indeed in his previous letter; he now takes up the other. And the second head of* Heloise's *petition had been that he would write a Rule for the nuns of Paraclete, which he admirably does in this, a book rather than a letter, many opinions of the Holy Fathers being scattered through it like flowers. And he calls it a tripartite treatise, because in it he treats chiefly of the three principal monastic virtues, to wit continence, voluntary poverty and silence. He establishes for the whole of their college seven office-bearing sisters, who shall prudently preside over the rest both in those things which are of the soul and in those which relate to temporal or bodily matters. The eating of flesh on three days in each week, and the use of wine in moderation he allows them, and the other things that pertain to the order of the monastic life he diligently and harmoniously sets forth.*

SOME part of thy petition having been already, so far as we were able, acquitted, it remains for us, God being willing, to turn our attention to the fulfilment both of thine own desires and of those of thy spiritual daughters, touching that part which is left. For there remains, following the order of your demand aforesaid, that some institute for you, as it were a rule of your calling, be written by us, and delivered to you, that ye may have more certainty from the written word than from custom of what it becomes you to follow. And so we, relying partly upon good customs, partly upon the testimony of the Scriptures or the support of reason, have decided to embody all these together, that, having to decorate the spiritual temple of God which ye are, we may contrive to adorn it as though with certain choice pictures, and out of many imperfect elements be able to fashion one perfect work. At the which task indeed, imitating the painter *Zeuxis*, we intend so to work in the spiritual temple as he arranged his work in the material. For him, as *Tully* records in the Rhetoric, the men of Crotona engaged for the decoration with most excellent pictures of a certain temple which they regarded with the greatest veneration. And that he might do this the more diligently he chose to himself five most beautiful virgins from among that people, looking upon whom as they sat by him painting he might in his painting imitate their beauty. Which very credibly may have been done for two reasons: both because, as the aforesaid doctor remarks, he had acquired the greatest skill in the portrayal of women, and also because, naturally, maidenly beauty is considered more elegant and more delicate than the male figure. And the aforementioned philosopher says that several virgins were chosen by him because he did not believe that he could find in one girl all the members equally comely, so much grace of beauty having never been conferred by nature upon any that she should have equal beauty in all her members; for nature herself produces nothing in the composition of bodies that is perfect in every part, as though if she were thus to confer all her benefits upon one she would have nothing left to bestow upon the rest. So also we, in depicting the beauty of the soul, and describing the perfection of the Bride of Christ, in which ye, as in a mirror of one spiritual virgin ever held before your eyes, may ascertain your own beauty or blemish, propose out of the many documents of the Holy Fathers or of the best customs of monasteries to intruct your conversation, plucking each blossom as it comes to mind, and gathering all together as though in a single garland that I shall see to accord with the sanctity of your calling.

And not those things only that have been instituted for nuns, but also those concerning monks. For as in name and in the profession of continence ye are conjoined with us, so also well-nigh all our institutions are competent to you. From these therefore, as we have said, gathering many thing as they were blossoms, wherewith we may adorn the lilies of your chastity, we ought with far greater zeal to describe the virgin of Christ than the aforesaid *Zeuxis* used to depict the likeness of an idol. And he indeed believed five virgins, whose beauty he should imitate, to suffice. But we, having an exuberant store in many documents of the Fathers, trusting in divine aid despair not of leaving to you a more perfect work: whereby ye may be able to attain to the lot or to the description of those five wise virgins, whom, in depicting the virgin of Christ, the Lord sets before us in the Gospel. And, that we may be able to perform this as we wish, we crave your prayers. Greeting in Christ, ye Brides of Christ.

We have decided that the treatise for your instruction shall be tripartite, in describing and arming your religion, and in arranging the celebration of divine service; wherein I consider the sum of the monastic religion to consist, to wit that one may live continently and without possessions, and may greatly study silence. Which is indeed, according to the Lord's teaching of the Evangelical rule, to gird the loins, to forsake all that we have, and to avoid idle words. And continence is that use of chastity which the Apostle enjoins, saying: "The unmarried woman careth for the things of the Lord, that she may be holy both in body and in spirit." In body, he says, as a whole, and not in one member, that to no lasciviousness in deed or in word may any of her members fall. But in spirit she is then holy when neither consent defiles nor pride puffs up her mind, like the minds of those five foolish virgins who while they ran to them that sold oil were left outside the door. To whom, beating upon the door that was already shut, and crying: "Lord, Lord, open to us," terribly the Bridegroom Himself makes answer: "Verily I say unto you, I know you not." And then, forsaking all things, we follow naked a naked Christ, as did the Holy Apostles, when for His sake not only our earthly possessions or the affections of kinship in the flesh but our own will also we put behind us, that we may not live according to our own judgment, but may be governed by the command of our prelate, and may wholly subject ourselves for Christ to him who in the place of Christ presides over us, as though to Christ. And if so be, which God forbid, that he live evilly, while he orders well, yet is not the sentence of God to be despised for the vice of man. Whereof He Himself enjoins us, saying: "Whatsoever they bid you observe, that observe and do; but do not ye after their works." And this spiritual conversion from the world to God He Himself diligently describes, saying: "Whosoever he be of you that forsaketh not all that he hath, he cannot be my disciple." And again: "If any man come to me, and hate not his father, and mother, and wife, and children, and brethren, and sisters, yea, and his own life also, he cannot be my disciple." And this is it to hate father or mother, for a man to refuse to follow the affection of kinship in the flesh, as to hate his own life is to refuse to follow his own will. Which also He enjoins elsewhere, saying: "If any man will come after me, let him deny himself, and take up his cross daily, and follow me." For so do we drawing near come to Him, to wit by closely imitating follow Him Who says: "I came not to do mine own will, but the will of him that sent me." As though He should say: Do all things by obedience.

For what is it to deny himself, save that a man should put behind him carnal affections and his own will, and should commit himself to be governed by another's, not by his own judgment? And so his own cross he does not receive from another but himself bears; whereby he may be crucified to the world and the world to him, when by the free will offering of his own profession he forbids himself worldly and earthly desires, which is not to follow his own will. For what else do the carnal seek save to secure their will? And what is earthly happiness, save the fulfilment of our own will, even when we achieve that which we desire with the greatest labour or peril? Or what else is to bear the cross, that is to endure some torment, save to do something against our own will, howsoever easy it may appear to us or profitable? Of this the other *Jesus*, far the lesser, warns us in Ecclesiasticus, saying: "Go not after thy lusts, but refrain thyself from thine appetites. If thou givest thy soul the desires that please her, she will make thee a laughing stock to thine enemies." But when we thus wholly forsake both those things that are ours and ourselves, then all possessions being truly cast aside we enter upon that Apostolic life, which reduces all things into a common store, as it is written: "And the multitude of them that believed were of one heart and soul: neither said any of them that ought of the things which he possessed was his own; but they had all things common." For it was divided unto each according to his need, for they were not equally in want; and so it was not distributed among them equally, but unto each according to his need. One heart in faith, because it is with the heart that we believe: one soul because by charity there was the same will mutually, since each wished the same things for his neighbour as for himself, nor sought his own advantage rather than that of others, or because all things were brought together by them for the common good, none seeking nor pursuing those things that were his but rather those that were of Christ Jesus. Otherwise they could in no way live without property, which consists rather in ambition than in possession. An idle or superfluous word is the same as a multitude of words. Wherefore *Augustine* in the first book of the Retractations, in the proem, says: "Far be it from me to esteem it a multitude of words when things needful are spoken, with whatsoever multitude and prolixity of words they may be said." And of this it is said through *Solomon:* "In the multitude of words there wanteth not sin: but he that refraineth his lips is wise."

We must therefore greatly beware of that in which there wanteth not sin, and the more study to prevent this malady the more dangerous and difficult it is to avoid. Which Saint *Benedict* foreseeing says: "At all times monks ought to study silence." And evidently to study silence is more than to keep silence. For study is the vehement application of the mind to the doing of something. For many things we do negligently or unwillingly, but none studiously unless we be willing or intent. And how difficult it is, and how profitable to refrain the tongue the Apostle *James* diligently considering says: "For in many things we offend all. If any man offend not in word, the same is a perfect man." The same likewise says: "For every kind of beasts, and of birds, and of serpents, and of things in the sea, is tamed, and hath been tamed of mankind." Who at this point considering how great matter there is in the tongue for evil, and consumption of all good, says both before and after: "Even so the tongue is a little member, and boasteth great things. Behold how great a matter a little fire kindleth! And the tongue is a fire, a world of iniquity . . . it is an unruly evil, full of deadly poison."

And what is more perilous than poison, or more to be avoided? For as poison extinguishes life, so does chattering utterly overthrow religion. Wherefore the same Apostle says in a former place: "If any man among you seem to be religious, and bridleth not his tongue, but deceiveth his own heart, this man's religion is vain."

Of this also in the Proverbs it is written: "He that hath no rule over his own spirit is like a city that is broken down, and without walls." This that elder diligently considered who, when *Anthony* said to him, of the chattering brethren who had accompanied him on his way: "Thou hast found good brethren with thee, Father," answered: "Good are they indeed, but their habitation hath no door. Whosoever will enters into the stable and unties the ass." As though our soul were tethered to the Lord's Manger, refreshing itself there with a certain rumination of sacred meditation, from which manger it is loosed, and hither and thither over the whole world runneth by the way of its thoughts, unless the bar of silence keep it in. For words impart understanding to the soul, that it may tend towards that which it understands, and by thinking adhere thereto. For in thinking we speak to God, as in words to men. And while here we tend towards the words of men, it is needful that we be led away from thence. Nor can we tend at once towards God and towards men.

Neither are idle words only, but those also which seem to contain some profit to be avoided, inasmuch as it is easy to pass from the needful to the idle, and from the idle to the harmful. For the tongue being, as *James* says, "an unruly evil," the smaller it is or subtler than the other members, so much the more mobile is it, and, whereas the others are wearied by motion, it when it moves not grows weary, and rest becomes a burden to it. Which, the more subtle it is in us, and from the softness of our body more flexible, so much the more mobile is it and the more prone to words, and is clearly the seed-bed of all malice. Which vice in us the Apostle especially noting wholly forbids women to speak in the Church, even of those things which pertain to God, save that he permits them to ask their husbands at home. And in learning these things, or whatsoever things are to be done, he specially subjects them to silence, writing thus to *Timothy* on these matters: "Let the woman learn in silence with all subjection. But I suffer not a woman to teach, nor to usurp authority over the man, but to be in silence."

And if for lay and wedded women he thus provides touching silence, what is to be done by you? And again, in writing to the same, shewing wherefore he has ordered thus, he argues that they are tattlers and speak things which they ought not. So, for this great plague providing a certain remedy, let us at least in these places or times subdue the tongue with a continual silence, to wit in prayer, in the cloister, the dormitory, the refectory, and in all eating and cooking; and from Compline onwards let this be specially observed by all. And in these places or times, if it be needful, let us use signs in place of words. Of the teaching or learning of which signs also let diligent care be taken, for which, if there be any need also of words, let the speaker be invited to converse in a fitting place, and one set apart for that purpose. And those words that are needful being briefly said, let her return to her former duties, or to what may next have to be done. Nor leniently should excess of words or of signs be corrected, but especially excess of words, wherein lies the greater peril. Which great and frequent peril Saint *Gregory* vehemently desiring to prevent, in the seventh book of the Morals thus instructs us: "When we neglect to beware of idle words, we come to harmful. By these are sowed incitements, quarrels arise, the torches of hatred are kindled, the whole peace of the heart is extinguished." Wherefore is it well said through *Solomon:* "The beginning of strife is as when one letteth out water." And to let out water is to let loose the tongue in a flood of eloquence. On the other hand, and in good part he asserts, saying: "The words of a man's mouth are as deep waters." Who therefore letteth out water is the beginning of strife; for whoso does not refrain his tongue scatters concord. Wherefore is it written: "He that maketh a fool keep silence turneth away wrath." By which he manifestly admonishes us, that we should adopt the strictest censure especially in the correction of this vice, that the punishment thereof be not any time deferred, and religion thus greatly imperilled. Since from hence spring slanderings, strife, evil speaking and often conspiracies and plots which do not so much undermine as overthrow the whole structure of religion. Which vice indeed when it has been cut off, haply depraved thoughts are not wholly extinguished, but they will cease from the corruption of others. To flee this one vice, as though he deemed that to be sufficient for religion, the Abbott *Macharius* warned his brethren, as it is written, in these words: "The Abbot *Macharius* the elder in Scythia said to his brethren: After the Mass is said, brethren, flee the churches. And one of them said to him: Father, where have we a greater solitude than this whereto to flee? And he set his finger on his lips, saying: That is what I say that ye are to flee. And so saying he entered into his cell, and shutting the door sat down alone." And this virtue of silence, which, as *James* says, makes the perfect man, and of which *Esaias* prophesied: "The work of righteousness shall be peace, and the effect of righteousness, quietness," was seized by the Holy Fathers with so great fervour, that, as it is written, the Abbot *Agatho* for the space of three years held a stone in his mouth, until he should learn to be silent.

Albeit the place do not bring salvation, yet it furnishes many opportunities for the easier observance of religion and for guarding it more safely. And many aids or impediments to religion consist therein. Wherefore also the sons of the prophets, of whom, as *Jerome* says, we read as of monks in the Old Testament, removed themselves to the secret places of the wilderness, building huts for themselves beside the river Jordan. *John* also and his disciples, whom we regard as the first of our calling, and thereafter *Paul*, *Anthony*, *Macharius*, and all such as have principally flourished in our calling, fleeing from the tumult of the age and from a world filled with temptations, bore the bed of their contemplation to the resting-place of the wilderness, that they might with more sincerity devote themselves to God. The Lord Himself also, to Whom no prompting of temptation might have access, teaching us by His example, when He wished to do aught chose the secret places especially, and avoided the tumult of the crowd. In this way the Lord Himself consecrated the wilderness for us by the forty days of His fasting, refreshed the multitudes in the wilderness, and for greater purity of prayer withdrew not only from the multitudes but even from the Apostles. The Apostles themselves also on a mountain apart He instructed and established, and with the glory of His Transfiguration distinguished the wilderness, and by the manifestation of His Resurrection made glad the disciples gathered together upon a mountain, and from a mountain ascended into heaven, and whatsoever great things He did else He wrought in a wilderness or a solitary place. Who also appears to *Moses* or to the Patriarchs of old in a wilderness, and through the wilderness leading the people to the promised land, and there, to the people that had long been detained there, delivering the Law, raining down manna, drawing water from a rock, comforting them with frequent apparitions and working miracles, He plainly taught them how greatly His solitude loves a solitary place for us, where we can more purely devote ourselves to Him. Who also diligently describing in a symbol the freedom of the wild ass, which loves the wilderness, speaks to Holy *Job*, saying: "Who hath sent out the wild ass free? Or who hath loosed the bands of the wild ass? Whose house I have made the wilderness, and the barren land his dwellings. He scorneth the multitude of the city, neither regardeth he the crying of the driver. The range of the mountains is his pasture, and he searcheth after every green thing." As though he should say openly: Who hath wrought this, if not I? And the wild ass, which we call the ass of the woods, is the monk who, set free from the chains of worldly things, has withdrawn himself to the quiet freedom of the solitary life, and fleeing the world has not remained in the world. Hence he dwells in a barren land, when his members through abstinence are parched and dry. He regards not the crying of the driver, but hears his voice, because he provides for his belly not things superfluous but things needful. For who is so importunate a driver, and so daily a driver as the belly? This makes its crying, that is its immoderate demands in superfluous and delicate foods wherein it must never be regarded.

The mountains of pasture are to him the lives or doctrines of the sublime Fathers, by reading and meditating upon which we are refreshed. Every green thing he calls the whole Scripture of the heavenly and unfading life.

Whereunto specially exhorting us Saint *Jerome* writes thus to the monk *Heliodorus:* "Interpret the word monk, which is thy name. What doest thou in the multitude who art alone?" The same also distinguishing our life from that of the clergy, writes to *Paul* the presbyter in these words: "If thou wilt exercise the office of a priest, if either the work or perchance the burden of the episcopate please thee, live in cities and towns, make the salvation of others a profit to thy soul. If thou desire to be what thou hast said, a monk, that is alone, what doest thou in the cities, which are the habitations not of the lonely but of the multitudes?" Each and every calling has its chiefs. And, to come to our own, let bishops and priests have as their example the Apostles and apostolic men, possessing whose honour let them strive also to acquire their merit. And we should have the chiefs of our calling, the *Pauls,* the *Anthonies,* the *Hilarions,* the *Macharies.* And, that I may return to the matter of the Scriptures, let our chief be, *Elias,* and *Eliseus,* our leaders also the sons of the prophets who dwelt in the fields and in the wilderness and made for themselves tabernacles by the river Jordan. Of these are also those sons of *Rechab* who drank neither wine nor strong drink, who dwelt in tents, who are praised by the voice of God through *Jeremy,* saying that they shall not want a man to stand before the Lord for ever. And let us therefore, that we may stand before the Lord, and being prepared may be the better able to take part in His worship, erect for ourselves tabernacles in the wilderness, lest the society of men shake the bed of our repose, disturb our rest, breed temptations, pluck our mind away from our holy calling.

Of which free tranquillity of life indeed to Saint *Arsenius,* under the Lord's guidance, was given a manifest example in one man to us all. Of whom it is written: "The Abbot *Arsenius,* when he was still in the palace, prayed to the Lord, saying: Lord, guide me to salvation. And there came a voice to him, saying: *Arsenius*, flee from men, and thou shalt be saved." And the book further relates: "And departing again to the monastic life he prayed the same prayer, saying: Lord, guide me to salvation. And he heard a voice saying unto him: *Arsenius*, flee, be silent, be at peace. For these are the roots of not sinning." He therefore, instructed by this one rule of the divine precept, not only fled from men but drave them away from him. To whom one day the Archbishop came with a certain judge, and, they requiring of him a counsel of edification, he said: "And if I shall tell you, will ye keep it?" And they promised that they would keep it. And he said to them: "Wheresoever ye shall hear of *Arsenius*, do not approach." And another time again the Archbishop visiting him sent first to see whether he would open. And he sent word to him, saying: "If thou comest, I open to thee, but if I shall have opened to thee, I open to all, and then I can no longer abide here." Hearing this the Archbishop said: "If by going I persecute him, I will never go to the holy man." The same also to a certain Roman matron visiting his sanctity said: "Wherefore hast thou presumed to undertake so great a voyage? Knowest thou not that thou art a woman and oughtest never to travel, or is it that thou mayest return to Rome and say to other women, I have seen *Arsenius*, and they may make the sea a highway for women coming to me?" But she said: "If the Lord should will that I return to Rome, I do not allow anyone to come hither. But pray for me, and be mindful of me always." And he answering said to her: "I pray God that He may wipe out the memory of thee from my heart." Hearing which she went away dismayed. He also, as it is written, being asked by the Abbott *Mark* wherefore he fled from men, replied: "God knows that I love men, but with God and with men equally I cannot be."

But to such an extent did the Holy Fathers shun the conversation and the notice of men, that many of them, that they might utterly remove men from them, feigned themselves to be mad, and, what is marvellous to relate, professed even that they themselves were heretics. Which who will may read in the Lives of the Fathers, of the Abbot *Simon*, how he prepared himself for the judge of the province coming to him: who to wit covering himself with a sack, and holding in his hand bread and cheese, sat in the door of his cell and began to eat. Let him read also of that anchorite who, when he had perceived certain men coming his way with lanterns, taking off his garments, cast them into the river; and standing there naked began to wash them. And he who ministered to him seeing these things was ashamed, and asked the men, saying: "Turn back, for our old man has lost his senses." And coming to him he said to him: "Wherefore hast thou done this thing, Father? For all who saw thee said, The old man has a devil." But he answered: "And I also wished to hear that." Let him read moreover of the Abbot *Moses*, who that he might wholly remove from him the judge of the province, rose up to flee into a marsh. And there came to him that judge with his company, and questioned him, saying: "Tell us, old man, where is the cell of the Abbot *Moses*?" And he said to them: "Wherefore do ye wish to seek him? The man is mad and a heretic." And what of the Abbot *Pastor*, who also would not allow himself to be seen by the judge of the province, that he might set free from prison the son of his own sister who besought him? Behold, the great ones of the world with great veneration and devotion seek the presence of the Saints, and there study, even with the greatest disrespect for themselves, to keep them utterly away from them.

But that we may know the virtue of your sex also in this matter, who could be found worthy to tell of that virgin who rejected even the visit of the most holy Saint *Martin*, that she might have leisure for contemplation? Whereof *Jerome* writing to the monk *Oceanus* says: "In the life of Saint *Martin* we have the testimony of *Sulpitius*, that Saint *Martin* journeying in the desire to greet a certain virgin pre-eminent in morals and chastity, she refused, but sent him a vail, and looking out from the window said to the holy man: Where thou art, Father, pray, for I have never been visited by a man. Hearing which Saint *Martin* gave thanks to God, that a woman imbued with such morals should have kept her chaste desire. He blessed her, and went his way full of joy." This woman indeed, disdaining or fearing to rise from the bed of her contemplation, was prepared to say to a friend knocking at her door: "I have washed my feet, how shall I defile them?" Oh, what an insult to themselves would the bishops or prelates of our day consider it if they had borne such a repulse from *Arsenius* or from this virgin! Let them blush for these things, if any monks yet remain in the wilderness, when they rejoice in the society of bishops, when they build for them special houses wherein they may be entertained, when the great ones of the world, whom a crowd accompany or follow, they not only do not shun but invite, and, multiplying their dwellings on the pretext of hospitality, turn to a city that solitude which they have sought. Verily, by this machination of the old and cunning temper, well-nigh all the monasteries of these days, after they had first been established in the wilderness, that men might be avoided, thereafter, the fervour of religion growing cold, have invited men, and gathering together menservants and maidservants, have built great villages in monastic places; and thus have returned to the world, nay, have drawn the world after them. Who involving themselves in the greatest miseries, and binding themselves in the greatest slavery both to ecclesiastical and to worldly powers, while they sought to live at their ease, and to enjoy the fruits of the labour of others, have lost the very name of monk, that is of solitary, as well as the life. Who also are often oppressed by such troubles that while they labour to protect the persons and the possessions of their followers they lose their own, and by the frequent conflagrations of the adjoining houses the monasteries also are burned.

Yet not even thus is their ambition refrained. These also not enduring any restriction whatsoever of the monastery, but dispersing themselves through villages, towns and cities, or even dwelling alone without any observance of a rule, are so much the worse than men of the world the more they fall away from their profession. Who, abusing the habitation of their people also, as well as their own, name their places Obediences wherein no rule is kept, wherein nothing save the belly and the flesh is obeyed, wherein abiding with their kinsmen or friends, they do the more freely what they will the less they fear their own conscience. Verily, in these most shameless apostates there can be no doubt that those excesses are criminal which in the rest of men are venial. The example of such lives let you not endure not only to follow but even to hear. But to your infirmity so much the more is solitude necessary, the less we are here assailed by the warfare of carnal temptations, and the less we stray towards bodily things through the senses. Wherefore also Saint *Anthony* says: "Whoso dwelleth in solitude and is at rest, is snatched from three wars, namely the wars of hearing, of speech and of sight. And against one only shall he have to fight, that is the war of the heart." These indeed, or the other advantages of the desert that famous Doctor of the Church Saint *Jerome* diligently pursuing, and vehemently extorting thereunto the monk *Heliodorus*, exclaims, saying: "O desert rejoicing in the presence of God! What doest thou, brother, in the world, who art greater than the world?"

And now that we have spoken of where it is fitting that monasteries should be built, let us shew what the position also of the place self ought to be. In determining the place of the monastery itself, as Saint *Benedict* also counselled, it is thus if possible to be provided that within the precincts of the monastery there may be contained those things especially which are necessary to monasteries; namely a garden, water, a mill, a bakehouse with oven, and places wherein the sisters may perform their daily tasks, that no occasion be furnished for straying without.

As in the camp of the world, so in the Camp of the Lord, that is in monastic congregations, certain persons are to be set up who shall preside over the rest. Just as there a single commander, at whose nod all things shall be done, is over them all. Who also, on account of the multitude of his army or the diversity of functions, distributing his duties, appoints certain magistrates under himself who may look after the different troops of men or offices. So also must it be done in monasteries, that there one matron shall preside over all, under whose consideration or judgment all the rest shall do all their work, nor any presume to oppose her in aught, or even murmur against any of her precepts. For no congregation of men, nor any household however small in one house can remain entire unless unity be preserved therein, to wit the whole governance thereof consist in the magistracy of one person. Wherefore also the ark, bearing a type of the Church, while it was of many cubits as well in length as in breadth, was finished in one point. And in the Proverbs it is written: "For the transgression of a land many are the princes thereof." Wherefore also when *Alexander* was dead, kings being multiplied, evils were multiplied likewise. And Rome being entrusted to many rulers could not maintain concord. Wherefore *Lucan* in his first book reminds us: "Thou, O Rome, hast been the cause of thine evils, being delivered to three Lords; for ever have the pacts of a kingdom entrusted to a multitude proved fatal." And a little later: "While the earth beareth the tide and the air the earth, and his long labour makes the sun revolve, and night followeth day through each house of heaven, there shall be no good faith among partners in a realm, and all powers shall be impatient of a consort."

Such, assuredly, were those disciples of Saint *Frontonius* the Abbot, whom he, when, in the city wherein he had been born, he had gathered them together to the number of seventy, and had won great favour there both before God and among men, leaving their monastery in the city with their portable goods bore naked with him into the wilderness. Which afterwards, in the manner of the children of Israel murmuring against *Moses*, because he likewise had led them out of Egypt, leaving the fleshpots and the abundance of the land, into the wilderness, murmuring vainly said: "Is chastity to be found only in the wilderness, and not in cities? Wherefore now do we not return to the city out of which for a time we have come forth? Or is it in the wilderness alone that God will give ear to prayers? Who can live by the bread of angels? Who finds pleasure in becoming the companion of herds and wild beasts? What need have we to linger here? Wherefore then do we not turn back to bless the Lord in the place wherein we were born?" And for this reason the Apostle *James* warns us: "My brethren, be not many masters, knowing that we shall receive the greater condemnation." For this reason also *Jerome* writing to the monk *Rusticus* of the conduct of his life says: "No art is learned without a master. Even the dumb animals and herds of wild beasts follow their leaders. Among the bees, one going before the rest follow. Cranes follow one of their number in good order. There is one Emperor, one judge of a province. Rome when it was founded could not have two brothers at the same time as kings, and was dedicated by parricide. In *Rebecca*'s womb *Esau* and *Jacob* waged war. All bishops of churches, all archpriests, all archdeacons, and every order in the church depend on their rulers. In a ship there is one steersman. In a house there is one master. In an army however great they look to the orders of one man. By all these examples my prayer tends to this, that I may teach thee that thou oughtest not to be governed by thine own judgment, but to live in a monastery under the discipline of one Father and in the company of many."

That concord therefore may be preserved in all things it is proper that one woman be over all, whom all may obey in all things. Under her also certain other persons, as she herself shall decide, ought to be set up, as they were so many magistrates. Who shall preside over such offices as she may have ordered and so far as she wishes, that they may be, as it were, captains or consuls in the Lord's army; but all the rest as soldiers or infantry, the care of these former looking after them, shall fight freely against the enemy and his satellites. And seven persons out of your number we consider to be necessary for the whole administration of the monastery, and to suffice, namely the Portress, the Cellaress, the Wardrober, the Infirmarian, the Chantress, the Sacristan and lastly the Deaconess, whom they now call Abbess. And so in this camp, and in this kind of divine host, as it is written: "The days of man upon earth are as an host," and again: "Terrible as an army with banners," the place of a commander, who is obeyed in all things by all, the Deaconess holds. And the other six under her, whom we call office-bearers, take the places of captains or consuls. But all the other nuns, whom we call the cloistral, expeditiously perform the divine service after the manner of soldiers. And the converts, who also forsaking the world have dedicated themselves to the service of the nuns, in a certain religious, yet not monastic habit, like infantry hold the lower rank.

And now it remains, the Lord inspiring me, to order the several ranks of this host, that against the assaults of devils it may be in very truth that which is called "an army with banners." From the head herself, I say, which we call the Deaconess, tracing the beginning of this institution, let us first dispose of her by whom all things are to be disposed. And her sanctity, as we have recalled in the preceding letter, Saint *Paul* the Apostle writing to *Timothy* diligently describes how eminent and tried it ought to be, saying: "Let not a widow be taken into the number under threescore years old, having been the wife of one man. Well reported of for good works; if she have brought up children, if she have lodged strangers, if she have washed the saints' feet, if she have relieved the afflicted, if she have diligently followed every good work. But the younger widows refuse." The same earlier of deaconesses, when also he was ordering the life of the deacons, says: "Even so must their wives be grave, not slanderers, sober, faithful in all things." And how greatly we esteem the intelligence or reason that there is in all these sayings we have sufficiently expounded in our last letter. Especially wherefore the Apostle wishes her to have been the wife of one husband, and to be advanced in years. Whereat we wonder not a little how this pernicious custom has begun to stink in the Church, that those who are virgins are elected to this office rather than those that have known men, and that often the younger are set above the elder. Albeit the Preacher says: "Woe to thee, O land, when thy king is a child," and we all alike approve that saying of Holy *Job:* "With the ancient is wisdom, and in length of days understanding." Hence also it is written in the Proverbs: "The hoary head is a crown of glory, if it be found in the way of righteousness." And in Ecclesiasticus: "O how comely a thing is judgment for gray hairs, and for ancient men to know counsel. O how comely is the wisdom of old men, and understanding and counsel to men of honour. Much experience is the crown of old men, and the fear of God is their glory." Likewise: "Speak, thou that art the elder, for it becometh thee. Speak, young man, if there be need of thee: and yet scarcely when thou art twice asked. Let thy speech be short, comprehending much in few words. But as one that knoweth, and yet holdeth his tongue. If thou be among great men, make not thyself equal with them, and when ancient men are in place, use not many words." Wherefore also the presbyters who in the Church are set over the people are interpreted as *elders*, that by the name itself it may be taught what they ought to be. And they who wrote the Lives of the Saints named them whom we now call *Abbots*, *Elders*.

And so in every way is care to be taken that in the election or consecration of the Deaconess that counsel of the Apostle be kept in mind, to wit that such an one be elected as ought to be over the rest by her life and doctrine, and by age also promises ripeness of morals, and by obedience shall have learned to govern, and by work rather than by hearsay shall have learned the Rule, and shall know it more thoroughly. And if she be not lettered, let her know that she is to accustom herself not to philosophical studies, or dialectical disputations, but to the doctrine of life and the display of works. As it is written of the Lord: "Began both to do and teach," to wit first to do, and afterwards to teach. In that better and more perfect is the teaching of works than that of speech; of the deed than of the word. Let us diligently pay heed to what, as it is written, the Abbot *Ipitius* said: "He is truly wise who by his deed teaches others, not by his words." And not a little comfort and confidence does he afford in this matter.

Let us pay heed also to that argument of Saint *Anthony* wherewith he confounded the wordy philosophers, to wit those who laughed at his rule as at that of a foolish and unlettered man: "And answer ye me," he said, "which cometh first, sense or letters, and which is the beginning of either, does sense spring from letters or do letters from sense?" And they asserting that sense was the author and inventor of letters, he says: "Then he that is whole in sense requireth not letters." Let us hear also the words of the Apostle and be strengthened in the Lord: "Hath not God made foolish the wisdom of this world?" And again: "But God hath chosen the foolish things of the world to confound the wise; and God hath chosen the weak things of the world to confound the things which are mighty; and base things of the world, and things which are despised, hath God chosen, yea, and things which are not, to bring to nought things that are: that no flesh should glory in His presence." For the Kingdom of God, as he himself afterwards says, is not in word, but in power. And if, to gain a better knowledge of anything, she consider that she ought to turn to the Scripture, let her not be ashamed to ask and to learn this of the lettered, nor in these matters let her despise the teaching of letters; but devoutly and diligently receive it, as he also the Prince of the Apostles diligently received public correction from his Brother Apostle *Paul*. For, as Saint *Benedict* also remarks, the Lord often reveals to the lesser man that which is better. And that we may more fully follow the divine provision which the Apostle also has recorded above, let this election never be made from among the noble or great ones of the world unless under pressure of the greatest necessity, and for the most assured reason. For such, easily confident in their race, become boastful, or presumptuous, or proud; and especially when they are natives of the place their prelacy becomes harmful to the monastery. For care must be taken lest the neighbourhood of her own kindred make her more presumptuous, and their company burden or disquiet the monastery, and she herself by her people bring about a detriment to religion, or come under the contempt of others, according to the words of the Truth: "A prophet is not without honour, save in his own country." Which Saint *Jerome* also foreseeing, writing to *Heliodorus*, when he has enumerated divers things which obstruct the way of monks who dwell in their own country, says: "The sum of these considerations is as follows: That a monk in his own country cannot be perfect. And not to wish to be perfect is a sin."

But what a perdition of souls, if she should be less forward in religion who presides in the mastery of religion! For to each of the subordinates it is sufficient that she display a single virtue. But in her examples of all the virtues ought to shine, that all those things which she enjoins on the others she may foreshew by her own example, lest she run counter in her morals to those things which she enjoins, and what she builds up by her words destroy by her deeds, and out of her mouth the word of correction be taken away, when she is ashamed to correct in others the faults which she herself is known to commit. Whereof indeed the Psalmist, lest it befall him, prays to the Lord, saying: "And take not the word of truth utterly out of my mouth." For he had in mind that gravest punishment of the Lord, whereof he elsewhere also reminds us, saying: "But unto the wicked God saith, What hast thou to do to declare my statutes, or that thou shouldest take my covenant in thy mouth? Seeing thou hatest instruction, and castest my words behind thee. But I keep under my body, and bring it into subjection; lest that by any means, when I have preached to others, I myself should be a cast-away." For to him whose life is despised it remains that his preaching also or his doctrine be contemned. And when any man ought to heal another, if he have laboured in the same infirmity, rightly is the reproach made to him by the sick: "Physician, heal thyself." Let him carefully heed, whosoever is seen to preside in the Church, what ruin his own fall may bring about, when he draws his subordinates together with himself to the precipice. "Whosoever therefore," says the Truth, "shall break one of these least commandments, and shall teach men so, he shall be called the least in the Kingdom of Heaven." For he breaks a commandment who by acting contrary to it infringes it, and by his example corrupting others sits in his chair a teacher of pestilence.

And if whosever acts thus is called the least in the Kingdom of Heaven, that is in the Church here on earth, what are we to call that vilest prelate by whose negligence the Lord requires the life not of his own soul only but of all the souls subject to him? Wherefore the Book of Wisdom well curses such men: "Power is given you of the Lord, and sovereignty from the Highest, who shall try your works and search out your counsels. Because, being ministers of this kingdom, ye have not judged aright, nor kept the law, horribly and speedily shall he come upon you; for a sharp judgment shall be to them that be in high places. For mercy will soon pardon the meanest: but mighty men shall be mightily tormented, and a sore trial shall come upon the mighty." For it suffices for each of the subordinate souls to provide for itself against its own offence. But prelates in the sins of others also death threatens. For when gifts are increased the reasons of the gifts multiply also; and to whom more is committed, of him more is exacted. Against which so great peril we are warned in the Proverbs to provide, where it is said: "My son, if thou be surety for thy friend, if thou hast stricken thy hand with a stranger, thou art snared with the words of thy mouth, thou art taken with the words of thy mouth. Do this now, my son, and deliver thyself, when thou art come into the hand of thy friend; go, humble thyself, and make sure thy friend. Give not sleep to thine eyes, nor slumber to thine eyelids." For then do we become surety for a friend, when our charity receives anyone into the conversation of our congregation. To whom we promise the care of our provision, as he also promises his obedience to us. And thus also do we strike our hand with him, when by becoming surety we establish the solicitude of our working on his behalf. And then do we come into his hand, because unless we shall have made provision for ourself against him we shall find him to be the slayer of our soul. Against which peril counsel is furnished when it is added: "Go, humble thyself," and the rest.

And so now hither, now thither, after the manner of a provident and a watchful captain, let him carefully go round his camp, or examine lest through any neglect a way lie open to him who, as a roaring lion, walketh about seeking whom he may devour. All the evils of her house let her be the first to know, that by her they may be corrected before they be known to the others, and taken as an example. Let her beware of that wherewith Saint *Jerome* charges the foolish or negligent: "We are always the last to learn of the evils of our own house, and remain ignorant of the vices of our children and wives when they are a song among the neighbours." Let her pay heed, who thus presides, that she has undertaken the custody as well of bodies as of souls. And of the custody of bodies she is warned, where it is said in Ecclesiasticus: "Hast thou daughters? Have a care of their body, and shew not thyself cheerful toward them." And again: "The father waketh for his daughter when no man knoweth; and the care for her taketh away sleep, lest she should be defiled." But we defile our bodies not only by fornication, but by working anything indecent in them, as well with the tongue as with any other member, or in whatsoever member abusing the bodily senses for any vanity. As it is written: "For death is come up into our windows," that is sin to the soul by the instruments of the five senses.

And what death is more fearful, or what custody more perilous than that of souls? "Fear not," says the Truth, "them which kill the body, but are not able to kill the soul." If any hear this counsel, who does not rather fear the death of the body than that of the soul? Who does not avoid a sword rather than a lie? And yet it is written: "The mouth that belieth slayeth the soul." What can so easily be slain as the soul? What arrow can be fashioned more swiftly than a lie? Who can safeguard himself if only against thought? Who is able to provide against his own sins, let alone those of others? What shepherd in the flesh is strong enough to guard spiritual sheep from spiritual wolves, things invisible from things invisible? Who would not fear the robber who does not cease to prow around, whom we can with no wall shut out, with no sword kill or wound? Of whom, incessantly laying snares, and especially persecuting the religious, in the words of *Habakkuk:* "Their portion is fat, and their meat plenteous," the Apostle *Peter* exhorts us to beware, saying: "Your adversary the devil, as a roaring lion, walketh about seeking whom he may devour." And how great is his presumption of devouring us the Lord Himself says to Holy *Job:* "He drinketh up a river, and hasteth not: he trusteth that he can draw up Jordan into his mouth." For what may he not presume to assail, who assailed the Lord Himself even, to tempt Him? Who straight from Paradise led our first parents into captivity, and from the company of the Apostles snatched away an Apostle even, whom the Lord had chosen? What place is safe from him, what gates stand not open to him? Who can provide against his snares, who is able to resist his strength? It is he who at one stroke smiting the four corners of the house of the holy man *Job*, crushed his innocent sons and daughters and slew them. What will the weaker sex be able to avail against him? By whom is his seduction so greatly to be feared as by woman? For her he first of all seduced, and through her her husband likewise, and led all their posterity captive. Greed of a greater deprived woman of a lesser good. By this art also will he now easily seduce a woman, when she desires rather to govern than to serve, driven thereto by ambition of wealth or honour.

And which of these it has been, the sequel shall prove. For if she have lived more delicately as a prelate than as a subordinate, if she have claimed for herself anything peculiar, beyond her needs, there can be no doubt that she desired this. If she have sought more costly ornaments after than before, assuredly she is swollen with vainglory. What at first lay hidden will afterwards appear. What aforetime she displayed, whether it were virtue or a feint, her prelacy will indicate. Let her be led to the prelacy rather than come to it, for upon the Lord's saying: "All that ever came before me are thieves and robbers," "Who came," comments *Jerome*, "not who were sent." Let her be assumed rather to the honour than assume the honour to herself. For "no man," says the Apostle, "taketh this honour unto himself, but he that is called of God, as was *Aaron*." If called, let her mourn as though she were being led out to death; if rejected, let her rejoice as though delivered from death. We are ashamed at the words, when we are said to be better than the rest. But when in our election this is made manifest in very fact, we are shamelessly devoid of shame. For who does not know that the better are preferred to the rest? So in the twenty-fourth book of the Morals: "He ought not to undertake the leadership of men, who knows not how to rebuke men well by admonition. Nor ought he who is chosen to this office, that he may correct the faults of others, himself to commit what ought to have been rooted out." In which election, however, if haply we avoid this shamelessness with some light refusal in words, yet only to the ear reject the dignity that is offered us, assuredly we bring this accusation against ourselves, that we are striving to appear more righteous and more worthy.

Oh, how many in their election have we seen to weep with their eyes and to laugh in their heart! To accuse themselves as being unworthy, and thereby to hunt the more after approval and human favour for themselves! Paying heed to what is written: "The just man is first in his own accusation." Whom afterwards when it befell them to be accused, and an occasion for retiring offered itself to them, most importunately and impudently strove to defend their prelacy which they had shewn themselves unwilling to undertake, by feigned tears and by truthful accusations of themselves.

In how many churches have we seen canonical persons resist their bishops, when they were urged by them to take holy orders, and profess themselves to be unworthy of so great a ministry, nor at all willing to acquiesce? And should the clergy thereafter elect them to the episcopate, they meet with none or with but a light refusal. And they who yesterday, as they said, avoiding a peril to their soul were shunning the diaconate, now almost in a night become justified of the higher order, do not fear the precipice. Of whom indeed it is written in the same Book of Proverbs: "A man void of understanding striketh hands, and becometh surety in the presence of his friend." For then does the wretch rejoice at that whereat he ought rather to mourn, when coming to the governance of others he is bound by his own profession to the care of his subordinates, by whom he ought to be loved rather than feared.

Against which pestilence providing so far as we can, we wholly forbid that the superior live more delicately or more softly than the subordinate: let her not have private chambers for eating or for sleeping, but let her do all things with the flock committed to her, and so much the more make provision for them, the more she is present constantly among them. We know indeed that Saint *Benedict*, greatly solicitous concerning pilgrims and strangers, set up a table apart for the abbot with them. Which albeit it was then piously established, yet latterly, by a most useful dispensation of monasteries, has been so amended that the abbot may not retire from the convent, but may provide a faithful dispenser for the pilgrims. For at table it is easy to fall, and then should discipline keep a stricter watch. Many also at the coming of strangers are propitious to themselves rather than to the strangers, and here by the gravest suspicion the absent are offended and murmur. And so much the less is the authority of the prelate, the more his life is unknown to his people. Then also whatsoever poverty there may be is more endurable, when it is shared by all alike, but especially by the prelates. As we have learned also in the example of *Cato*. For he, as it is written, when the people with him were thirsty, rejected and poured away a little water that was offered him, and all were satisfied.

Since therefore sobriety is most necessary to prelates, so much the more sparingly should they live as through them provision is to be made for the rest. Who also, lest they turn the gift of God, that is the prelacy conferred upon them into pride, and by this greatly insult their subordinates, let them hear what is written: "Be not as a lion in thy house, nor frantic among thy servants." "Pride is hateful before God and man." "The Lord hath cast down the thrones of proud princes, and set up the meek in their stead." "If thou be made the master of the feast, lift not thyself up, but be among them as one of the rest." And the Apostle instructing *Timothy* with regard to his subordinates says: "Rebuke not an elder, but entreat him as a father; and the younger men as brethren; the elder women as mothers; the younger as sisters." "Ye have not chosen me," says the Lord, "but I have chosen you." All other prelates are chosen by their subordinates, and by them are created and established, because they are chosen not to be Lord, but to serve. For He alone is truly Lord, and it is for Him to choose His servants for His service. Nor yet did He shew Himself Lord, but a servant, and His disciples, when they were already aspiring to the high places of dignity, rebuked by His Own example, saying: "Ye know that the princes of the Gentiles exercise dominion over them, and they that are great exercise authority upon them. But it shall not be so among you." He therefore imitates the princes of the Gentiles who seeks dominion over his subordinates rather than service, and works rather to be feared than to be loved, and, being swollen with the authority of his prelacy, loves "the uppermost rooms at feasts, and the chief seats in the synagogues, and greetings in the markets, and to be called of men, Rabbi, Rabbi." And of the honour of this title, that we should not glory in names, but look to humility in all things, "But be not ye," says the Lord, "called Rabbi: and call no man your father upon the earth." And thereafter, forbidding all glorying, He says: "Whosoever shall exalt himself shall be abased."

Care must be taken also lest through the absence of the shepherds the flock be imperilled, and lest when the prelates stray without the discipline within grow slack. And so we order that the Deaconess, looking after spiritual rather than bodily things, for no care of things without leave the monastery, but be the more solicitous for her subordinates the more assiduous she is; and so among men also shall her presence be more venerable, the rarer it is, as it is written: "If thou be invited of a mighty man, withdraw thyself, and so much the more will he invite thee." But if the monastery need any mission, let the monks or their converts perform it. For always it behoves the men to provide for the needs of the women. And the greater their religion is, the more they devote themselves to God, and need more assistance of men. Wherefore also *Joseph* is warned by the angel to take care of the Lord's Mother, Whom nevertheless he is not permitted to know. And the Lord Himself when He was dying provided as it were a second son for His Mother, who should take care of her in temporal things. Nor is there any question what great attention the Apostles paid to the devout women, as we have already recorded sufficiently elsewhere: to whose service also they appointed the seven Deacons. And we indeed, following this authority, the very necessity of the matter also requiring it, have decided that monks and their converts, after the manner of the Apostles and Deacons, shall provide for monasteries of women in those things that pertain to outward charges. Wherein the monks are necessary principally for the masses, but for works the converts.

And so it is fitting, as we read that it was done in Alexandria under *Mark* the Evangelist, in the very beginning of the infant Church, that monasteries of men should not be wanting from the monasteries of women, and that by men of similar religion all things without be administered to the women. And then certainly we believe that monasteries of women more firmly observe the religion of their calling if they are governed by the rule of spiritual men, and the same shepherd is set as well over the sheep as over the rams, to wit when he that is over the men presides likewise over the women, and always, according to the Apostolic institution, the head of the woman is the man, as the head of every man is Christ, and the head of Christ is God. Wherefore also the monastery of Saint *Scholastica*, being situated on the lands of a monastery of brethren, was governed also by the rule of a brother, and by the frequent visitation of himself or his brethren instructed and comforted. Of the provision also of this government the Rule of Saint *Basil* in a certain passage instructing us, contain these words: "*Question.* Whether it befits him who presides, apart from her who presides over the sisters, to say anything that may pertain to edification to the virgins. *Answer.* And how shall that precept of the Apostle be observed, which says: Let all things be done decently and in order?" Likewise in the following chapter: "*Question.* Whether it is seemly for him who presides to converse frequently with her who presides over the sisters, and especially if some of the brethren are thereby offended. *Answer.* Albeit the Apostle says: For why is my liberty judged of another man's conscience? it is good to imitate him when he says: Nevertheless we have not used this power; but suffer all things, lest we should hinder the gospel of Christ. And so far as may be the sisters are to be seen seldom, and the discussion is to be briefly ended." Of this also is that decision of the Council of Seville: "By common consent we have decreed that the monasteries of virgins in the Baetic province be ruled by the ministration and presidency of monks. For then do we provide things salutary for the virgins dedicated to Christ, when we choose for them spiritual fathers, by whose guidance they may not only be protected, but edified also by their doctrine."

Yet this caution is to be observed with regard to the monks, that they shall be kept apart from the privacy of the sisters, nor have familiar permission to approach even to the vestibule, and that neither the Abbot nor he that is set over them shall in the absence of her that presides be allowed to say aught to the virgins of Christ that pertains to the institution of morals. Nor with her that presides ought he to converse frequently alone, but in the presence of two or three sisters. So, as the access is rare, let the speech be brief. For God forbid that we should wish the monks, which even to say is shameful, to be familiar with the virgins of Christ. But, according to what the ordinances of the Rule and of the Canons lay down, keeping the men separate and far apart, we commit the sisters to their guidance only, ordaining that one man most proved of the monks be chosen, in whose charge shall be the management of their lands, in the country or in the town, the erection of buildings, or the provision of whatsoever else it may be for the needs of the monastery, that the handmaids of Christ, solicitous for the welfare of their souls alone, may live in divine worship, and serve their own works. Clearly he who is set over them by his Abbot, shall be approved by the judgment of his Bishop. And let the sisters make the clothing for those same communities wherefrom they expect tutelage. Receiving from them in turn, as has been said, the fruits of their labour, and the support of their protection.

And so we, following this provision, wish monasteries of women to be so ever subject to monasteries of men that the brethren may take care of the sisters, and one man preside as a father over both, to whose dispositions either monastery shall look, and that over both in the Lord, as there is one fold, there may be one shepherd. Which society indeed of spiritual brotherhood has been so much the more pleasing as well to God as to man, the more perfectly it is able to suffice for either sex coming to conversion, to wit that the monks take in the men, and the nuns the women, and the society itself can provide for every soul that is thinking of its own salvation. And whosoever with either a mother or a sister or a daughter, or any woman else of whom he has charge, shall seek to be converted, may find there a complete solace. And that both monasteries may be joined together by so much the greater mutual affection, and be the more solicitous one for the other, the more closely the persons that are in them are united by some propinquity of affinity. And the Provost of the monks, whom they name Abbot, we wish so to preside over the nuns also that he may regard them, that are the Brides of the Lord, Whose servant he is, as his own mistresses, nor rejoice to be over them, but to be of service to them. And let him be like the steward in a king's palace, who does not oppress the mistress with his power, but acts providently towards her, that he may straightway obey her in things needful, and in harmful things not give ear to her, and so minister to all things without that he may never, unless ordered, enter into the secrecy of the bride-chamber.

In this manner therefore we wish the servant of Christ to provide for the Brides of Christ, and to take charge of them faithfully for Christ, and to treat of all things that are proper with the Deaconess. Nor without consulting her shall he decide aught touching the handmaids of Christ, or those things that pertain to them, nor shall he order aught of any of them save through her, nor presume to speak to them. But whensoever the Deaconess shall have summoned him, let him not delay to come, and whatsoever she shall have advised him touching those things whereof she or her subordinates have need, let him not delay to carry out, so far as he is able. And being summoned by the Deaconess, let him say nought to her save openly and in the presence of approved persons, nor let him draw near to her, nor detain her with copious speech. But all things that pertain to food or to clothing, and the money also, if there be any, shall be gathered together among the handmaids of Christ, or set aside, and from thence shall things needful be made over to the brethren, of those which the sisters may have in excess. And so the brethren shall procure all things without, and the sisters those things only that are proper to be done within by women, to wit the putting together of the garments, those of the brethren also, or the washing of them, the kneading of bread also, and the handing of it to be baked, and taking of it when baked. To them shall pertain also the charge of the milk, and of those things that are made therefrom, and the feeding of hens or geese and what things soever woman can do more conveniently than men.

And the Provost himself when he shall have been appointed, in the presence of the Bishop and of the sisters shall swear that he will be to them a faithful steward in the Lord, and will solicitously preserve their bodies from carnal contagion. Wherein if peradventure, which God forbid, the Bishop shall find him negligent, let him straightway depose him as guilty of perjury. All the brethren also, in making their profession, shall bind themselves to the sisters, that they will in no way consent to their suffering, and will provide, within their power, for their bodily purity. None of the men therefore, save by leave of the Provost, shall have access to the sisters, nor shall any missive be received by them, unless it be transmitted by the Provost. None of the sisters shall ever leave the precincts of the monastery, but all things without, as has been said, the brethren shall procure, and in strong works the strong shall swink. None of the brethren shall ever enter these precincts, unless the leave of the Provost and Deaconess have been obtained, when some necessary or honest reason shall have required this. If any perchance shall have presumed against this, let him without delay be expelled from the monastery. Lest however the men, being stronger than the women, presume to burden them in aught, we order that they also shall presume nothing against the will of the Deaconess, but shall do all things at her nod, and all alike, men as well as women, make profession to her, and promise obedience, that the peace may be so much the more lasting, and concord better preserved, the less licence is allowed to the stronger; and that the strong be so much the less burdened by obedience to the weak, the less they have to fear their violence. And the more a man shall have humbled himself here before God, be it certain that he shall be the more highly exalted. Let these things that have been presently said concerning the Deaconess suffice. Now let us turn our pen to the office-bearers.

The Sacristan, who is also the Treasurer, shall provide for the whole oratory, and shall herself keep all the keys that pertain thereto, and such things as are necessary to it; and if there be any offerings, she shall receive them, and shall have the charge of fashioning or refashioning those things that are needed in the oratory, and of its whole adornment. It is her duty also to see to the Hosts, the vessels. and the books of the altar, and the whole adornment thereof, the relics, the incense, the lights, the clock, the striking of the bells. And the Hosts, if it be possible, let the virgins prepare, and let them purify the flour whereof they are made, and wash the palls of the altar. But the relics, and the vessels of the altar, it shall never be permitted to her nor to any of the sisters to touch, nor the palls even, unless they have been handed over to them to be washed. But to this office the monks or their converts shall be summoned, and their coming awaited. And if it shall be needful, let certain of them be appointed under her to this office, who may be worthy, if the need should arise, to touch those things, and from the chests unlocked by her let the men take them out or replace them there. She indeed who presides over the sanctuary ought to be pre-eminent in purity of life; if it be possible let her be whole in mind as in body, and let her abstinence and her continence alike be proved. She ought to be learned especially in the computation of the moon, that according to the order of the seasons she may provide for the oratory.

The Chantress shall provide for the whole choir, and shall arrange the divine offices, and shall have the mastery in the teaching of singing or of reading, and of those things that pertain to writing or to dictation. She shall keep also the aumbry of the books, and shall take them out thence and receive them again, and shall undertake the charge of writing or adorning them, or shall see to this. She shall ordain how they are to sit in choir, and shall give the seats, and shall make provision who are to read or sing, and shall compose the list to be recited on Saturdays in Chapter, wherein all the weekly duties shall be described. On this account it is most fitting that she be lettered, and especially that she be not ignorant of music. She also after the Deaconess shall see to all the discipline. And if haply the Deaconess be occupied with other matters, she shall take her place in this.

The Infirmarian shall provide for the sick, and shall preserve them as well from sin as from want. Whatsoever their sickness shall demand, as well of food as of baths, or aught else that may be, is to be allowed them. For there is a proverb known in such cases: "The law was not made for the sick." Let flesh meat in no way be denied them, save on the sixth day of the week or on the chief vigils or the fasts of the Four Seasons, or of Lent. But from sin let them be so much the more urged, the more it is incumbent upon them to think of their departure. And then especially is silence to be studied, wherein we may most exceed, and they shall be instant in prayer, as it is written: "My son, in thy sickness be not negligent: but pray unto the Lord, and He will make thee whole. Leave off from sin, and order thy hands aright, and cleanse thy heart from all wickedness." There must also be always a careful guardian present by the sick, who, should the need arise, may straightway come to them, and the house must be furnished with all things that are necessary to their infirmity. Of medicines also, if need be, provision shall be made according to the resources of the place. Which can more easily be done if she who is over the sick is not lacking in knowledge of medicine. And to her also the charge shall pertain of those that have an issue of blood. But there ought to be some one skilled in bleeding, lest it be necessary for a man to enter among the women for this purpose. Provision is to be made also for the offices of the Hours, and for Communion, lest these be wanting to the sick, that on the Lord's Day at least they may communicate, confession always, and satisfaction so far as may be preceding. Touching the anointing also of the sick, let the precept of Saint *James* the Apostle be carefully observed, for the execution of which, especially when they despair of the sick person's life, let there be brought in from the monks two of the elder priests with a deacon, let them bring the consecrated oil with them, and the convent of sisters being present, yet with a partition set between, let them celebrate the sacrament. Similarly, when the need shall arise, let the Communion be administered. And thus it is necessary that the sickhouse be so arranged that the monks, to do these things, may have an easy access and egress, neither seeing the convent nor being seen by them. And once on every day at the least let the Deaconess with the Cellaress visit the sick person, as she were Christ, that they may carefully provide for her needs as well in bodily as in spiritual things, and may deserve to hear it said by the Lord: "I was sick, and ye visited me."

And if the sick person shall have drawn near to her departure, and have come to the agony of death, straightway let some one that is by her run to the convent with a board, and beating upon it announce the sister's departure, and let the whole convent, whatsoever be the hour of day or night, hasten to the dying unless they be prevented by the offices of the Church. And should this befall, since nothing is to be set before the work of God, it is enough that the Deaconess with certain others, whom she shall choose, go in haste, and the convent follow after. But whosoever shall go running at the beating of the board, let her straightway begin the Litany, until the invocation of the Saints, male and female, be completed, and then let the Psalms or other things that pertain to exsequies follow. And how salutary it is to go to the sick or to the dead, the Preacher diligently pursuing says: "It is better to go to the house of mourning than to go to the house of feasting: for that is the end of all men; and the living will lay it to his heart." Likewise: "The heart of the wise is in the house of mourning." And straightway let the body of her that is dead be washed by the sisters, and, being clad in some cheap but clean garment and in sandals, let it be laid on a bier, the head being wrapped in the veil. And let these garments be strongly stitched or tied to the body nor let them be moved thereafter. But let the burial of the Deaconess have this honour only above the others, that her whole body be wrapped in a shroud alone, and therein be sewn up as in a sack.

The Wardrober shall provide all that regards the charge of clothing, to wit in shoes as well as in all things else. She shall cause the sheep to be shorn, and shall receive the hides for the sandals. The flax or wool she shall spin and store and shall have the whole charge of the woven stuffs. Thread and needle and scissors she shall supply to all. She shall have the whole charge of the dormitory, and shall provide beds for all. Of the coverings also of the tables and of the towels and of all the cloths she shall have charge, of the cutting and of the sewing and of the washing. To her especially the words apply: "She seeketh wool and flax, and worketh willingly with her hands. She layeth her hands to the spindle, and her hands hold the spindle. She shall not be afraid of the snow for her household: for all her household are clothed with scarlet. She looketh well to the ways of her household, and eateth not the bread of idleness. Her children arise up, and call her blessed." She shall have the instruments of her work and shall provide out of her work that which she ought to enjoin upon her sisters severally. For she shall have the charge of the novices, until they be received into the congregation.

The Cellaress shall have charge of all those things that pertain to victuals, of the cellar, the refectory, the kitchen, the mill, the bakehouse with the oven, the gardens also and the orchards, and the whole cultivation of the fields; of all bees also, herds and flocks; or of the necessary birds. Of her shall be required whatsoever shall be necessary in the matter of food. Her it becomes especially not to be a miser, but ready and willing to furnish all things needful. "For God loveth a cheerful giver." Whom we utterly forbid that in the dispensing of her administration she be more propitious to herself than to others, or prepare private dishes for herself, or reserve aught for herself defrauding others. "The best steward," says *Jerome*, "is he that reserves nothing for himself."

Judas abusing the office of his stewardship, when he had the bag, perished out of the company of the Apostles. *Ananias* also and *Sapphira* his wife, by keeping back the part, received sentence of death.

To the Portress, or Ostiary, which is the same, pertains the reception of guests, or of any comers, and the announcement of them or conducting of them to the proper place, and the charge of hospitality. It is well that she be discreet in years and in mind, and that she know how to receive and to give answer, and to determine who are and who are not to be taken in, and how. By her especially as by the vestibule of the Lord the religion of the monastery ought to be adorned, since with her the discovery of it begins. Let her therefore be gentle in words, mild in speech, that in them also whom she debars she may study to edify their charity by giving a fitting reason. For thus it is written: "A soft answer turneth away wrath: but grievous words stir up anger." And elsewhere: "Sweet language will multiply friends." She also, seeing the poor more often and knowing them better, if there be aught of food or clothing to be distributed among them, let her distribute it; but both to her and to the other office-bearers, should they need the support or comfort of others, let vicars be given by the Deaconess. Which should generally be taken from among the converts, lest any of the nuns be absent ever from the divine offices, or from the chapter or the refectory. Let her have a lodge by the gate, wherein she or her vicar may ever be ready for all comers, where also let them not sit idle, and all the more let them study silence, the more easily their talking may reach the ears of them also that are without. Verily her duty is not only to shut out the men who must be debarred; but also utterly to exclude rumours, that they be not wantonly carried into the convent, and whatsoever excess there may be in this matter is to be visited on her. But if she should hear what may need to be made known, let her report it secretly to the Deaconess, that she may, if it please her, deliberate thereon. And so soon as there shall be a knocking or a clamour at the door, let her that is at hand ask of the comers who they be or what is their will, and straightway, if need be, let her open the door that she may receive the incomers. And women only shall be entertained within. But the men shall be directed to the monks. And so no man for any reason shall be admitted within, unless the Deaconess have first been consulted, and order it. But to women the gate shall at once be opened. But the women who are taken in, or the men who upon any occasion enter, the portress shall cause to wait in her cell, until the Deaconess or the sisters, if it be necessary or opportune, may come to them. But to poor women who require washing of their feet let the Deaconess herself, or the sisters diligently perform this grace of hospitality. For the Apostle also principally from this service of humanity was called Deacon. As in the Lives of the Fathers also one of them records, saying: "For thee, O man, the Saviour becoming a Deacon, girding Himself with a towel, washed the disciples' feet, ordering them also themselves to wash one another's feet." Therefore the Apostle says of the Deaconess: "If she have lodged strangers, if she have washed the saints' feet." And the Lord Himself says: "I was a stranger, and ye took me in." Let all the office-bearers save the Chantress be attached to these duties, who study not letters, if such may be found as are suited for this, that they may more freely devote themselves to letters.

Let the ornaments of the oratory be necessary, not superfluous; clean rather than costly. Let there be nothing therefore in it fashioned of gold or of silver, save one silver chalice, or more even, if need be. Let there be no ornaments of silk, save the stoles or maniples. Let there be no carven images in it. Let a wooden cross only be set up there over the altar, whereon if haply it please them to paint the image of the Saviour, it is not forbidden. But no other images let the altars know. With a pair of bells let the monastery be content. Let a vessel filled with holy water be set without, at the entrance of the oratory, that they may bless themselves with it going in in the morning or coming out after

Compline. Let not any of the nuns be absent from the Canonical Hours; but so soon as the bell shall have been rung, putting aside all things else let her hasten to the divine office, yet with a modest gait. And entering into the oratory secretly, let them say that can: "I will come into thy house in the multitude of thy holy mercy: and in thy fear will I worship toward thy holy temple." Let no book be kept in the choir save it be necessary to the present office. Let the Psalms be said openly and distinctly so as to be understood, and let the psalmody or singing be so moderated that those who have a feeble voice may be able to sustain it. Let nothing be said or sung in the church, unless it be taken from the authentic Scripture, but chiefly from the Old or the New Testament. Each of which shall be distributed over the lessons so that in their entirety they may be read in church during the year. But let expositions thereof or sermons of the Doctors, or whatsoever writings contain some edification be recited at table or in chapter, and, wheresoever there may be need, let the reading of all things be allowed. But let none presume to read or to sing save what she has first prepared. If haply any of them have pronounced anything faultily in the oratory, let her there by supplication in the presence of all give satisfaction secretly, saying: "Pardon, Lord, this time also, my neglect." And at midnight, according to the Apostolic institution, they must rise for the nocturn vigils, wherefore they must so timeously retire to bed that weak nature may be able to sustain these vigils. And all things that pertain to the day may be done with the daylight, as also Saint *Benedict* instituted. And after the vigils let them return to the dormitory, until the hour strike of the matutinal Lauds.

And if any of the night still remain, let sleep not be denied to weak nature. For sleep greatly refreshes weary nature, and makes it patient of toil and keeps it sober and alert. Yet if any need meditation of the Psalter or of any lessons, as Saint *Benedict* also states, they ought so to study that they may not disturb the sleepers. For thus he has said *meditation* in this passage, rather than *reading*, lest the reading of some prevent the sleep of others. Who also when he said: "By the brethren that are in need," did not, certainly, compel any to this meditation. At times, however, if there be need also of teaching of singing, provision is to be made of this in like manner for those to whom it is necessary. But let the morning Hour be performed so soon as the day begins to shine; and on the sun's rising, if it can be arranged, let the bell be rung. Which Hour ended, let them return to the dormitory. And if it be in the summer, because the night-time is then short, and the morning long, we do not forbid them to sleep for a little before Prime, until they are aroused by the ringing of the bell. Of which sleep also, to wit after the morning Lauds, Saint *Gregory* in the second chapter of the Dialogues, where he speaks of the venerable man *Libertinus*, makes mention, saying: "But on the following day there was a cause to be heard for the benefit of the monastery. The morning hymns therefore having been sung, *Libertinus* came to the bedside of the Abbot, and humbly sought a blessing for himself." Let this morning sleep therefore, from Easter until the autumnal equinox, when the night begins to exceed the day, be not denied. And coming out of the dormitory let them wash themselves, and taking books let them sit in the cloister reading or singing, until Prime be rung. But after Prime let them go to Chapter, and all seating themselves there let a lesson of the Martyrology be read, the state of the moon being first given out. Where afterwards let there be some edifying discussion, or let some of the Rule be read and expounded. Then if there are things to be corrected, or ordered, let them proceed to these.

But it must be known that neither a monastery nor any house ought to be called disordered if things be done there disorderly, but if when they have been done they be not carefully corrected. For what place is entirely free from sin? Which Saint *Augustine* diligently pursuing when he is instructing his clergy, in a certain passage remarks, saying: "For howsoever vigilant be the discipline of my house, I am a man, and among men I dwell. Nor do I dare to claim for myself that my house is better than *Noe*'s Ark, where nevertheless among eight persons one was found reprobate, nor better than the house of *Abraham*, where it was said: Cast out this bond-woman and her son; nor better than the house of *Isaac:* I loved *Jacob* and I hated *Esau;* nor better than the house of *Jacob*, wherein a son defiled his father's bed; nor better than the house of *David*, of whose sons one lay with his sister, another rebelled against the so holy meekness of his father; nor better than the company of *Paul* the Apostle, who if he dwelt among good men would not say: Without were fightings, within were fears. Nor would he say: For I have no man like-minded, who will naturally care for your state. For all seek their own; nor better than the company of Christ Himself, wherein eleven good men must tolerate the traitor and thief *Judas;* nor better lastly than heaven, wherefrom angels fell." Who also greatly exhorting us to the discipline of the monastery added this, saying: "I confess before God, from the day on which I began to serve God, with what difficulty I have found men better than those who have advanced in monasteries. So have I not found men worse than those who in monasteries have fallen." So that of this, I judge, is it written in the Apocalypse: "He which is filthy, let him be filthy still: and he that is righteous, let him be righteous still."

Let the strictness of correction therefore be such, that whosoever shall have seen in another what is to be corrected, and have concealed it, shall be subjected to a graver discipline than she who committed it. Let none therefore delay to accuse either her own or another's fault. But whosoever accusing herself shall have come before the others, as it is written: "The just man is first in his own accusation," deserves a milder discipline, if her negligence have ceased. But let none presume to excuse another unless haply the Deaconess question her as to the truth of a matter which is unknown to the rest. Let none ever presume to strike another for what fault soever, unless she have been so ordered by the Deaconess. And it is written, concerning the discipline of correction: "My son, despise not the chastening of the Lord; neither be weary of his correction; for whom the Lord loveth he correcteth, even as a father the son in whom he delighteth." Likewise: "He that spareth the rod hateth his son: but he that loveth him chasteneth him betimes. Smite a scorner, and the simple will beware. When the scorner is punished, the simple is made wise. A whip for the horse, a bridle for the ass, and a rod for the fool's back. He that rebuketh a man, afterwards shall find more favour than he that flattereth with the tongue. Now no chastening for the present seemeth to be joyous, but grievous: nevertheless afterward it yieldeth the peaceable fruit of righteousness unto them which are exercised thereby." And again: "An evil-nurtured son is the confusion of his father that begat him, and a foolish daughter is born to his loss. He that loveth his son, causeth him oft to feel the rod, that he may have joy of him in the end. He that chastiseth his son, shall have joy in him, and shall rejoice of him among his acquaintance. An horse not broken becometh headstrong, and a child left to himself will be wilful. Cocker thy child and he shall make thee afraid: play with him and he will bring thee to heaviness." But in the discussion of counsel it shall be open to any to offer her opinion, but whatsoever may appear to all let the decree of the Deaconess be held fast, in whose judgment all things consist, even if, which God forbid, she be mistaken, and decide upon that course which is the worse. Whereof is that saying of Saint *Augustine* in the book of Confessions: "He sins greatly who is disobedient to his superiors in aught, even if he choose things better than those that are ordered of him." For it is far better for us to do well, than to do good. Nor ought we to consider so much what is done as in what manner or spirit it is done. A thing is well done which is done in obedience, even if what is done seem to be least good.

And so in all things superiors are to be obeyed, however great be the material harm, if no peril is apparent to the soul. Let the superior see that he orders well, since to the subordinates it is sufficient to obey well; and not to follow their own will, as they have professed, but the will of their superiors. For we utterly forbid that custom be ever set above reason, than anything be ever defended because it is the custom, but because it is of reason; nor because it is in use, but because it is good: and so much the more readily let it be received the better it shall appear. Otherwise let us as the Jews prefer the antiquity of the Law to the Gospel. Whereto Saint *Augustine* adding many testimonies from the counsel of *Cyprian*, says in a certain passage: "Whoso, despising truth, presumes to follow custom, either is odious and malicious towards his brethren, to whom the truth is revealed; or he is ungrateful to God, by Whose inspiration His Church is instructed." Likewise: "In the Gospel the Lord says: I am the Truth. He did not say: I am the custom. And so, the truth being made manifest, let custom yield to truth. Likewise revelation being made of the truth let error yield to truth, as also *Peter*, who at first circumcised, yielded to *Paul* preaching the truth." The same in the fourth book, Of Baptism: "Vainly indeed do those who are vanquished by reason plead custom against us, as though custom were greater than truth, or that were not to be followed in spiritual things which has been revealed by the Holy Ghost for the better." This plainly is true, that reason and truth are to be set above custom. *Gregory* the Seventh writes to Bishop *Wimund:* "And certainly, if we may use the words of Saint *Cyprian*, no custom, however ancient, however widespread, is to be set above the truth: and the use of which is contrary to the truth is to be abolished." And with what love truth in words even is to be embraced, we are admonished in Ecclesiasticus, where it is said: "Be not ashamed when it concerneth thy soul." Likewise: "In no wise speak against the truth." And again: "Let reason go before every enterprise, and counsel before every action."

Let nothing either be taken as authority because it is done by the many, but because it is proved by the wise and the good. "That which is wanting cannot," says *Solomon*, "be numbered."

And according to the assertion of the Truth: "For many are called, but few are chosen." Costly things are rare; and those which abound in number are diminished in price. For let none in taking counsel follow the greater part of the company, but the better. Nor let a man's age, but let his wisdom be considered; nor let friendship, but let truth be regarded. Wherefore also is that saying of the poet:

'Tis right even from our foe to learn.

But so often as there is need of counsel, let it not be deferred. And if important matters are to be discussed, let the convent be assembled. But in the discussion of minor matters the Deaconess shall suffice, a few of the major persons being assembled with her. It is written also of counsel: "Where no counsel is, the people fall: but in the multitude of counsellors there is safety. The way of a fool is right in his own eyes: but he that hearkeneth unto counsel is wise. He that believeth in the Lord taketh heed to the commandment; and he that trusteth in him shall fare never the worse." If perchance anything done without counsel has a prosperous outcome, the benefit of fortune does not excuse the presumption of the man. But if after taking counsel men sometimes err, the power that sought counsel is not to be held guilty of presumption. Nor is he so to be blamed that believed, as are they with whom he agreed in their error.

And coming out from Chapter, let them attend to those works that are proper, to wit reading or singing, or handiwork until Terce. And after Terce let the mass be said, for the celebration whereof let one of the monks be appointd priest by the week. Who moreover, if the company be so great, should come with a deacon and subdeacon, who may minister to him what is necessary, or themselves perform their own offices. Let their coming in and their going out be so arranged that they are in no way visible to the convent of sisters. But if more have been necessary, provision shall be made for them also, and if it be possible always so made that monks, on account of the nuns' masses, are never wanting in their own convent for the divine offices. But if Communion is to be made by the sisters, let a priest of ripe age be chosen, who after the mass may communicate them; the deacon and the subdeacon having first withdrawn, to remove any occasion of temptation. And thrice at least in the year let the whole convent communicate, that is at Easter, at Pentecost and at the Lord's Nativity, as was instituted by the Fathers for the laity also. And for these Communions let them so prepare themselves that on the third day preceding they may all repair to confession and make fitting atonement, and by three days of fasting on bread and water and by frequent prayer purify themselves with all humbleness and trembling, applying to themselves those terrible words of the Apostle: "Wherefore whosoever shall eat this bread, and drink this cup of the Lord, unworthily, shall be guilty of the body and blood of the Lord. But let a man examine himself, and so let him eat of that bread and drink of that cup. For he that eateth and drinketh unworthily, eateth and drinketh damnation to himself, not discerning the Lord's body. For this cause many are weak and sickly among you, and many sleep. For if we would judge ourselves, we should not be judged."

After mass also let them return to their work until Sext, and at no time let them live idly, but let each and every one do that which she can and which is fitting. But after Sext, they are to take their nuncheon, unless it be a fast. For then they must wait until None, and in Lent until Vespers even. But at no time let the convent lack reading. Which when the Deaconess may wish to end, let her say: "Enough." And immediately let all rise to give thanks to God. In the summer-time after nuncheon until None they are to rest in the dormitory, and after None to return to their work until Vespers. But after Vespers they are straightway either to eat or to drink. And then also, according to the custom of the season, to go to collation. But on Saturday before collation let them be made clean, to wit by washing of the feet and of the hands. In which office indeed let the Deaconess serve with the sisters of the week, who have served in the kitchen. But after collation they are to come straightway to Compline, and thereafter to go to sleep.

In food and clothing, moreover, let the Apostolic sentence be observed, wherein it is said: "And having food and raiment let us be therewith content." To wit that necessary things shall suffice, superfluous things not be sought. And let that which can more cheaply be bought, or more easily had, and without offence taken, be given them. For only the offence of his own or of his neighbour's conscience does the Apostle avoid in food, knowing that not the food is at fault, but the appetite. "Let not him," he says, "that eateth despise him that eateth not. And let not him which eateth not judge him that eateth. Who art thou that judgest another man's servant? He that eateth, eateth to the Lord, for he giveth God thanks; and he that eateth not, to the Lord he eateth not, and giveth God thanks. Let us not therefore judge one another any more: but judge this rather, that no man put a stumblingblock, or an occasion to fall, in his brother's way. I know, and am persuaded by the Lord Jesus, that there is nothing unclean of itself: but to him that esteemeth any thing to be unclean, to him it is unclean. For the kingdom of God is not meat and drink; but righteousness, and peace, and joy in the Holy Ghost. All things indeed are pure, but it is evil for that man who eateth with offence. It is good neither to eat flesh, nor to drink wine, nor any thing whereby thy brother stumbleth, or is offended." Who also after the offence to his brother adds the offence to himself of him who eats against his own conscience, saying: "Happy is he that condemneth not himself in that thing which he alloweth. And he that doubteth is damned if he eat, because he eateth not of faith: for whatsoever is not of faith is sin." For in all that we do against our conscience, and against that which we believe, we sin. And in that which we prove, that is by the law which we approve and receive, we judge and condemn ourselves, if forsooth we eat those foods which we distinguish, that is exclude by the law, and set apart as being unclean. For such is the testimony of our conscience, that it greatly accuses or excuses us before God.

Wherefore also *John* writes in his First Epistle: "Beloved, if our heart condemn us not, then have we confidence toward God. And whatsoever we ask, we receive of him, because we keep his commandments, and do those things that are pleasing in his sight." And so it is well said by *Paul* above: "that there is nothing unclean of itself; but to him that esteemeth any thing to be unclean," that is if he believes it to be unclean and forbidden to himself. For we call foods unclean which according to the Law are called clean, because the Law cutting them off from its own may yet expose them publicly to those that are without the Law. Wherefore also common women are unclean, and common things or things that are made public are cheap, or less dear. And so he asserts through Christ that no food is common, that is unclean, because the Law of Christ forbids nothing, save as has been said for the removing of offence whether to a man's own conscience or to another's. Whereof also he says elsewhere: "Wherefore, if meat make my brother to offend, I will eat no flesh while the world standeth, lest I make my brother to offend. Am I not an Apostle? Am I not free?" As who should say: Have I not that freedom which the Lord gave to the Apostles, to eat whatsoever I will or to take alimony from others? For thus, when He was sending for the Apostles, in a certain passage He says: "Eating and drinking such things as they give." To wit distinguishing no kind of food from the others. Which the Apostle diligently heeding carefully proceeds to say that all kinds of food, even if they be the food of infidels and idolaters, are lawful to Christians, only, as we have said, avoiding offence in food. "All things," he says, "are lawful for me, but all things are not expedient: all things are lawful for me, but all things edify me not. Let no man seek his own, but every man another's wealth. Whatsoever is sold in the shambles, that eat, asking no question for conscience' sake: for the earth is the

Lord's, and the fulness thereof. If any of them that believe not invite you to a feast, and ye be disposed to go, whatsoever is set before you eat, asking no question for conscience' sake. But if any man say unto you, This is offered in sacrifice unto idols, eat not for his sake that showed it, and for conscience' sake. Conscience, I say, not thine own, but of the other. Give none offence, neither to the Jews, nor to the Gentiles, nor to the Church of God."

From which words of the Apostle it is plainly gathered that nothing is forbidden us which we may eat without offence to our own conscience, or to another's. But without offence to our own conscience we then act, if we believe that we are keeping that calling in life whereby we may be saved. And without offence to another's if we are believed to be living in that manner whereby we may be saved. We shall indeed live in this manner, if, allowing all the things necessary to our nature, we avoid sin, nor presume upon our strength to bind ourselves by profession to that yoke of life whereby overburdened we may fall; and so much the heavier be the fall, the higher was the degree of our profession. Which fall, indeed, and vow of a foolish profession the Preacher foreseeing says: "When thou vowest a vow unto God, defer not to pay it; for he hath no pleasure in fools: pay that which thou hast vowed. Better is it that thou shouldest not vow, than that thou shouldest vow and not pay." Which danger the Apostolic counsel meeting says: "I will therefore that the younger women marry, bear children, guide the house, give none occasion to the adversary to speak reproachfully. For some are already turned aside after Satan." Considering the remedy of a feeble age, he opposes the remedy of a looser life to the peril of a better. He counsels us to abide in the low places, lest we be made to fall from the high.

Following this counsel, Saint *Jerome* also, instructing the virgin *Eustochium*, says: "But if they that are virgins, yet on account of other faults be not saved, what shall become of those that have prostituted the members of Christ, and have turned the temple of the Holy Ghost into a brothel? Better were it for a man to undergo matrimony, to have trodden the level ground, than, straining after the heights, to fall into the depths of hell." And if we search through all the words of the Apostle never shall we find him to have allowed a second marriage, save to women. But men especially exhorting to continence, he says: "Is any man called being circumcised? Let him not become uncircumcised." And again: "Art thou loosed from a wife? Seek not a wife." Whereas *Moses*, more indulgent to men than to women, allows one man to have many wives at a time, not one woman many husbands, and punishes the adulteries of women more strictly than those of men. A woman, says the Apostle, "if her husband be dead, is loosed from the law of her husband; so that she is no adulteress, though she be married to another man." And again: "I say therefore to the unmarried and widows, It is good for them if they abide even as I. But if they cannot contain, let them marry: for it is better to marry than to burn." And again: "The wife, if her husband be dead, is at liberty to be married to whom she will; only in the Lord. But she is happier if she so abide, after my judgment." Not a second marriage only does he allow to the weaker sex, he makes bold to set no limit to the number, and when their husbands are dead permits them to marry others. He fixes no limit to their marriages so long as they escape the sin of fornication. Let them marry often rather than fornicate once, that if they be prostituted to one they pay not the debt of carnal commerce to many. Albeit the payment of this debt is not wholly free from sin, but lesser sins are allowed that greater may be avoided.

What wonder therefore if that wherein there is no sin is allowed them, lest they incur sin; that is whatsoever foods are necessary, not superfluous? For not the food, as we have said, is at fault, but the appetite, to wit when that attracts us which is not lawful, and that is desired which is forbidden, and at times shamelessly snatched, whereby the greatest offence is created. But what among all the foods of man is so perilous or so destructive and contrary to our religion or to holy quiet as wine? Which that wisest of men diligently heeding, strongly warns us from it, saying: "Wine is a mocker, strong drink is raging; and whosoever is deceived thereby is not wise. Who hath woe? who hath sorrow? who hath contentions? who hath babbling? who hath wounds without cause? who hath redness of eyes? They that tarry long at the wine; they that go to seek mixed wine. Look not thou upon the wine when it is red, when it giveth his colour in the cup, when it moveth itself aright: at the last it biteth like a serpent, and stingeth like an adder. Thine eyes shall behold strange women, and thine heart shall utter perverse things: yea, thou shalt be as he that lieth down in the midst of the sea, or as he that lieth upon the top of a mast. They have stricken me, shalt thou say, and I was not sick; they have beaten me, and I felt it not: when shall I awake? I will seek it yet again." Likewise: "It is not for kings, O *Lemuel*, it is not for kings to drink wine, nor for princes strong drink; lest they drink, and forget the law, and pervert the judgment of any of the afflicted." And in Ecclesiasticus it is written: "A labouring man that is given to drunkenness shall not be rich; and he that contemneth small things shall fall by little and little. Wine and women will make men of understanding to fall away, and expose men of sense."

Esaias also, passing over all other foods, as a cause of the captivity of his people mentions wine only: "Woe unto them that rise up early in the morning, that they may follow strong drinks; that continue until night, till wine inflame them! And the harp and the viol, the tabret and the pipe, and wine, are in their feasts: but they regard not the work of the Lord, neither consider the operation of his hands. Therefore my people are gone into captivity, because they have no knowledge; and their honourable men are famished, and their multitude dried up with thirst." Who also extending his complaint from the people to the priests and prophets, says: "But they also have erred through wine, and through strong drink are out of the way; the priest and the prophet have erred through strong drink, they are swallowed up of wine, they are out of the way through strong drink; they err in vision, they stumble in judgment. For all tables are full of vomit and filthiness, so that there is no place clean. Whom shall he teach knowledge? and whom shall he make to understand doctrine?" The Lord says through *Joel:* "Awake, ye drunkards, and weep; and howl, all ye drinkers of wine." Not that he forbids wine in necessity, as the Apostle thereof counsels *Timothy,* "for thy stomach's sake and thine often infirmities;" not infirmities only, but often. *Noe* first planted the vine, still ignorant perchance of the evil of drunkenness, and when drunken uncovered his nakedness; because there is joined with wine the filthiness of lechery. Who also being mocked by his son put a curse upon him and bound him by a sentence of servitude: which before that time we know not ever to have been done. *Lot,* being a holy man, his daughters saw could never be drawn into incest save by drunkenness. And the holy widow believed that proud *Holofernes* could not, save by this artifice, be cozened and brought low. The angels that appeared to the Patriarchs of old, and were received by them with hospitality used meat, we read, but wine never. And to that greatest and first of our chiefs, *Elias,* hiding himself in a solitary place, the ravens ministered alimony of bread and flesh in the morning and in the evening, but not of wine. The children of Israel also we read to have been fed in the wilderness principally upon the most delicate meat of quails, but not to have used wine, nor to have wished for it. And those refections of loaves and fishes, wherewith the people were sustained in the wilderness, are nowhere said to have included wine. Only marriage, which has an indulgence of incontinence, had the miracle of wine, wherein is luxury. But the wilderness, which is the proper habitation of monks, has known the benefit of flesh rather than that of wine.

That cardinal point also in the law of the Nazarites, whereby they consecrated themselves to God, forbade only wine and strong drink. For what strength, what good remains in the drunken? Wherefore not wine only, but all that can make a man drunken, we read to have been forbidden to the priests of old also. Wherefore *Jerome* writing to *Nepotian* of the life of the clergy, and greatly indignant that the priests of the Law, abstaining from all that might make them drunken, surpass our priests in this abstinence, says: "Never smell of wine, lest thou hear said of thee those words of the philosopher: This is not offering a kiss, but proffering a cup." Priests given to wine the Apostle also condemns, and the Old Law forbids: "Do not drink wine nor strong drink, when ye go into the tabernacle of the congregation." By strong drink in the Hebrew tongue is understood every potion that may inebriate, whether that which is produced by fermentation; or from the juice of apples, or of the hive, is decocted into sweetness, and potions of herbs, or when the fruit of the palm is pressed into liquor, or water enriched with boiled grain. Whatsoever inebriates and upsets the balance of the mind, shun thou as it were wine. By the Rule of Saint *Pacomius*, none shall have access to wine and liquor save in the sickhouse. Who among you has not heard either that wine is utterly not for monks, and was so greatly abhorred by the monks of old, that vehemently warning us from it, they called it Satan? Wherefore we find it written in the Lives of the Fathers: "Certain persons told the Abbot Pastor of a certain monk that he did not drink wine, and he said to them that wine was not for monks." And again: "Once upon a time there was a celebration of masses on the mount of *Anthony* the Abbot, and there was found there a jar of wine. And one of the elders taking up a small vessel bore the cup to the Abbot *Sisoi* and gave it to him. And he drank once; and a second time, and he took it and drank. He brought it to him also a third time, but he took it not, saying: Peace, brother, knowest thou not that it is Satan?" And furthermore of the Abbot *Sisoi*: "*Abraham* says therefore to his disciples: If it come to pass on the Sabbath and the Lord's Day at church, and he shall drink three cupfuls, is it overmuch? And the old man said: If it were not Satan it would not be overmuch." Nor was Saint *Benedict* unmindful of this when by a certain dispensation he allowed wine to monks, saying: "Albeit we read that wine is not for monks, yet because in our times it is wholly impossible to persuade monks of this."

What marvel then, if to monks it is not to be allowed, that to women also, whose nature is in itself weaker, albeit stronger against wine, Saint *Jerome* wholly forbids it? For he instructing *Eustochium* the virgin of Christ of the preservation of her virginity, vehemently exhorts her, saying: "And so if there can be any counsel in me, if my experience is trusted, this first of all I warn and testify, that the Bride of Christ shun wine as it were poison. These are the first weapons of desire against youth. Not so does avarice shake, pride puff up, ambition flatter. Easily we forego other vices. This enemy is shut up within us. Whithersoever we may tend, we carry the enemy with us. Wine and youth are a twofold fire of lust. Wherefore do we throw oil on the flame? Why do we minister fuel of fire to the ardent body?" And yet it is clear from the teaching of those who have written of physic, that the strength of wine can prevail far less over women than over men. Inducing the reason whereof, *Macrobius Theodosius* in the fourth book of the Saturnalia says thus: "*Aristotle* says that women are rarely inebriated, old men often. The woman is of an extremely humid body. This we learn from the lightness and brilliancy of her skin. We learn it especially from the regular purgations, relieving the body of its superfluous humours. When therefore wine that has been drunk falls into so general an humour, it loses its strength; nor does it easily strike the seat of the brain, its strength being extinguished." Likewise: "The woman's body is cleansed by frequent purgations, it is pierced with many holes, that it may open channels and provide a way for the humours flowing into the issue of egestion. By these holes the vapour of wine is speedily released."

On what grounds then is that allowed to monks which to the weaker sex is denied? What madness to grant it to those whom it may more gravely harm and to deny it to others. What, lastly, more foolish than that religion should not abhor this which is so contrary to religion, and most makes us fall away from God? What more shameless, than that a thing which to the kings even and priests of the Law is forbidden the abstinence of Christian perfection should not avoid; nay, should greatly delight in it? For who knows not how greatly in these days the zeal of clerics especially or of monks turns towards the cellars, to wit that they may fill them with divers kinds of wine? That they brew it with herbs, with honey, and with other kinds, that so much the more easily they may make themselves drunken, the more pleasurably they drink? And so much the more incite themselves to lust, the more they burn with wine? What error, or rather what madness is this that they who most bind themselves by the profession of continence should less prepare themselves for the observance of their vow? Nay, so do that it may least be observed? Whose bodies, forsooth, if they are kept in the cloister, their hearts are filled with lust, and their mind is inflamed towards fornication. Writing to *Timothy*, the Apostle says: "Drink no longer water, but use a little wine for thy stomach's sake and thine often infirmities." To whom on account of his infirmities a little wine is allowed, clearly because, were he whole, he would take none. If we profess the Apostolic life, and especially vow the form of abstinence, and are called to flee the world: wherefore do we most delight in that which we see to be most adverse to our calling, and which is more delectable than all foods?

The diligent describer of penitence, Saint *Ambrose*, condemns nothing in the diet of the penitent save wine, saying: "And who considers that penitence where there is ambition of acquiring dignity, where there is pouring out of wine, where there is conjugal use of the marriage-bed? We must forsake the world; they are more easily found who have kept their innocence than who have done fitting penance." Likewise in the book, Of Fleeing the World: "Thou fleest well," he says, "if thine eye flee cups and flagons, nor become lustful while it lingers over wine." Alone of all foods in fleeing the world he mentions wine, and if we flee this wine he says that we flee well the world, as though all the pleasures of the world depend on this one; nor does he say even, if the palate flee the taste of it, but if the eye the sight, lest it be caught by the desire and delight of that whereupon it looks often. Whereof also are those words of *Solomon* which we have quoted above: "Look not thou upon the wine when it is red, when it giveth his colour in the cup." But what, I ask, are we to say here, who that we may be delighted as well by the taste as by the sight of it, when we have brewed it with honey, with herbs, or with divers kinds, wish also to drink of it from flagons? Saint *Benedict* under compulsion making an indulgence of wine, says: "Let us to this at least consent, that we drink not to satiety, but sparingly: for wine will make men of understanding to fall away." Oh, would that it were sufficient to drink only to satiety, lest guilty of a greater transgression we be carried to superfluity.

Saint *Augustine* also ordering the monasteries of clerks, and writing a Rule for them, says: "On the Sabbath only and on the Lord's Day, as the custom is, let who will take wine"; then, to wit, out of reverence for the Lord's Day and its vigil, which is the Sabbath, and also because then the brethren dispersed among their cells were gathered together. As also in the Lives of the Fathers Saint *Jerome* records, writing of the place which he names Cellia, in these words: "They remain severally in their cells. Yet on the Sabbath and the Lord's Day they come together into the church, and there see themselves restored one to another as though in heaven." Wherefore surely this indulgence was convenient, that coming together they might rejoice in some recreation, not saying so much as feeling: "Behold how good and how pleasant it is for brethren to dwell together in unity." Behold, if we abstain from flesh meat, wherefore is it imputed to us a great thing, when we feed with any superfluity upon things else? If at great cost we procure divers plates of dishes, if we mix with them the savours of peppers and spices, if when we are drunken with wine we add cups of herbs and flagons of juices. All this is excused by abstinence from common flesh, while in public we do not eat it, as though the quality rather than the superfluity of our food were at fault. Which also diligently following Saint *Augustine*, fearing nothing in food save wine, nor distinguishing any quality of food, held this to be enough in abstinence which he briefly expressed, saying: "Subdue your flesh by fasting, and by abstinence from meat or drink so far as your health is able." He had read, if I be not mistaken, that passage of Saint *Athanasius* in his exhortation to monks: "Of fasts also let there be no fixed measure for the willing, but so far as possibility allows, unless they be extended by effort: and except on the Lord's Day let these always be solemn, and not votive." As though he should say: If they are undertaken because of a vow, let them be devoutly performed at all times, save on the Lord's Day. No fasts are here fixed, but so far as health allows. For it is said: "He regards the capacity of nature alone, and permits it to set a measure for itself; knowing that there is failure in nothing if moderation be kept in all things." To wit that we be not relaxed by our pleasures more remissly than is right, as it is written of the people nourished upon the kidneys of wheat and the pure blood of the grape: "Thou art waxen fat, thou art grown thick, thou hast kicked." Nor let us, famished by abstinence beyond measure or wholly vanquished, succumb, nor by murmuring throw away our gain, nor glory in our singularity. Which the Preacher foreseeing says: "There is a just man that perisheth in his righteousness. Be not righteous overmuch; neither make thyself over wise: why shouldst thou destroy thyself?" that is to say by marvelling at thine own singularity. But over this diligence let discretion, the mother of all virtues, so preside, that she look carefully upon whom she may impose what burdens, namely to each according to his own strength, and following nature rather than drawing it, let her not at all remove the use of satiety but the abuse of superfluity; and let vices be so rooted out that nature be not injured. It is enough for the weak, if they avoid sin, albeit they do not rise to the height of perfection. It is enough also to dwell in a corner of Paradise, if thou canst not take thy place with the martyrs. It is safe to vow in moderation, that grace may add more, over and above what we owe. For of this it is written: "When ye shall have done all those things which are commanded you, say, We are unprofitable servants: we have done that which was our duty to do." "Because the law," says the Apostle, "worketh wrath: for where no law is, there is no transgression." And again: "For without the law sin was dead. For I was alive without the law once: but when the commandment came, sin revived, and I died. And the commandment, which was ordained to life, I found to be unto death. For sin, taking occasion by the commandment, deceived me, and by it slew me; that sin, by the commandment, might become exceeding sinful."

Augustine writes to *Simplician:* "By prohibition desire being increased has become more sweet, and so has deceived me." The same in the second book of Questions, and at the eighty-third question. "The persuasion of pleasure to sin is more vehement when there is prohibition." And "we strive ever after the forbidden, and desire things denied to us." Let him pay heed to this and tremble, whosoever seeks to fasten himself to the yoke of any rule, as though to the profession of a new law. Let him choose what he can, fear what he can not. None is made guilty by the law unless he have already professed it. Before thou profess, deliberate. When thou hast professed, observe. That is voluntary before which afterwards becomes necessary. "In my Father's house," says the Truth, "are many mansions." So also are there very many ways whereby we may approach thither. The married are not condemned, but the continent are more easily saved. Not for this reason, that we might be saved, were the Rules of the Holy Fathers given to us, but that we may be saved more easily, and may be able more purely to devote ourselves to God. "And if," says the Apostle, "a virgin marry, she hath not sinned; nevertheless such shall have trouble in the flesh: but I spare you." Likewise:

"The unmarried woman careth for the things of the Lord, that she may be holy both in body and in spirit: but she that is married careth for the things of the world, how she may please her husband. And this I speak for your own profit; not that I may cast a snare upon you, but for that which is comely, and that ye may attend upon the Lord without distraction." And this is most easily done when withdrawing in body even from the world we shut ourselves up in the cloisters of monasteries, lest the tumults of the world disturb us.

Nor let him only that receives the law, but let him that makes the law take heed, lest by multiplying precepts he multiply transgressions. The Word of God, coming to earth, has curtailed the word upon earth. *Moses* spake many things; and yet, as the Apostle says, "the law made nothing perfect." Many things, indeed, and so burdensome that the Apostle *Peter* professes that no man could endure his precepts, saying: "Men and brethren, why tempt ye God, to put a yoke upon the neck of the disciples, which neither our fathers nor we were able to bear? But we believe that through the grace of the Lord Jesus Christ we shall be saved, even as they." In a few words Christ instructed the Apostles touching the edification of morals and holiness of life, and taught the way of perfection. Putting aside the austere and heavy, He taught the easy and light, wherein He summed up the whole of religion: "Come unto me, all ye that labour and are heavy laden, and I will give you rest. Take my yoke upon you, and learn of me; for I am meek and lowly in heart; and ye shall find rest unto your souls. For my yoke is easy, and my burden is light." For so do we act often in good works as in the things of the world. For many in their business labour more and gain less. And many afflict themselves more outwardly, and inwardly advance less before God, Who regards the heart rather than works. Which also, because they are more taken up with outward things, can devote themselves less to things within; and the more they shine among men, who judge of outward things, the greater the glory they seek out among them, and the more easily they are led astray by elation.

Which error the Apostle meeting vehemently belittles works, and, extending justification by faith, says: "For if *Abraham* were justified by works, he hath that whereof to glory; but not before God. For what saith the scripture? *Abraham* believed God, and it was counted unto him for righteousness." And likwise: "What shall we say then? That the Gentiles, which followed not after righteousness, have attained to righteousness, even the righteousness which is of faith; but Israel, which followed after the law of righteousness, hath not attained to the law of righteousness. Wherefore? Because they sought it not by faith, but as it were by the works of the law." These cleaning the outside of the cup or platter, to its inward cleanness pay less heed, and watching over the flesh rather than the soul are fleshly rather than spiritual. But we, desiring that Christ should dwell in the outward man by faith, are but little concerned with outward things, which are common to the reprobate as to the elect, paying heed to what is written: "Thy vows are upon me, O God: I will render praises unto thee." Wherefore also we do not follow that outward abstinence of the law, which certainly confers no righteousness. Nor does the Lord forbid us anything in the way of food, save surfeiting and drunkenness, that is, superfluity. Who also what He did allow us was not ashamed to display in Himself, albeit many being thereby offended reproached Him not a little. Wherefore, also, speaking with His Own lips, He said: "For *John* came neither eating nor drinking, and they say, He hath a devil. The Son of man came eating and drinking, and they say, Behold a man gluttonous and a wine-bibber." Who also excusing His Own disciples, because they did not, like the disciples of *John*, fast, nor even, when they sat down to eat, cared greatly for that bodily cleanness of the washing of hands, said: "Can the children of the bride-chamber mourn, as long as the bridegroom is with them?" And elsewhere: "Not that which goeth into the mouth defileth a man; but that which cometh out of the mouth, this defileth a man. But those things which proceed out of the mouth come forth from the heart; and they defile the man. But to eat with unwashen hands defileth not a man." Food therefore defiles not the soul; but the appetite for forbidden food. For as the body is not defiled save by bodily filth, so is not the soul save by spiritual. Nor need we fear whatsoever is done in the body, if the mind is not betrayed into consenting. Nor should we trust in the cleanness of the flesh, if the mind is corrupted by the will.

In the heart, therefore, consists the whole death of the soul, and its life. Wherefore *Solomon* in the Proverbs: "Keep thy heart with all diligence; for out of it are the issues of life." And according to the utterance of the Word which we have quoted, out of the heart proceed those things which defile a man; inasmuch as the soul is lost or saved by good or evil desires. But inasmuch as the union of soul and body conjoined in one person is close, we must take especial care lest the pleasure of the flesh lead the soul to consent, and lest, while too great indulgence is given to the flesh, it grow lascivious and strive against the spirit, and where it should be subject begin to rule.

But this we shall be able to avoid if, conceding all things needful, superfluity, as has often been said, we utterly cut off, and to the weak sex deny not the use of any food, but the abuse of all. Let all things be allowed to be taken but none to be taken beyond measure. "For every creature of God," says the Apostle, "is good, and nothing to be refused, if it be received with thanksgiving. For it is sanctified by the word of God and prayer. If thou put the brethren in remembrance of these things, thou shalt be a good minister of Jesus Christ, nourished up in the words of doctrine, whereunto thou hast attained." And let us therefore with *Timothy* following this teaching of the Apostle, and, according to the words of the Lord, avoiding nought in food save surfeiting and drunkenness, so temper all things that with all things we may sustain weak nature, not nurture vices. And let those things which by their superfluity are more able to harm us, receive a greater tempering. For it is a greater thing and more praiseworthy to feed temperately, than to abstain altogether. Wherefore also Saint *Augustine*, in the book Of the Good of Marriage, where he deals with bodily sustenance, says: "In no wise does a man use these things well, unless he can also refrain from using them. Many indeed more easily abstain that they may not use than temper that they may use well. Yet no man can use these things wisely, unless he can also continently not use them." Of this practice *Paul* also said: "I know how both to abound and to suffer need." And to suffer need is the lot of all men; but to know how to suffer need is that of the great. So also any man can begin to abound. But to know how to abound is given to none save those whom abundance does not corrupt.

From wine therefore, since, as has been said, it is a luxurious thing and a tumultuous, and so greatly contrary as well to continence as to silence, let women either abstain altogether in God's Name, as the wives of the Gentiles are forbidden this, from fear of adultery; or so temper it with water that it may at once satisfy their thirst and their health, and not have strength to harm them. And this we believe to be secured if a fourth part at the least of this mixture be water. But it is most difficult for us, when drink is set before us, so to observe that we drink not of it to satiety, as Saint *Benedict* ordered concerning wine. And so we think it safer that we should not forbid satiety, lest thereby we incur peril. For not in satiety, as we have often said, but in superfluity lies the crime. But that wine of herbs be prepared as medicaments, or even pure wine be taken, is not to be forbidden. Yet let the convent never use these, but let them be drunk separately by the sick. The pure flour of wheat also we utterly forbid, but always when they have flour let a third part at the least of coarser grain be mixed with it. Nor let them ever be regaled with hot loaves from the oven, but with such as have been baked at least one day before.

And of the other foods let the Deaconess have such care that, as we have already said, what can be most cheaply bought or most easily had may meet the needs of the weaker sex. For what more foolish than, when our own things suffice us, to purchase others?

And when there are the needful things at home, to seek superfluous things without? And when we have to our hand what may suffice, to labour for those things that are superfluous? Of which necessary moderation of discretion indeed instructed not so much by human as by angelic, or indeed by the Lord's Own teaching, let us know in the satisfying of the needs of this life not so much to seek quality in food as to be content with those things that are at hand. Wherefore both angels were fed upon the flesh set before them by *Abraham*, and the Lord Jesus refreshed a hungry multitude with fishes found in the wilderness. Whereby we are plainly taught that the eating indifferently of flesh or of fishes is not to be rejected, and that those things especially are to be taken which both avoid the offences of sin and, since they offer themselves freely, are more easily prepared, and involve less expense. Wherefore also *Seneca*, that greatest follower of poverty and continence and, among all philosophers, the chief teacher of morals, says: "Our duty is to live according to nature. This is against nature, for a man to torment his body, and to hate easy cleannesses, and to seek after filth, and to use not cheap food merely, but revolting."

And in so far as to long for delicate things is luxury, so to shun things commonly used and prepared at no great cost is folly. Philosophy demands frugality, not penance. Yet there can be a not unstudied frugality; this mean pleases me. Wherefore also *Gregory*, in the thirtieth book of the Morals, where he teaches that we must give heed to the quality not so much of our food as of our minds, and distinguishes the temptations of the palate, says: "At one time it seeks more delicate meats, at another it desires that whatsoever is to be taken be more scrupulously prepared." But often both that which it desires is more abject, and yet it sins by the very heat of its immense desire. The people when they had been led out of Egypt fell in the wilderness, because despising manna they sought flesh meat, which they thought more delicate. And *Esau* lost the pride of the firstborn, because with a great heat of desire he longed for a cheap food, to wit lentils, when by setting it above even his birthright which he sold he shewed with what an appetite he yearned after it. For not the food is at fault, but the appetite. Wherefore also we often take the more delicate foods without blame, and not without guilt of conscience feed on the more abject. For this *Esau* of whom we have spoken lost his eldership for lentils, and *Elias* in the wilderness kept the virtue of his body by eating flesh. Wherefore also the old enemy, because he knows not food but the desire of food to be the cause of damnation, both subjugated the first man to himself not with flesh but with an apple, and not with flesh but with bread did tempt the Second. Hence is it that often the sin of *Adam* is committed even when abject and cheap things are consumed.

And so those things are to be taken which the necessity of nature seeks, and not those which the lust of eating suggests. But we long with less desire for those things which we see to be less costly, and which more abound, and are more cheaply bought; as is the meat of common flesh, which both strengthens weak nature far more than do fishes, and involves less expense and an easier preparation. But the use of flesh and wine, like that of marriage, is considered intermediate between good and evil, that is indifferent. Albeit the use of the marriage tie be not wholly free from sin, and wine be more perilous than all other foods. So, surely, if the temperate use of this be not forbidden to religion, wherefore do we fear the use of other foods, so long as in them moderation be not exceeded? If Saint *Benedict* professes of wine, that it is not for monks, yet by a certain dispensation to the monks of his time, when the fervour of the primitive charity was already growing cold, is obliged to allow it, wherefore should not we allow those other things to women, which at present no profession forbids them? If to the Pontiffs themselves and to the Rulers of Holy Church, if moreover to monasteries of clerks it is allowed without offence to eat even flesh, to wit because they are held from such things by no profession, who can blame the allowing of these things to women, especially if in the rest they endure a greater strictness? For it is enough for the disciple that he be as his master. And it seems great foolishness if what is allowed to monasteries of clerks be forbidden to monasteries of women. Nor is it to be reckoned a small thing if women, with the other restrictions of the monastery, in this one indulgence of flesh meat be not inferior to the faithful laity in religion, especially since, as *Chrysostom* bears witness, nothing is lawful to the secular that is not lawful to monks, save only to lie with a wife. Saint *Jerome* also, judging the religion of clerks to be not inferior to that of monks, says: "As though whatsoever is said against monks did not redound upon clerks, who are the fathers of monks." Who is there either that does not know it to be contrary to all discretion if as heavy burdens are laid upon the weak as upon the strong? If as great abstinence is enjoined upon women as upon men? Whereof also if any seek out an authority beyond the evidence of nature, let him consult Saint *Gregory* also upon this matter. For this great Ruler (rather than Doctor) of the Church, diligently instructing the other Doctors in this matter, in the twenty-fourth chapter of his Pastoral, writes thus: "In one way therefore are men to be admonished, in another women: for heavy burdens are to be laid on the former, but on the latter things lighter; and let great things exercise the one, but light things convert the other gently. For those things which are of little account in the strong are reckoned great in the feeble." Albeit this licence to eat common flesh affords less pleasure than the flesh of fishes or of birds, yet even these Saint *Benedict* nowhere forbids us. Of which also the Apostle, where he distinguishes the sundry kinds of flesh, says: "All flesh is not the same flesh: but there is one kind of flesh of men, another flesh of beasts, another of fishes, and another of birds."

Now the flesh of beasts and of birds the Law of the Lord includes in the sacrifice; but fishes not at all, that none may suppose the eating of fishes to be cleaner before God than the eating of flesh. Which also is so much the more burdensome to poverty, or the dearer, inasmuch as there is less abundance of fish than of flesh, and as it strengthens weak nature less, so that in one respect it burdens us more, in the other helps us less. And so we considering at once the means and the nature of men, forbid nothing in food, as we have said, save superfluity. And so we temper the eating of flesh or of whatsoever else, that, with all things allowed them, the abstinence of the nuns may be greater than that of monks, to whom certain things are forbidden. We wish therefore the eating of flesh to be so tempered that they may not take it more than once in the day, nor may several dishes of it be prepared for the same person; nor any sauces be added to it separately, nor it be ever allowed to be eaten more than thrice in the week, to wit upon the first, third and the fifth days, whatsoever the feasts be that may intervene. For the greater the solemnity, with the greater devotion of abstinence is it to be celebrated. Whereunto that famous Doctor *Gregory Nazianzen* vehemently exhorting us in the third book Of Lights, or the Second Epiphany, says: "Let us celebrate the festal day not indulging the belly but exulting in the spirit." The same in his fourth book Of Pentecost and the Holy Ghost, says: "And this is our festal day; let us put away in the soul's treasure-house something perennial and perpetual, not those things that perish and are dissolved. Sufficient for the body is its malice, it needs not more copious material, nor needs the insolent beast more abundant foods that he may become more insolent, and more violently urge." Therefore the solemnity is to be kept rather spiritually; which also Saint *Jerome*, his disciple, following in his letter on the acceptance of gifts, writes in a certain passage thus: "Wherefore we ought to take more anxious care, that we celebrate the solemn day not so much with abundance of food as with exultation of spirit; since it is plainly absurd to seek to honour by over-saturation a martyr whom we know to have found favour with God by his fasting." *Augustine*, Of the Medicine of Penitence: "Consider all the thousands of martyrs. For wherefore does it please us to celebrate their nativities with vile banquets, and not please us to follow their example in honest ways?"

But so often as they shall want flesh meat, we allow them two dishes of any vegetables, nor do we forbid fish meat in addition. But let no costly spices be applied to the food in the convent; rather let them be content with such things as grow in the country wherein they dwell. Fruit, however, let them not eat save at supper. As medicine, however, for those who may need it, we never forbid that herbs or roots, or any fruits or other things of the sort be brought to table. If peradventure any pilgrim nun received in hospitality be present at table, let her taste the humanity of charity in some dish given to her over and above. Whereof indeed if she be minded to distribute aught, she may. But she, or however many there be, shall sit at the high table and the Deaconess shall serve them. Afterwards she shall eat with the rest of those that serve the tables. But if any of the sisters have wished to subdue the flesh by a more sparing diet, let her on no account presume to do this save by way of obedience, and let it on no account be refused to her, if she seem to desire it not from levity but from virtue, and her strength be sufficient to endure it. Yet let it never be permitted to any that for this cause she go outside the convent, nor that she pass any day without food. Condiment of fat on the sixth day let them never use, but, contenting themselves with Lenten food, shew compassion, by a form of abstinence, for their Bridegroom, Who upon that day suffered death. And this practice is not only to be forbidden, but is vehemently to be abhorred which is the custom in many monasteries, to wit that on some part of the bread which is left over and is to be kept for the poor, they are wont to clean and to wipe their hands and knives, and, that they may spare the table-cloths, pollute the bread of the poor. Nay, His bread, Who, indicating Himself by the poor, says: "Inasmuch as ye have done it unto one of the least of these my brethren, ye have done it unto me."

Touching the abstinence of fasts, let the general institution of the Church suffice them; nor do we presume to burden them in this matter beyond the religion of the faithful laity, nor dare we in this set their infirmity above the strength of men. But from the autumnal equinox until Easter, on account of the shortness of the days, we consider that one meal in the day is enough. And because we say this on account not of religious abstinence but of the shortness of the season, we here distinguish no kinds of food.

Let costly garments, which the Scripture utterly condemns, be carefully avoided. Against which the Lord especially warning us, both denounces the pride in them of damned Dives, and on the contrary commends the humility of *John*. Which Saint *Gregory* diligently following, in his sixth Homily on the Gospels, says: "What is it to say, They that wear soft clothing are in kings' houses, unless to shew by open expression that they fight not in the heavenly but in an earthly kingdom, who refuse to suffer hardships for God, and given to outward shows alone seek the softness and delicacy of this present life." The same in his fortieth Homily: "Some there are who think the love of fine and costly garments to be no sin. Which if it were not blameworthy, never would the Word of God so vigilantly express that Dives, who was tormented in hell, had been clothed in purple and fine linen. For no one seeks especial raiment save for vainglory, to wit that he may appear more honourable than the rest. For from vainglory alone is a costly garment sought. As the fact proves, that no one wishes to be clad in costly raiment in a place where he cannot be seen by others." From this fault also the First Epistle of Peter warning lay and wedded women says: "Likewise, ye wives, be in subjection to your own husbands; that, if any obey not the word, they also may without the word be won by the conversation of the wives; while they behold your chaste conversation coupled with fear. Whose adorning let it not be that outward adorning of plaiting the hair, and of wearing of gold, or of putting on of apparel; but let it be the hidden man of the heart, in that which is not corruptible, even the ornament of a meek and quiet spirit, which is in the sight of God of great price." And rightly did he consider that women rather than men ought to be warned from this vanity, whose weak mind more strongly desires it, that by them and in them luxury may have a firmer hold.

But if lay women are to be forbidden these things, what care must women take that are devoted to Christ. Whose fashion in dress is that they have no fashion. Whosoever therefore seeks that fashion, or refuses it not when offered,* loses the testimony of chastity. And whosoever is such, let her be thought to be preparing herself not for religion, but for fornication, and be reckoned less a nun than a whore. To whom also fashion itself is as the badge of whoredom, which betrays an unchaste mind, as it is written, "A man's attire, and excessive laughter, and gait, shew what he is." We read that the Lord in *John*, as we have already recorded above, commended the cheapness or roughness of his raiment rather than of his food, and praised the same, saying: "What went ye out for to see? A man clothed in soft raiment?" For at times the use of costly food serves some useful purpose, but of raiment never. Which raiment, forsooth, the more costly it is, the more jealously it is kept, and the less it serves, and burdens the purchaser more, and because of its fineness can be more easily spoiled and furnishes less warmth to the body. And no clothes better than black befit the mournful garb of penitence, nor does any wool so become the Brides of Christ as that of lambs, that in their very habit even they may be seen to have put on, or be warned to put on the Lamb, the Bridegroom of Virgins. And let their veils be made not of silken, but of some flaxen cloth dyed. And we wish that there be two kinds of veil, that one kind may be for the virgins already consecrated therewith, the other not. But let those that are the veils of modest virgins bear the emblem of the Cross imprinted on them; whereby they may be shewn to pertain especially to Christ by the integrity of their bodies, and as in their consecration they are set apart from the rest, so let them be distinguished by this marking of their habit, and taking alarm thereat let it be more abhorrent to any of the faithful to burn with lust after them. And this sign of virginal purity the virgin shall wear on the top of her head, marked with white threads, and let her not presume to wear it before she have been consecrated by the Bishop. But let no other veils be marked with this sign.

Let them wear clean shifts nigh to their flesh, clad in which also let them always sleep. The softness also of mattresses and sheets we do not refuse to their weak nature. But let them sleep and eat each by herself. Let none presume to be indignant, if the garments or aught else that are bestowed on her by any be made over to another sister, that has more need of them. But then let her greatly rejoice, when in the need of her sister she shall enjoy the fruits of charity, or see herself to be living not for herself alone but for others. Else, she pertains not to the brotherhood of the holy society, nor is she wanting in the sacrilege of having possessions. And we consider to suffice for the covering of the body a shift, a woollen gown; and, when it shall be very cold, a mantle thereover. Which mantle forsooth they may use also for a covering when they lie down. But in view of the infestation of vermin or the accumulation of dirt that must be washed off, all these garments shall be in pairs, according to the letter of *Solomon*, saying in praise of the strong and provident wife: "She is not afraid of the snow for her household: for all her household are clothed with scarlet." Let the length of these garments be so moderated that they extend not beyond the heels, lest they stir up dust. And let the sleeves not exceed the length of the arms and hands. And let their legs and feet be fitted with shoes and stockings. Nor ever on account of religion let them go barefoot. On the beds let one mattress, a blanket, a pillow, a counterpane and a sheet suffice. And on the head let them wear a white band, and over it a black veil, and for the tonsure of their hair let them put on a bonnet of lamb's wool, if need be.

Nor in diet alone or in clothing let superfluity be avoided, but also in buildings or in any possession soever. In buildings indeed this is plainly discerned if they are made greater or finer than need be, or if we adorning them with sculptures or paintings do not build habitations of the poor, but erect kings' palaces. "The Son of Man," says *Jerome*, "hath not where to lay his head, and dost thou measure out wide porches and spacious roofs?" When we take pleasure in costly or beautiful equipages, not superfluity only but the elation of vanity is displayed. And when we multiply herds of animals or earthly possessions, then is our ambition swollen towards outward things: and the more things we possess on earth, the more we are obliged to think of them, and are called away from the contemplation of heavenly things. And albeit we be shut up in the body in cloisters, yet those things that are without the mind loves, is compelled to follow, and scatters itself hither and thither with them, and the more things are possessed that may be lost, the greater the fear with which they torment us; and the more costly they are, the more they are loved, and by ambition for them more ensnare the wretched mind. Wherefore every care is to be taken that we fix a certain measure to our household and to our expenses, nor beyond what is needful either desire aught, or receive offerings, or retain what we have received. For whatsoever is over and above our needs we possess by fraud; and are guilty of the death of so many of the poor as we might have sustained therewith. Every year, therefore, when the victuals shall have been gathered in, provision is to be made for as much as may suffice for the year; and if aught be over, it is not so much to be given as to be restored to the poor. Some there are who, knowing not the measure of provision, when they have but small revenues rejoice that they have a great household. And when they are burdened with the provision for them they go shamelessly begging, or extort by violence from others what they themselves have not.

Of this sort we even see not a few Fathers of monasteries, who boasting of the multitude of their convent, seek not to have good but to have many sons, and seem great in their own eyes if they are held the greater among many. Whom indeed that they may draw under their rule, when they ought to preach to them harsh things they promise smooth, and by no examination first proving those whom they undiscerningly take in, easily lose backsliders. Such men, as I see it, the Truth rebuked, saying: "Woe unto you, for ye compass sea and land to make one proselyte; and when he is made, ye make him twofold more the child of hell than yourselves." Who surely would boast less of their multitude if they sought the salvation rather than the number of souls, and presumed less upon their strength in giving an account of their rule. Few Apostles the Lord chose, and of that His choosing one so far fell away that of him the Lord said: "Have I not chosen you twelve, and one of you is a devil?" And as from the Apostles *Judas*, so from the Deacons *Nicolas* fell. And when the Apostles had as yet gathered together but a few, *Ananias* and *Sapphira* his wife earned sentence of death. As also aforetime when from the Lord Himself many Apostles had gone backward, a few remained with Him. For narrow is the way that leadeth to salvation, and few there be that find it. As on the contrary broad is the way and spacious that leadeth to destruction; and many there be which go in thereat. For as the Lord testifies elsewhere: "Many be called, but few chosen." And according to *Solomon:* "That which is wanting cannot be numbered."

Let him fear therefore, who rejoices in the multitude of his subordinates, lest among them, according to the Lord's saying, few be found chosen, and he himself unduly multiplying his flock suffice less for their custody, so that rightly to him may those words of the Prophet be said: "Thou hast multiplied the nation, and not increased the joy." Such indeed as glory in numbers, while as well for their own needs as for those of their people they are obliged more often to issue forth, and to return to the world, and to go about begging, involve themselves in bodily rather than in spiritual cares, and acquire for themselves infamy rather than fame. Which indeed among women is so much the more shameful, the less safe it is seen to be for them to wander about the world. Whosoever, therefore, desires to live quietly or honourably and to devote himself to the divine offices, and to be held dear as well by God as by the world, let him fear to gather together those for whom he cannot provide, nor in his expenditure let him rely upon the purses of others; nor let him watch over seeking but over giving of alms. The Apostle, that great preacher of the Gospel, having power also from the Gospel to receive gifts, labours with his hands; because he would not be chargeable to any, or make his glorying void. We, therefore, whose business is not to preach, but to bewail our sins, with what boldness or shamelessness do we go about begging; that we may be able to sustain those whom inconsiderately we gather together? Who also often break forth into such madness that when we know not how to preach we take about with us preachers and false apostles, carry crosses and phylacteries of relics, that we may sell both these and the Word of God, or even figments of the devil, to simple and foolish Christians, and promise them whatsoever we believe to be profitable for the extortion of money. By which shameless cupidity indeed, seeking those things that are its own and not of Jesus Christ, how greatly our Order and the very preaching of the Divine Word have been debased is known, I ween, to all. Hence also Abbots themselves, or they who seem to be in authority in monasteries, importunately betaking themselves to the great ones of the world and to earthly courts, have already learned to be carnal rather than cenobite. And hunting the favour of men by any artifice, they are accustomed more frequently to gossip with men than to speak with God. Reading often vainly and ignoring, or hearing but hearkening not to the warning which Saint *Augustine* gives us, saying: "As fishes, if they remain on dry ground, die; so also monks, remaining outside their cell, or sojourning among men of the world, are loosened from their vow of quiet."

It is proper therefore, as for a fish to the sea, so for us to hasten back to our cell, lest haply, lingering without, we forget the custody of things within. Which also the writer of the Monastic Rule, namely Saint *Benedict*, diligently heeding, as though he wished Abbots to be assiduous in their monasteries, and to keep a solicitous watch over their flocks, openly taught both by his example and in his writings. For he, when he had gone forth from his brethren to visit his most holy sister, and when she wished to detain him for one night at least for her edification, openly professed that he could on no account remain away from his cell. Nor indeed does he say: "We cannot," but, "I cannot," because the brethren might, by his leave, do so, but he himself might not, unless by a revelation from the Lord, as afterwards befell. Wherefore also, when he wrote the Rule, he made no mention of the Abbot's leaving the monastery, but only of the brethren's. And for the Abbot's assiduous presence he so cautiously provided, that on the vigils of Sundays and Feasts he orders the reading of the Gospel, and those things that are joined thereto, to be done by the Abbot only. Who also instituting that the Abbot's table shall ever be with the pilgrims and guests, and that as often as guests shall be wanting he shall bid to it such as he pleases of the brethren, one only or two of the elders being left with the rest, evidently suggests that never at mealtimes ought the Abbot to be absent from the monastery, or, as being accustomed to the delicate meats of princes, leave the daily bread of the monastery to his subordinates; like those of whom the Truth says: "They bind heavy burdens and grievous to be borne, and lay them on men's shoulders; but they themselves will not move them with one of their fingers." And elsewhere, of false preachers: "Beware of false prophets, which come to you." They come, he says, of themselves, not sent of God, or expecting to receive something. *John* the Baptist, our chief, to whom the priesthood passed by inheritance, went forth once only from the city to the wilderness, leaving, to wit, the priesthood for the monkhood, the cities for the solitary places. And to him the people went out, nor did he go in to the people. Who when he was so great that he was believed to be the Christ yet could correct nothing in the cities: he was already upon that bed, wherefrom he was prepared to answer to the knocking of the Beloved: "I have put off my coat; how shall I put it on? I have washed my feet; how shall I defile them?"

And so whosoever desires the secret of monastic quiet, let him rejoice that he has a narrow bed rather than a wide. For from the wide bed, as the Truth says, "the one shall be taken, and the other shall be left." But the narrow bed we understand to be that of the Bride, that is of the contemplative soul more straitly joined to Christ, and with the strongest desire adhering to Him. Which whosoever may have entered, we do not read that any left. Whereof also the Bride herself speaks: "By night on my bed I sought him whom my soul loveth." From which bed also she declining, or fearing to rise, answers to the knocking of the Beloved as we have set forth above. For she does not believe that there is dirt save outside her bed, in which she is afraid to defile her feet. *Dinah* went forth that she might see strange women, and was defiled. And as it was foretold by his Abbot to *Malchus*, that evil monk, and as he himself afterwards found; the sheep that goes out from the fold is speedily exposed to the bite of the wolf. Let us not therefore gather together a multitude, for which we may seek an occasion for going out, nay, be compelled even to go out, and with detriment to ourselves acquire wealth for others; after the manner of the lead, which, that the silver may be saved, is consumed in the furnace. We must rather beware lest the lead and the silver alike the vehement furnace of temptations consume. The Truth, they will argue, says: "And him that cometh to me I will in no wise cast out." Nor do we wish that those who have been taken in be cast out, but that provision be made in the taking of them in, lest, when we have taken them in, we cast out ourselves for their sake. For the Lord Himself we read not to have cast out him that had been taken in, but to have rejected him that offered himself. To whom, indeed, saying: "Master, I will follow thee whithersoever thou goest," He answered: "The foxes have holes," and the rest. Who also diligently warns us to look first to the cost, when we think to do any thing, saying: "Which of you, intending to build a tower, sitteth not down first, and counteth the cost, whether he have sufficient to finish it? Lest haply, after he hath laid the foundation, and is not able to finish it, all that behold it begin to mock him, saying, This man began to build, and was not able to finish." It is a great thing, if any one be sufficient to save himself alone, and it is a perilous thing for him to provide for many who is barely able to watch over himself. And no one is zealous in watching, unless he have been timid in receiving. And no one so perseveres in what he has begun, as he that is slow and provident in beginning. Wherein indeed so much the greater is the providence of women, the less their infirmity is able to bear great burdens, and the more they have to cultivate quiet.

It is agreed that the Holy Scripture is a mirror of the soul, wherein whoso lives by reading, advances by understanding, learns the beauty of his own ways, or discovers the blemish, that he may labour to increase the one, to remove the other. Recalling to us this mirror, Saint *Gregory* says in the second book of the Morals: "The Holy Scripture is set before the mind's eye as a sort of mirror, that our inward face may be seen therein. For there we both discover our blemishes and behold our beauty. There we perceive how far we are advancing, and how far we have failed to advance. But whoso studies a Scripture which he understands not, like a blind man holds it before his eyes, wherein he is not able to discern what manner of man he is, nor does he seek that doctrine in the Scripture, wherefore alone it was made; and like an ass set before a lyre, sits idly before the Scripture, and has it set before him like bread, whereby, being anhungered, he is not refreshed, while, neither penetrating the Word of God himself by understanding it, nor breaking it by another's teaching him, he has food to no purpose which profits him nothing. Wherefore also the Apostle exhorting us generally to the study of the Scriptures says: "Whatsoever things were written aforetime were written for our learning; that we through patience and comfort of the scriptures might have hope." And elsewhere: "Be filled with the Spirit; speaking to yourselves in psalms and hymns and spiritual songs." For to himself or with himself he speaks who understands what is said to him, or by understanding gathers fruit of his own words. The same says to *Timothy:* "Till I come, give attendance to reading, to exhortation, to doctrine." And again: "But continue thou in the things which thou hast learned and hast been assured of, knowing of whom thou hast learned them; and that from a child thou hast known the holy scriptures, which are able to make thee wise unto salvation through faith which is in Christ Jesus. All scripture is given by inspiration of God, and is profitable for doctrine, for reproof, for correction, for instruction in righteousness: that the man of God may be perfect, throughly furnished unto all good works." Who also encouraging the Corinthians to an understanding of the Scripture, to wit that they may be able to expound what others speak concerning the Scripture, says: "Follow after charity, and desire spiritual gifts, but rather that ye may prophesy. For he that speaketh in an unknown tongue speaketh not unto men, but unto God: but he that prophesieth, edifieth the church. Wherefore let him that speaketh in an unknown tongue pray that he may interpret. I will pray with the spirit, and I will pray with the understanding also; I will sing with the spirit, and I will sing with the understanding also. Else, when thou shalt bless with the spirit, how shall he that occupieth the room of the unlearned say Amen at thy giving of thanks, seeing that he understandest not what thou sayest? For thou verily givest thanks well, but the other is not edified. I thank my God, I speak with tongues more than ye all: yet in the church I had rather speak five words with my understanding, that by my voice I might teach others also, than ten thousand words in an unknown tongue. Brethren, be not children in understanding: howbeit in malice be ye children, but in understanding be men."

By speaking with tongues is meant he who with his lips alone forms words, and does not minister to the undersatnding by expounding them. But he prophesies or interprets who, *after the manner of the Prophets,* which are called seers, that is understanders, understands those things which he says, that he may be able to expound them. He prays or sings with the spirit who with the breath of utterance only forms his words, and does not apply the understanding of his mind. And when our spirit prays, that is the breath of our utterance alone forms words, nor is that which the mouth utters conceived in the heart, our mind is without the profit which it ought to receive in prayer, to wit that by its understanding of the words it should be urged and inflamed towards God. Wherefore he admonishes us to have this perfection in words, that we may not, like so many, know only how to utter the words but also may have some sense of understanding in them, and otherwise he protests that we pray or sing to no profit. Whom also Saint *Benedict* following says: "Let us so apply ourselves to singing that our mind may be in harmony with our voice." This too the Psalmist enjoining, says: "Sing ye praises with understanding," to wit that from the utterance of the words the condiment and savour of understanding be not wanting, and that with him we may be able truthfully to say to the Lord: "How sweet are thy words unto my taste." And elsewhere he says: "He taketh not pleasure in the legs of a man." For *tibia,* the leg-bone, that is the flute, emits a sound for the delectation of the sense, not for the understanding of the mind. Wherefore they are said to sing well to the flutes, and not thereby to please God, who so delight in the melody of their song that no understanding may be built up thereon. And with what reason, says the Apostle, when blessings are given in church, shall a man answer Amen, if he do not understand what is prayed for in the blessing? To wit, whether it be a good thing that the prayer bids, or no. For thus we see often in church many unlearned persons, and persons who know not the sense of letters, pray for things harmful to themselves rather than helpful, as when it is said: "That we may so pass through things temporal, that we lose not the things eternal." Easily the close similarity of the words so deceives them that they say either: "that we lose now the things eternal," or else, "that we love not the things eternal." Against which peril also the Apostle providing says: "Else, when thou shalt bless with the spirit," that is, with the breath of thine utterance only form the words of blessing, not instruct the mind of thine hearer in the sense, "how shall he that occupieth the room of the unlearned," that is any of the congregation, whose office it is to respond, so act in responding as an unlearned man is not able, nay ought not to act? "How shall he say Amen," when forsooth, he knows not whether thou be not leading him to curse rather than to bless?

Moreover, they that have not understanding of the Scripture, how shall they minister edifying discourse unto themselves, or be able either to expound or understand the Rule, or to correct things faultily uttered? Wherefore we wonder not a little what suggestion of the enemy has brought to pass in monasteries that there is no study there of the understanding of the Scripture, but instruction is given in singing alone, or discipline exercised only in the forming, not in the understanding of words, as though the bleating of the sheep were more useful than the feeding of them. For the food of the soul, and its spiritual refreshment, is the understanding of Holy Scripture. Wherefore the Lord also, when he appoints the Prophet *Ezekiel* to be a preacher, feeds him first upon a roll, which straightway was in his mouth as honey for sweetness. Of which food also it is written by *Jeremy*: "The young children ask bread, and no man breaketh it unto them." For he breaks bread unto the young children who reveals the sense of the letter to the more simply minded. And these young children ask for bread to be broken, when they long to feed their soul on the understanding of the Scripture, as elsewhere the Lord bears witness: "I will send a famine in the land, not a famine of bread, nor a thirst for water, but of hearing the words of the Lord."

But on the other hand the old enemy has instilled into monasteries a famine and thirst of hearing the words of men, and the rumours of the world, that giving ourselves over to vain speaking we may find the word of God so much the more wearisome, the more tasteless it becomes to us lacking the sweetness or condiment of understanding. Wherefore also the Psalmist, as we have said above, cries: "How sweet are thy words unto my taste! Yea, sweeter than honey to my mouth!" And in what this sweetness consisted he straightway added, saying: "Through thy precepts I get understanding." That is, through God's rather than through man's precepts I have received understanding, being made wise and instructed by them. Nor did he omit to say what was the profit of this understanding, adding: "Therefore I hate every false way." For many false ways lie open so of themselves that easily they come into hatred or contempt among all, but only by the Word of God do we know every false way, that we may be able to avoid them all. Wherefore is it written: "Thy word have I hid in mine heart, that I might not sin against thee." It is hidden in the heart rather than sounding upon the lips, when our meditation retains an understanding of it. And the less we study the understanding thereof, the less we see and avoid these false ways, and the less we are able to guard ourselves against sin. Which negligence indeed is so much the more to be rebuked in monks, who aspire to perfection, the easier this teaching is for them, who both abound in sacred books, and enjoy the leisure of quiet. Whom indeed boasting of the multitude of their books, but abstaining from the reading thereof, that elder in the Lives of the Fathers vehemently rebukes saying: "The Prophets wrote books; our Fathers came after them and wrought many things in them. Their followers also committed them to memory. But then came the generation that now is, and wrote them upon paper and upon parchment, and set them back idle on the shelves." Wherefore also the Abbot *Palladius*, vehemently exhorting us to learning and to teaching alike, says: "It befits the soul that would follow after the will of Christ either to learn faithfully what it knows not, or to teach openly what it knows. But if, when it can, it will not do either, it labours under the disease of madness. For the beginning of a withdrawal from God is a weariness of teaching, and when he has no appetite for that for which the soul ever hungers, how shall a man love God?"

Wherefore also Saint *Anastasius*, in his exhortation of monks, so commends the study of learning or reading that for this purpose he even allows the prayers to be interrupted. "Let me trace," he says, "the course of our life. First, the care of abstinence, endurance of fasting, instance in prayer and reading, or if any be still without knowledge of letters, let the desire to learn inspire an eagerness to hear. For these are the first stages, as though of sucking children, in the knowledge of God." And a little later, after he had first said: "But we must be so instant in our prayers that scarcely any time be interposed between them," he straightway added: "These, if it be possible, let only the intervals of reading interrupt." Nor would the Apostle *Peter* counsel aught else: "Be ready always to give an answer to every man that asketh you a reason of the hope that is in you." And the Apostle: "We do not cease to pray for you, and to desire that ye might be filled with the knowledge of his will in all wisdom and spiritual understanding." And again: "Let the word of Christ dwell in you richly in all wisdom." And in the Old Testament the Word instilled into men a like care for holy precepts. For thus says *David:* "Blessed is the man that walketh not in the counsel of the ungodly, nor standeth in the way of sinners, nor sitteth in the seat of the scornful; but his delight is in the law of the Lord." And to *Joshua* the Lord speaks: "This book of the law shall not depart out of thy mouth; but thou shalt meditate therein day and night." Moreover among these occupations the slippery courses of evil thoughts often work their way, and albeit our very sedulity present the mind ready to God, yet the gnawin care of the world makes it anxious in itself. And if he that is dedicated to the toil of religion must frequently and importunately suffer this, surely the idle man shall never be free from it. And the Pope Saint *Gregory*, in the nineteenth book of the Morals, says: "We lament that those times are already begun, when we see many placed within the Church who will not perform that which they understand, or who even scorn to understand and to know the Word of God. For turning away their ears from the Truth, they hearken unto fables, when all seek those things that are their own, not of

Jesus Christ. The Scriptures of God are found everywhere and known, and are set before their eyes. If men scorn to read these, none almost will seek to know that which he has believed."

Whereunto also both the Rule of their own profession and the examples of the Holy Fathers greatly exhort them. For *Benedict* prescribes nought touching the teaching or study of singing, when he lays down much concerning reading, and diligently appoints the times for reading, as also for working: and so provides for the teaching of dictation or writing, that among the necessities for which the monks are to look to the Abbot, he does not omit tablets and pens. And when, among other things, he orders that at the beginning of Lent all the monks shall receive each a manuscript from the library, which they shall read through in due order, what could be more absurd than to give time to reading and not to take pains to understand? For that proverb of the Sage is well known: "To read and not to understand is to misread." To such a reader is that saying of the philosopher rightly applied: "An ass before a lyre." For as an ass is before a lyre so is a reader holding a book and unable to do that for which the book was made. Far more profitably would such readers attend to other things, in which there might be some advantage, than idly either regard the letters of the Scripture, or turn the pages. In which readers surely, we see openly fulfilled that prophecy of *Esaias:* "And the vision of all is become unto you as the words of a book that is sealed, which men deliver to one that is learned, saying, Read this, I pray thee: and he saith, I cannot; for it is sealed: and the book is delivered to him that is not learned, saying, Read this, I pray thee: and he saith, I am not learned. Wherefore the Lord said, Forasmuch as this people draw near me with their mouth, and with their lips do honour me, but have removed their heart far from me, and their fear towards me is taught by the precept of men: therefore, behold, I will proceed to do a marvellous work among this people, even a marvellous work and a wonder; for the wisdom of their wise men shall perish, and the understanding of their prudent men shall be hid." For they are said in the cloisters to know letters, whosoever have learned to pronounce them. Which indeed, so far as understanding is concerned, professing themselves to be ignorant of the law, the book that is delivered to them is as much sealed as to those whom they there call unlearned. Whom indeed the Lord rebukes, saying that they draw near Him with their mouth and lips rather than their heart, because those words which they are able after a fashion to pronounce they cannot in the least understand. Who while they lack the knowledge of the Word of God, follow in their obedience the custom of men rather than the utility of the Scripture. Wherefore the Lord threatens that they also, who are reckoned learned among them, and sit as doctors, shall be blinded.

That greatest Doctor of the Church and glory of the monastic profession, *Jerome*, who, exhorting us to the love of letters, says: "Love the knowledge of letters and thou wilt not love the vices of the flesh," what labour and expense he used in the teaching of them, we have learned also from his own testimony. Who among the other things that he writes of his own study, to wit that he may instruct us also by his example, addressing *Pammachius* and *Oceanus*, in a certain passage, says thus: "When I was young, I burned with a marvellous love of learning. Nor after the presumption of some men did I teach myself; I heard *Apollinaris* frequently at Antioch, and cherished him, while he was making me learned in the Holy Scriptures. Already my head was grizzled, and I ought to have been a teacher rather than a disciple. Yet I went to Alexandria. I heard *Didymus*, for many things I am thankful to him; what I did not know, that I learned. Men thought that I had made an end of learning. Returning to Jerusalem and Bethlehem, with what labour, at what a cost, did I have *Barannias*, a Hebrew, as my teacher by night. For he feared the Jews, and shewed himself to me a second *Nicodemus*." Surely he had stored that in his memory which he had read in Ecclesiasticus: "My son, gather instruction from thy youth up: so shalt thou find wisdom in thine old age." Wherein he, instructed not only by the words of the Scriptures, but by the example of the Holy Fathers, among the other praises of that excellent monastery has added the following, of its singular practice in the Holy Scriptures: "But in the meditation and understanding of the Holy Scriptures, and of divine learning, never did we see so great a practice, so that thou mightest believe each and all of them to be orators in divine learning." Venerable *Bede* also, as he relates in his History of the English, having been taken as a boy into a monastery, says: "Passing the whole space of my life from that time in the habitation of the same monastery, I gave my whole attention, in meditation, to the Scriptures, and between the observance of the regular discipline and the daily duty of singing in church, I ever held it sweet either to learn or to write." But now they that are taught in monasteries persist in such folly that, content with the sound of letters, they pay no heed to the understanding of them, nor study to instruct the heart, but the tongue. Which plainly that Proverb of *Solomon* rebukes: "The heart of him that hath understanding seeketh knowledge: but the mouth of fools feedeth on foolishness," to wit, when it takes pleasure in words which it does not understand. Who surely are so much the less able to love God, and to be kindled towards Him, the more remote they are from an understanding of Him, and from the sense of the Scripture that teaches us of Him.

And this we believe to have come about in monasteries for two reasons chiefly; either from the envy of the lay brethren, that is the converts, or of the superiors themselves; or from the vain speaking of idleness, to which in these days we see monastic cloisters much abandoned. There, surely, desiring to attach us with them to earthly rather than to spiritual things, are those who like the Philistines persecute *Isaac* when he is digging wells: and filling them with earth strive to prevent his work. Which Saint *Gregory* expounding in the sixteenth book of the Morals, says: "Often when we attend to the Word of God, we are more gravely burdened by the wiles of evil spirits, because they scatter the dust of earthly thoughts upon our mind, that they may darken the eyes of our intention from the light of inward vision." Which the Psalmist had suffered beyond measure when he said: "Depart from me, ye evil-doers, for I will keep the commandments of my God." To wit openly suggesting that he could not keep the commandments of God, when he was suffering in his mind from the wiles of evil spirits. Which also in the work of *Isaac* we understand to be meant by the naughtiness of the Philistines, who filled with earth the wells that *Isaac* had dug. For we dig wells, indeed, when we penetrate deeply into the hidden meaning of the Holy Scripture. Which wells, however, the Philistines secretly fill up, when, as we are tending to higher things, they throw in the earthly thoughts of an unclean spirit, and as it were take away the water of divine learning which we have found.

But that none overcomes these enemies by his own strength is said by *Eliphaz:* "Yea, the Almighty shall be thy defence, and thou shalt have plenty of silver." As though it were said: When the Lord shall have driven off from thee evil spirits by His Own strength, the talent of the Divine Word grows more bright in thee. He had read, if I be not mistaken, the homilies of that great philosopher of the Christians, *Origen*, upon Genesis, and had drawn from his wells what now he says of those others. For that zealous digger of spiritual wells, vehemently exhorting us not to drink of them only but also to dig others for ourselves, in the twelfth homily of the aforesaid exposition, speaks thus: "Let us try also to do that which Wisdom advises us, saying: Drink waters out of thine own cistern, and running waters out of thine own well. Let them be only thine own. Do thou therefore also try, my hearer, to have thine own well, and thine own cistern, that thou also when thou takest up a book of the Scriptures mayest begin of thine own sense to proffer some understanding thereof, according to that which thou hast learned in the Church. Do thou also try to drink of the well of thine own spirit. Thou hast within thee a spring of living water, there are perennial veins, and flowing channels of reasonable sense, if only they be not filled with earth and stones. But strive to dig thy ground, and to cleanse it of its filth, that is thy spirit, to remove sloth, and to shake off torpor of heart. For hear what the Scripture saith: "He that pricketh the eye will make tears to fall; and he that pricketh the heart maketh it to shew her knowledge. Purge thou then thy spirit, that in good time thou mayest drink of thy cisterns, and from thy wells mayest draw living water. For if thou hast received the Word of God into thyself, and hast received from Jesus living water, and hast faithfully received it, it shall be in thee a fountain of running water to life everlasting." The same, in the following homily, of the wells of *Isaac* aforementioned, says: "Those which the Philistines had filled with earth are, without doubt, those who shut up their spiritual understanding, so that they neither drink themselves, nor allow others to drink." Hear the Word of the Lord saying: "Woe unto you, lawyers, for ye have taken away the key of knowledge: ye entered not in yourselves, and them that were entering in ye hindered."

But let us never cease from digging wells of living water, and by the discussion, now of new things, now of old, let us be made like unto that Scribe in the Gospel, whereof the Lord said: "Which bringeth forth out of his treasure things new and old." Let us return again to *Isaac*, and dig with him wells of living water, even if the Philistines obstruct us, even if they fight, let us neverless persevere with the digging of our wells, that to us also it may be said: "Drink waters out of thine own cistern, and running waters out of thine own well;" and so let us dig that not to ourselves alone may the knowledge of the Scriptures suffice, but that we may teach others also, and instruct them how to drink. Let men drink and beasts, as also the Prophet says: "O Lord, thou preservest man and beast." And later he says: "He that is a Philistine, and knows earthly things, knows not in all the earth where to find water, where to find reasonable sense." What does it profit thee to have learning, and know not how to use it? To have speech and know not how to speak? That is verily to be as the sons of *Isaac*, who over all the earth dig wells of living water.

Ye, however, be not so, but abstaining from all vain speech, whosoever have obtained some grace of learning, let them study to be instructed in the things that pertain to God. As it is written of the man that has blessedness: "But his delight is in the law of the Lord, and in his law doth he meditate day and night." And what is the profit that follows upon the assiduous study of the law of God is straightway added: "And he shall be like a tree planted by the rivers of water." Inasmuch as a dry tree is not fruitful, because it is not watered by the streams of the Word of God. Whereof it is written: "Out of his belly shall flow rivers of living water." These are those rivers, whereof, in praise of the Bridegroom, the Bride sings in the Song of Songs, describing him: "His eyes are as the eyes of doves by the rivers of waters, washed with milk and fitly set." And do ye, therefore, being washed with milk, that is shining with the whiteness of chastity, abide by those rivers like doves, that drawing thence draughts of wisdom ye may be able not only to say but to teach also, and to shew to others, as it were, whither to turn their eyes, and may have power not only to behold the Bridegroom himself, but to describe him to others. Of whose especial Bride, whose honour it was to conceive Him by the ear of the heart, we know it to be written: "But *Mary* kept all these things, and pondered them in her heart."

So the Mother of the Supreme Word, having His Words in her heart rather than upon her lips, pondered them also diligently, because she studiously considered each, and compared them one with another; to wit, how harmoniously they all agreed together. She knew that, according to the mystery of the Law, every animal is called unclean, save those that chew the cud and divide the hoof. And so no soul is clean, unless by meditating, so far as it is able, it chew the cud of divine precepts, and in the following of them have discretion, that it may do not good things only, but may do them well, that is with a right intention. For the division of the hoof is the discretion of the mind, whereof it is written: "If thou offerest rightly, but dividest not rightly, thou hast sinned." "If a man love me," says the Truth, "he will keep my words." But what words or precepts of his Lord can he keep by obeying them, unless he have first understood them? No one will be studious in following save he that has been attentive in hearing. As also we read of that holy woman who, laying aside all things else, and sitting at the Lord's feet, heard His Words: to wit, with those ears of the understanding which He Himself requires, saying: "He that hath ears to hear, let him hear." And if ye are not able to be kindled to such a fervour of devotion, do ye at least imitate, both in the love and in the study of Holy Writ, those blessed disciples of Saint *Jerome*, *Paula* and *Eustochium*, at whose request, chiefly, the aforesaid Doctor enriched the Church with so many volumes.